D0432469

ENSLAVED

GORDON THOMAS

An Investigation into Modern~Day Slavery

ENSLAVED

BANTAM PRESS

LONDON · NEW YORK · TORONTO · SYDNEY · AUCKLAND

TRANSWORLD PUBLISHERS LTD
61-63 Uxbridge Road, London W5 5SA

TRANSWORLD PUBLISHERS (AUSTRALIA) PTY LTD
15-23 Helles Avenue, Moorebank, NSW 2170

TRANSWORLD PUBLISHERS (NZ) LTD
Cnr Moselle and Waipareira Aves,
Henderson, Auckland

Published 1990 by Bantam Press
a division of Transworld Publishers Ltd
Copyright © Gordon Thomas 1990

The right of Gordon Thomas to be identified
as author of this work has been asserted in accordance
with sections 77 and 78 of the Copyright Designs and
Patents Act 1988

British Library Cataloguing in Publication Data
Thomas Gordon, *1933-*
    Enslaved.
    1. Slavery
    I. Title
    306.362

ISBN 0–593–01688–2

Printed in Great Britain
by Mackays of Chatham, PLC, Chatham, Kent

For
Edith, Alexander, Lucy,
Nicholas, Natasha and Catherine

The light side of a dark world

Contents

FOR THE MOMENT

A Note To The Reader

Of all the truths in this book, none is more sobering than this: the number of slaves continues to grow. All the major human rights organizations concur that there are over 200 million people enslaved in 1990. Slavery remains the largest single source of labour in the world. There are more slaves than the entire work forces of North America or Western Europe. For every male slave, there are twice the number of women and child slaves; the vast majority are used for sexual exploitation.

In the closing decade of the twentieth century, slavery is established as the largest growth industry on earth. US agencies estimate its global profits at around an annual US $1 trillion. This is greater than the value of all American currency in circulation in 1990.

By the time you finish reading this book, there will assuredly be more slaves: those sold, coerced, inveigled or simply driven by economic necessity into becoming enslaved.

This is their testament – and our shame. It is also a real opportunity to join forces with those fighting to end slavery. This book should be read with that constantly in mind.

Prologue

The urge to enslave remains the dark side of human nature and is common to all races and peoples. It is the treadmill of human miseries from which no nation can be absolved. Today slavery transcends not only national borders, but race and colour. It remains, as always, the product of lust, greed and the love of power, of owning another human being, and being able to do to that human whatever forms of abuse satisfy the basic feelings.

> Excerpt from author's interview with Maureen Alexander-Sinclair, Deputy Director, The Anti-Slavery Society for the Protection of Human Rights; 14 March 1988.

ONE

A Boy Called Shambu

It is that most magical of all hours on the sub-continent of India. The hour when the glare and the heat of the summer sun lessens, and the light is a soft reddish-gold flood bathing the land. That hour before darkness once more claimed Shambu's world. It was also the hour when the slavers sent one of their own to buy the boy.

Other villagers would later remember Shambu as a child with a shy smile and possessed of a quick and natural intelligence, though he could neither read nor write, and that he was also physically small for his age, seven, and alarmingly thin. Despite that, he was strong and able to control his father's water-buffalo, expertly steering it past the little altar at the entrance to the rice field. The family regularly came to the altar to say their *puja*, and make their offerings to the gods.

In recent times, after sprinkling a few grains on the altar, Shambu's father had again prayed for help to find the money to buy a little more land to feed the family. He had said similar *pujas* just before Shambu's brother, Puli, a year older, had suddenly gone from home.

No villager discussed Puli's fate or that of other boys who had similarly disappeared. The police had not been called to investigate. Everyone knew what had happened.

Like Puli, the other boys were light-boned, and aged between six and eight years, and just as was Shambu, physically strong for their years. In the past twelve months as many as a dozen boys had disappeared from Shambu's village. It was the same in other villages throughout the land. From many of them had gone a handful of boys – gone, never to return.

No one will ever know, not now, what Shambu was thinking as he drove the beast along a track hemmed-in on either side by creeper, more scarlet than ever in the brilliant golden light. If he was hurrying, it could be because, like so many little boys in this part of the world, the approach of sunset still held its precursor of private terror.

But that final brilliant moment when the sun, with a sudden plunge, dropped behind the horizon and left Shambu's world in darkness – that moment was still a little while away. Meanwhile the golden light gave the land a very special kind of beauty, softening its harshness. This was the hour when the air became still and the scent, not only from the scarlet creeper, but from all the other flowers and plants, was so heavy and heady, that Shambu might indeed have thought this the most perfect part of his long day.

But then, on such an evening, Samina, Shambu's eldest sister, had also abruptly gone from home. She would be fourteen now.

As with Puli, in the weeks following Samina's departure, the tension in his parents had grown. It was not the tension which the dreadful heat brought every summer, wearing adult nerves finer and finer. It was something else. At night his parents would whisper fiercely to each other, thinking the children were asleep. Shambu, too tired to make out the words, had nevertheless detected the tension in their voices.

On the way to the fields, Shambu would ask his two remaining sisters, both older than him, what was happening. They only shrugged. Shambu did not bother enquiring of his three younger brothers: they were of an age when children were still allowed to play, chasing lizards, or using slingshots to try and bring down the flying foxes, as large as falcons, which circled and wheeled above the surface of the pond where the women beat their clothes and the sacred cows walked, spattering the banks with dung.

Ahead the track forked, one path heading for the village, the other leading down to the river which fed the pond. For ten months of the year it was a sluggish canal, covered with algae. When the rains came it became a brown torrent, overflowing into the village, a rush of stagnant water turning dust into mud, which in turn was turned by the sun back into dust.

Beyond the river, partly hidden by the mango trees, was a glow from the ghats, the embers of a funeral pyre for the latest death in the village, a still-born baby.

From the track Shambu could make out the small group of mourners, the men naked in the heat save for their trousers, the women huddled together. Later, one of them would remember him standing there, the setting sun giving him an ethereal-like quality.

Shambu watched one of the men, perhaps the father of the dead infant, prodding the pile of burning wood to encourage the flames to consume the tiny corpse, so that the family could go home.

In this community death is something to be quickly disposed of, the body to be turned into ash before the sun sets. What visible grief there is, is brief: from the moment of death there is nothing left of the person which, in life, has been loved, or perhaps hated.

From the time he could comprehend, Shambu had been told by his parents that his body was only a form which might give him pleasure, but more likely pain. They had said that on his way back from his first family funeral pyre – lit to mark the death of another sister. She had been a year younger than Samina.

Soon there would be another mouth to feed; his mother was once more heavy with child.

Perhaps, Shambu had suggested to his sisters, this was the reason for their parents' tension. The girls had still only shrugged. Shambu had persisted, saying he could not remember his mother and father behaving like this in the months before his little brothers were born. His sisters told him to stop such foolish talk. Yet he should have remembered a similar tension in his parents prior to Puli going. But the family had never eaten better than in those weeks afterwards.

Nor was there a mystery any longer over what had happened to Samina. In this community there are no secrets for long.

His sister had been sold by their father to a relative in that place which for centuries has made Lahore renowned throughout India. Samina had become a whore in the walled city's Heera Mandi, the district first described by Rudyard Kipling, whose pen gave its opium dens and brothels a glamour which has never quite faded. Many an impoverished Indian parent still arranges for an unwanted daughter to be sent to Heera Mandi. It has long been an outpost of slavery.

The girls remain what they were in Kipling's day – among the youngest, most attractive and highly trained of Asia's millions of prostitutes. But where their predecessors had entertained the officers of the Raj, their clients nowadays are rich Arabs from the Gulf States, Saudi Arabia, Iraq and Syria. They often arrive in Lahore aboard their private aircraft, prepared to pay from eight thousand rupees (£260) up to twenty thousand rupees (£660) for a night with a girl. Occasionally, an unusually pretty child is bought outright for a substantial sum and flown to a desert palace. No one ever hears of her again.

Once past their prime, those who remain in Heera Mandi find their life is brutish and generally short-lived. Most die in their late teens from disease or drugs and, more recently, AIDS. In an average year Heera Mandi turns over between fifteen to twenty thousand girls, bought-in and sold-off as casually as the sex on offer. Under the United Nations' definition of modern slavery, the girls are sexual slaves, totally owned and exploited by their keepers.

Shambu's sister would never return home, and her only contact with the family was the handful of rupees which arrived intermittently from the relative in Lahore. Samina had not been sold into prostitution for a single payment, but on a less favourable contract, which stipulated that a small proportion of her earnings would be sent to her family only as long as she worked. With so many parents prepared to sell-off their daughters it was still a buyer's market.

There was no news of Puli from the day he had gone. Shambu's first questions about his brother had been met by angry silence from his father. Finally, his mother had said Puli would also never return home, and there was no more to be said. Since then, within the family, no one spoke of either child.

Their *chakra*, the wheel of destiny which governs every member of the community, had turned beyond discussion.

The village stood in silhouette against the fading light. From the trees around the huts came a fearful row – an unorchestrated chorus of birdsong and animal sounds. The stillness of the evening was shattered by the infernal noise. Shambu quickened his step, knowing that the day was close to ending, as surely as the mongooses would end the lives of the first of the mice foolhardy enough to venture forth in the twilight in search of food.

There was a timelessness about it all, and Shambu, guiding the water-buffalo home, might reasonably have expected that the even routine of his own life would only be interrupted when the day came for him to marry, and later, with the birth of his first child. When old enough, that child would assume the responsibility for herding a beast.

This has been the way of life among the community for two thousand years and longer, a value-system which has survived invasion, pillage and civil war. Now to this world, once more, came the slaver.

In the last moments of light, the air grew still more pungent and heavy from the aroma of burning wood chips and cow dung the village women used to heat their ovens for the evening meal, and the yellow dust raised by animals being herded home a little faster.

During the three years he had driven the buffalo back and forth along the track, the great and greedy banyans which lined either side had sent down more branches. Each worked their way into the poor soil, taking root and claiming another piece of the ground. Further down the track, where it joined the surfaced road, there was a banyan which covered acres, a virtual forest which at the same time remained a single living tree.

Growing redder by the minute, Surya, the sun god, slipped towards the horizon, encouraged by the village flutists to go to his place of rest after another day of warming up the earth. Shambu could see the musicians squatting outside the mud-walled huts. In the failing light came the soft thumping of a hand drum, then another,

4

improvisations which blended with the fluting. It was a sound older than measured time.

At some point along the track Shambu saw something which was not a part of this familiar scene. Parked before his house was an old truck, with high sides and wire mesh across the top and back. It was like a cage on wheels.

A stranger stood talking to his father on the verandah running the length of the three-roomed hut. They were so deep in conversation they never so much as glanced up at his approach. Nevertheless, instinct may have told Shambu he should run and hide – but hide where? In the jungle the jackals would scream louder as they grew bolder and crept closer, the first of them making its sudden dart, tearing at his flesh. At dawn the greedy vultures would swoop down and pick over what was left. There was no hiding place. Shambu continued to drive the buffalo forward, anxious to reach the only place of safety he knew: the inside of his home.

One room was where all the children slept, a second, their parents' bedroom. The third was where they ate after Shambu's mother rang a small handbell to warn off the evil spirits, and his father trimmed the oil lamp so that its flame burned steadily before the tinted photographs of the tutelary Hindu gods in their gold-painted frames who, between them, managed the lives of every family member. There was Rama, the great and wise; Sita, goddess of all that was sown and harvested; Ganesh, the bringer of good fortune through his elephant head; Lakshmi, ready to dispense health upon all who gazed on her serene face. Set apart from them was a reproduction of Krishna, his face bent towards a bowl of butter, a reminder that the Cowhead god is the most dearly loved by all Hindus.

At this hour Shambu's mother should have been at the open-air clay oven. Instead, she sat idle before the rice-husking machine, not unlike an old-fashioned Singer sewing machine listening to what the stranger was saying.

Shambu may have wondered if the man was either the *zemindar*, the local landowner, or one of his representatives. But then, if he thought again, he would have realized this was an unlikely hour for such an exalted person to come calling to raise such questions of endless dispute as the price of land and rights of way. Such matters are discussed only at sunrise, when men have slept and can argue more calmly.

Then the sun disappeared, and night closed over the village as if it had suddenly and completely been enveloped in a heavy and impenetrable curtain.

Shambu guided the bullock to the lean-to at the back of the hut. He moved quickly, no doubt anxious to be done, possibly reassured by the familiar sounds and movements all around him in

5

the darkness. Men were going to borrow or settle with the *mahajan*, the village moneylender and pawnbroker, and often the community bloodsucker, who asked for and obtained, up to one thousand per cent interest on a loan. Women were busy at the *golas*, the small grain silos which were an integral part of every home. Children who did not yet have to work still had enough energy to play.

The mynah birds had started their nightly concert as Shambu drove the animal past the well his family shared with three others. The clumps of bamboo around the water-hole rustled in the breeze which briefly sighed across the land every nightfall. By the time Shambu tethered the animal the stars were out and the air was filled with the other sounds of the night: the rustling of a whole menagerie of small beasts and the hum of insects.

Shambu was still standing beside the bullock when the stranger appeared, followed by his father. The man was strong, lean and tall and wore a city dweller's suit, not a loin cloth like his father wore, tucked up between his legs to make it easier to walk. His father told Shambu that the stranger had come to take him to Puli. From inside the house came the sound of his mother crying. The stranger grasped Shambu firmly by the arm and led him to the truck.

Perhaps this was the moment Shambu would have remembered that on the nights Puli and the other boys disappeared, a truck like the stranger's had also been in the village. It had then driven away, gathering speed as it passed the smouldering funeral ghats. Even if he had remembered any of this, it would have made no difference. For his parents his body was already a thing of the past, like those of Puli and Samina, never to be spoken openly of again. For them to survive they had once more disposed of their own flesh and blood into slavery.

THE ENFORCERS OF HOPE

Some people look for motives. I just want results. Evil is evil. Corruption is corruption. Those who deal in it won't find me forgiving their actions or regretting their death. It may be true that life is not something that anyone can train for. But my job helps.

Excerpt from author's interview with John D (Jack) O'Malley, Special Agent, Department of the Treasury, US Customs Service, Office of Enforcement, 21 June 1988.

When I see a new case I always think of the two verses from the Book of Job. "Again there was a day when the sons of God came to present themselves before the Lord, and Satan came also among them to present himself before the Lord. And the Lord said unto Satan 'From whence cometh thou?' And Satan answered the Lord, and said, 'From going to and from in the earth, and from walking up and down in it'." And I say to myself that nowadays the Devil seems to do most of his walking among the kids of the world. That's the really scary part of life today.

Excerpt from author's interview with Charles Houston Pickett, Supervisory Technical Advisor and Director of Investigations, National Center for Missing and Exploited Children, Washington DC, 14 June 1988.

TWO

Susan And The Sting Master

In a comfortably old-fashioned family house in a suburb of Orange County, California, the kind of day it was shaping up to be, blue sky with only a tiny stack of clouds as far distant as San Diego and a cooling breeze from the Pacific, did nothing to hide the anger on Susan Davidson's face.

She now knew what had happened to Shambu. After the boy's father had sold him for US $70, the going price, to a trafficker named Gupta, the man had driven Shambu and other boys he had also bought, to Karachi. The port is an important centre for the trade in children. They are bought and sold in their thousands every year by men like Gupta – usually to work in factories, mines and brickyards or to stock the brothels of the Middle East. The most physically handsome are despatched to wealthy private owners needing a constant supply of young flesh to satisfy their sexual passions.

Before buying Shambu, Gupta already had a purchaser for the boy, Mohammed Saleem. The portly sleek-haired Saleem confines his operations to the Gulf States – in his case providing the desert princes and princelings with child jockeys for the camel races which are traditionally part of the winter festivals of the Arabian Peninsula.

Once the riders were young Arab warriors, volunteers skilled in the dangerous art of camel racing. Then, coinciding with the oil bonanza in the 1970s, the races were redesigned to amuse the rich but bored new Arab petrobillionaires – made more dangerous by introducing a wilder breed of camel and using children to ride them. The casualties were many. Unable to find native-born parents any longer willing to sacrifice their own bloodline, the tiny riders had to be imported from India and Pakistan. Saleem quickly established himself as the man for the job.

During the three winter months of the camel racing season in 1987, Susan's sources had reported that Saleem made US $700,000 from trafficking in children – even after he had paid-off the officials, police, customs and immigration officers, to look the other way as he went about his business.

Susan had no doubt they all had collaborated at every stage of Shambu's final journey – right up to the moment when the little boy was tied to the back of a camel and the beast began to race over the sands. After a short distance, the camel unseated Shambu. The boy fell in the path of following animals and was trampled to death on a day as warm and pleasant as this California one promised to be.

The details were there in yet another report Susan had received, this one from Defence For Children International, a Geneva-based child-care agency. The report ended by saying that since Shambu's death, there had been others. Each lost life served as a tiny example of how poverty not only leads to exploitation, but how slavery continues to capitalize on a strongly held belief in the psyche of poor nations – that children are merely chattels, to be used and abused at will.

Susan knew that Shambu's death would change nothing. Nor would the deaths of all the other camel jockeys. Men like Mohammed Saleem would swiftly replace them.

That knowledge had brought the look of anger to Susan's face.

Usually people notice her wide, laughter-prone mouth, which does nothing to take away from the poise which makes her look taller than five-six, younger than her forty-four years. Her hair is auburn; worn casually short and framing a narrow, fine-boned face.

She is Executive Director of the Adam Walsh Child Resource Center.

Now in 1989, she managed a team of doctors, therapists, counsellors, social workers, and what she called 'old-fashioned do-gooders', volunteers who turned their hand to anything she asked: visiting a distressed family, monitoring court proceedings, typing up reports, licking stamps. Susan presided over them all in a kindly but firm way. Though she has no formal medical training, she worked closely with the doctors, and often advised on cases where sexual abuse left children seriously traumatized.

Privately funded, the Center's income came mostly from gifts and solicitations, as it charged no fees. It also had its critics among law-enforcement agencies – primarily because they said the Center's constant warnings of an underground traffic in humans, mostly babies for human sacrifice, were really too fanciful, even for California.

Susan would quietly remind them how the Center came to be founded.

On 27 July, 1981, six-year-old Adam Walsh was abducted from a shopping mall in Hollywood, Florida. Two weeks later his partial remains were found 150 miles north of his home. He had been a victim of a human sacrifice. Adam's parents refused to let their son's death become just another statistic. They led a national campaign which resulted in the passage of the Missing Children's Act and the establishment of the National Center for Missing and Exploited Children in Washington DC.

In December, 1983 Adam's parents founded the first Center to bear their son's name. There are now five similarly named units across the United States. The one Susan ran had opened in 1984. Its mandate is enshrined in its Articles of Inauguration, 'to protect the children of Southern California'.

To do so she kept herself informed about abuse elsewhere. A week after Shambu died, she had the details. She knew about the child slave whores of Heera Mandi where his sister, Samina, still worked. She probably knew more about child exploitation of all kinds than anyone in North America. She used the information to try and warn of what was already happening in the United States because adults remained indifferent to the plight of American children. She believed that what happened to children in the Third World and also in one of the most affluent societies on earth, was already almost indistinguishable. The police kept on asking for more proof. She continued to gather evidence. She saw it as part of her job to be 'an alarm raiser. Not an alarmist. A realist.'

Susan felt life had channelled her into her present work. As a straight-A's student, she had written a term paper on Mexican migrant workers, a quarter of whom were children, describing how many suffered from food poisoning, sunstroke and illnesses caused by prolonged exposure to the chemical pesticides used in the fruit and vegetable growing industries in California, Ohio, Oregon, Maine and Washington. Migrant children from the age of six worked ten hours a day in summer temperatures of 100 degrees Fahrenheit. Maine farmers used Indian and French-Canadian children to pick potatoes from dawn to dusk. Every year in Ohio and Oregon, some forty thousand migrant families toiled to harvest the sugar beet and cucumber crops.

She had cited the relevant international conventions broken by the use of child labour in the United States. Widespread exploitation of this kind, she wrote, was caused by a blatant disregard of existing legislation by employers concerned only with profits, and by the desperate economic needs of the children's own parents, who saw their only hope of surviving was to commit the entire family to work from the earliest possible age.

Those who interviewed her for her present job said they were impressed by the way she had kept in touch with the matter. She replied it was only part of the activities of modern-day slavers which

11

concerned her, going on to explain that while there has always been a demand for children as cheap labour, they are now being increasingly exploited for sexual purposes.

She described how, in Brazil, wealthy families still bought infant girls from starving parents. As the children grew, they were used by the sons of the household to gain sexual experience. When the girls reached puberty they were sold off to procurers and ended their lives in prostitution. She explained why, in Thailand, the idea of giving away or selling a child was permissible, and even lauded; it was no more than an extension of the ancient Thai Buddhist-based tradition of presenting a boy to a monk. She told them about a brothel in Bangkok in which children had been chained to their beds between being forced to service customers for twenty hours a day. Their prison had caught fire and a number of the little girls, all under the age of ten, were burned to death.

Her listeners had shuddered and said thank God that was not happening in California.

She told them what was happening in California. They had sat, white faced and drained, as she outlined a number of scenarios.

A social service worker in Los Angeles receives information about the physical and sexual abuse of numerous children by the staff of a popular day center. A police officer in the backwoods of San Francisco discovers several children are victims of sexual mistreatment, including being posed for pornographic photographs. In Sacramento, the director of an emergency shelter reports an alarming rate of venereal disease among his wards. The children are selling themselves for money to buy drugs. In San Diego the police learn of a private club that promotes nude dancing by underage girls. These all appear to be separate cases. They are treated as such. No one looks to see the links. I want to make the connections. I want to show there may be as many as a million-and-a-half children in the United States who are being victimized. I want to fight for them. I want to fight all those who enslave them.

Without further deliberation, they said she could. She had got the job.

One of Susan's many guiding principles was that once she was convinced something was true, nothing would shake her. She was certain that slavery in all its forms was rampant throughout the State of California; that what was happening here and now was every bit as shocking and frightening as the fate of children in the Third World.

Susan was now certain among much else, that babies were being bred for sacrifice within the State, and more were also being smuggled into the country from Mexico and other Latin American countries for a similar purpose.

Such claims made her a further bane of law-enforcement and other child-care agencies in North America. They challenged her sources, doubted her evidence and scorned her as a populist. She resolutely ignored their criticism, simply asking: 'Why would I make any of it up? Why would anyone?' No one had yet answered those questions to her satisfaction.

She continued to lead a one-woman war against all sources of child exploitation. Though she kept the Center's activities at a low key level, there were regular threatening telephone calls and she and her staff had been followed to and from work. Most unsettling of all were the anonymous faces in parked cars, just watching the building for hours at a time. Some of the staff resigned. She respected their feelings: everybody had a threshold beyond which they could not go. Even when she told them, she realized only a few really understood what drove her – the visceral burning memory of what was done to her as a child, coupled with a commitment to stop it happening to other children. This driving force made her truly formidable.

Her growing conviction that something evil, almost unspeakably so, continued to happen out in the desert, where those babies were being bred, and other fearful things were going on at a place she simply called the Ranch, had once more preoccupied her from the time she woke up.

Susan had worked late, finalizing a solicitation to the board of a fruit company, trying to strike a balance between statistics and case histories. It was never easy. She had hesitated over whether to include a paragraph about the growing number of Roman Catholic priests convicted of gross child abuse. Recently the Church had paid $5 million to nine families whose sons were sexually violated by their parish priest in a remote township in Louisiana.

The image of what the boys had endured further focussed Susan's mind on what was happening out in the desert. She had been told that priests were involved in the Ranch, and had decided to leave in the paragraph. If the executives who read her report were shocked into asking questions, so much the better. It might lead to them calling for action from the police.

Learning to see the world as the law did had been a slow and painful process for her – just as knowing about the suffering of one child for a single hour longer than she could prevent it, affected her deeply.

Susan had no difficulty in imagining the look in the eyes of the children held at the Ranch. It would be the same terror-struck vulnerability she saw on faces of other children when they first came to the Center. Sometimes it almost made her physically ill to see the results of what had been done to them.

She spent hours with the children alone, coaxing them out of their listlessness and withdrawal, trying to make them eat, helping them cope with and understand their sudden outbursts of rage and violence, and those equally difficult periods of guilt-ridden silence.

Susan had told Lee, her husband, that having to confront human anguish, hour after hour, knowing how to ask a question and when to remain silent but still a sympathetic observer: that this kind of psychotherapy is perhaps the hardest work anybody can do.

Some nights when she returned home, Susan felt she had 'surfaced from a slime pit'. Lee would hold her close and say someone had to do it, and how proud he was it was her. He would remind her of her successes. How he had seen her work the miracle of bringing life back to dulled eyes, and hope to voices which had been without any when they had first spoken to her. She had shown families how to reach out and literally support each other, and begin to live again. It was very wonderful, the way she could do all that.

Next day she would plunge back into work, with her usual monomania, dealing with the kinds of abuse done to children which, when she began to tell others about it, frequently made them turn away, uncomfortable and guilty looking. She realized that while people were prepared to lend support – sending a cheque in the name of some corporation or chain store – they wanted to be spared the details. Her kind of work played on their primal fears: the there-but-for-the-grace-of-God-go-my-family syndrome.

But she still tried to make people face all kinds of unpleasant realities. Paedophiles could live next door, and often the only extraordinary thing about them was that they seemed so ordinary – they might be well-mannered and middle-aged or even elderly men with kindly smiles. Sometimes they were younger members of the professional classes, lawyers and doctors, stockbrokers and market analysts, and the hardest of all for Susan to convince people about, some among them were cops, clergymen and social workers.

Then there were the wives. All too often they were women who found sex or any form of physical intimacy repugnant, and in order to escape from it, encouraged their men to seek satisfaction elsewhere. Usually the men did so with children. There were a lot of theories why, none of them, in Susan's view, proven. All she knew was that the age and helplessness of the children made them easy targets. Susan knew, because it had happened to her.

Susan's first clear recollection was that her nightmare began in Prestcott, a small Arizona township. She was five-years-old and her

14

mother was already on the way to her own self-destruction, venting her dark anger and rage in rampages of violence. Little Susan had not known which was more frightening, her mother drunk and berserk, or maudlin.

On that night in Prestcott her mother was drunk again. From her bedroom Susan had heard raised voices and the sound of crashing glass and crockery. Then had come an extra loud bang, like someone falling, followed by silence. Susan had been too frightened to investigate. After a while, the silence ended with footsteps coming up the bare stairtreads and along the corridor to her bedroom. The man, whose name she had never known, stood in the doorway wearing only a shirt and socks. She tried to hide beneath the sheets, curling her feet inside her nightdress, calling for her Mommy. The stranger had pulled the covers aside and thrown himself on top of her, his weight crushing her, driving out the air from her body. She tried to force him away. He pinned her arms above her head with one hand. She had screamed: 'Mommy! Mo—mee.'

She was five-years-old, and did not know then that she had lost her virginity, because she did not know what a virgin was. Nor did she understand she had been sexually abused, because she did not know what sex was. All she knew was that she hated what the man did, and that it hurt her very much. In the years which followed, other men had also hurt her. No matter how loud she had screamed, her mother never came. One day as she had cried out, the man sprawled on top of her shouted. 'Your Ma ain't gonna help you, girl! She gave you to me.'

Susan had whimpered that could not be true, that her Mommy would never do such a terrible thing. The man had hurt her particularly badly.

After that experience, Susan had learned never again to shout for her mother. When she was nineteen she fled into marriage, accepting the proposal of the first man who asked her to be his wife. She divorced him after ten years. Seven years later, after a few brief and unsatisfactory relationships while setting down a basis for a successful business career, she married again, convinced she could save her new husband from his alcoholism and drug-taking. The marriage lasted only weeks. She divorced once more.

A year later she met Lee. Meeting him was still the best thing that had happened to her. It made all the past pain not only bearable but also, finally, understandable. They had explored together her past. She became secure enough to tell him of terrible things she had told no one about and, which were buried deep in her subconscious.

What Susan found so remarkable was that Lee knew, instinctively, how to respond. When the hideous dreams finally broke through into her consciousness, he sat with her through the long nights, a

15

fearful time as the nocturnal predators in her mind had emerged: razor-tongued serpents, slimy creatures, each with a human face, of the men who had abused her. For months Susan had poured out her recollections. Then one day the purging was over. 'The darkness no longer presses upon me. That awful fetid thing has gone from me,' she told Lee.

She had explained she felt different, a whole person. There and then, she had promised God she would try and devote the rest of her life to helping others to survive. Shambu, she could do nothing about, except include him in her prayers. But she could still fight for all the other children, especially those at the Ranch.

What was happening there was more frightening than anything she had ever encountered. This July morning in 1989 she wondered again if she should tell O'Malley. She hardly knew him. How would he respond? Would he listen politely – and then say she had better try some other agency to stop what was happening out in the desert? Or would he mobilize his powerful forces to fight with her?

Over a thousand miles away from where Susan pondered, O'Malley drove his unmarked government car through the outer suburbs of Chicago listening to the continuous cross-talk from the police radio under the dashboard.

He too waged war, day and night, months at a time without let-up, against child slavery. He did so in the name of the United States government, and in one particular area – against the world-wide production and distribution of child pornography. An estimated 95 per cent of all this pornography was targeted at the United States. There were various theories as to why this was happening, none of which O'Malley found plausible. For him it was enough it was happening.

Experience had taught him that those involved were cost-efficient, selecting their product with care and marketing it with skill. In everything they did, they were acquisitive and exploitive beyond belief. Untold tens of thousands of women and children were destroyed every year by pornographers. The vaults of the great financial houses in London, New York, Paris and Hong Kong all held their vast deposits of laundered money made from such trafficking in humans. O'Malley had read, in one of the statistical surveys which crossed his desk, that the global profits in 1988 from sexual slavery was an estimated $1 million an hour.

O'Malley liked his working life contained in more understandable measurables, in the same way he liked the faint hum of the air conditioning of his office, the click-clacking of computer keyboards, the muted ring of telephones, the state-of-the-art video players on which to view the latest seizures. He knew some agents felt uncomfortable in the hi-tech atmosphere. They never stayed long, transferring to drug enforcement or the Secret Service. It was not so much that he ever said anything, but rather they themselves sensed they did not belong.

It did not happen very often because he chose a man carefully, looking beyond whether he was a good investigator, to whether he could work well in a team. A newcomer must immediately understand that there was no scope for him unless he had worked out the fine balance between ruthlessness and conscience by the time he stepped out of the lift for the first time on the eighth floor of the building in downtown Chicago.

Forty-five agents worked on the other seven floors. Between them they dealt with arms smuggling, fraud, currency violations and drugs. They often worked closely together.

The men on the eighth floor were a team apart. Except for O'Malley, only two other men in the whole world knew everything about Special Operations. The Commissioner of Customs in Washington was one. John Sullivan, head of the Office of Enforcement, was the other. He rarely called to ask what was happening. His trust in O'Malley was total. O'Malley had told his superior that the minute he felt otherwise, he would quit. It was not a threat. Rather it was a statement that O'Malley could not operate in any other way.

Among themselves, its habitués call the eighth floor 'The Parish House', and O'Malley 'Father'. Recently, they had taken to calling him 'The Sting Master'. He liked that.

More formally, when an agent from one of the other Federal agencies came visiting, mostly men from the FBI or DEA, though sometimes from the CIA, the desk man solemnly asked if the visitor had come to see John D. O'Malley, Special Agent, Investigations Division, Department of the Treasury, United States Customs Service, Office of Enforcement.

O'Malley knew it was their knockabout way of showing respect for him.

As he drove to work, his mind was preoccupied with an operation centred on Germany, with links to the Philippines and perhaps other Asian countries.

O'Malley knew more than most men about how the hauntingly lovely women and girls of the Pacific Rim nations are bought or stolen to service the sex markets of the First and Second Worlds. There was now not a major city in Western Europe or North America which did not have its number of Asians sold into prostitution or the pornography industry.

Nor is it only heterosexuals the slavers cater for. Increasingly, with AIDS sweeping the Western world, they promote the boys and youths of the region.

17

Every day planes filled with American and European paedophiles land at Bangkok and Manila airports in search of under-age sex.

In Bangkok there are multi-floored massage parlours, employing up to a thousand girls and boys a day; brothels with hundreds of bedrooms; 'bondage centres' where men, women and even small children are regularly beaten with a variety of whips and instruments; clubs which specialize in animal sex floor shows – acts in which young girls and boys have oral sex with dogs or are penetrated by mules. Nothing is too gross.

In 1989 Japan's thriving sex-for-sale industry continued to depend on young foreign women and children, imported from Manila, Bangkok and Seoul. The older women were brought from Amsterdam, Stockholm and, not infrequently, London.

The slavers have purchased travel agencies, hotels and a financial interest in some of the charter airlines flying from Europe and North America to Asia. Their activities help to make sex tourism the third largest gross earner in Thailand, and the fourth in the Philippines in 1989.

In the private screening rooms of Europe's self-styled 'pornokings', the men and women who make fortunes out of sexual exploitation are always on the lookout for new faces and bodies. One company alone, ZBF, had a turnover of DM60 million in 1988 which included revenue from a catalogue of explicit material as thick as a London telephone directory. Twice a year buyers from all over the world travel to ZBF's headquarters near Wiesbaden to sample the company's newest range of pornographic magazines, books and films. It is all perfectly legal.

As West Germany firmly established itself in the forefront of sexual permissiveness, its underworld had developed close ties, in particular with the Philippines, to ensure a continuous supply of young women for the Federal Republic's legalized brothels and massage parlours.

The German traffic in women is often tacitly encouraged by those who should be fighting it. Some police officers argue that stocking-up brothels with Asian women is simply fulfilling the natural law of supply and demand, given that fewer German women wanted the work, and that, further, there is the bonus of keeping prostitution off the streets, out of sight of impressionable German youth. O'Malley thought it could not have been better expressed by any of the slavers.

He also found it ironic that West Germany, one of the richest countries on earth, continued to add to its wealth by allowing the trade in the poor, uneducated and invariably desperate women and children of the Third World – ironic that such a distinction fell to the nation which was responsible for the single most widespread use of slavery during this century. The slaves of the Third Reich were the

18

property of the State, and its industrial and manufacturing concerns. In 1989 the slaves of the Bundesrepublik remain the chattels of their sexual exploiters.

Now another of them had come to his notice. So far he had little more than a name to go on – Riki Sturmer – and an address in West Germany. But he had often begun an operation with a lot less and won. The trick was not to rush – just as he would not rush into deciding what he was going to do about Susan Davidson's request for help.

She had explained she was given his number by Charlie Pickett at the National Center for Missing and Exploited Children in Washington, DC. That was the first check made by the agent who took her call. Pickett described Susan as 'having an abundance of the two Cs – concern and commitment.'

A check was made on the Center. It was run like any other 'for profit' business; a franchise, with 20 per cent of its donations going to the Adam Walsh parent organization in Florida. The Center's supporters included the usual mix of California organizations who find it advantageous to be associated with a child-care agency. Disneyland, Hostess Cake, Polaroid, Toshiba and several banks were listed as contributors. Another was the Orange County Sheriffs Association.

The agent had written a short report on Susan's claim about the Ranch, and her request for an undercover operation to obtain evidence to convict its operators.

O'Malley continued to listen to the radio transmissions, dominated by the voice of the dispatcher. The car was his to use as he saw fit. The radio in case of trouble. He had never had to pick up the handset to patch himself into the net and give his call-sign to request urgent assistance. To summon help would probably mean he had not properly calculated beforehand the dangers. He came down hard on agents who failed to do that. But, of course, as a last resort he would use the police radio; he was not given to Hollywood heroics.

O'Malley listened to the dispatcher the way he would follow the action of a game on television, observing but not allowing it to involve him. He had once thought through the entire strategy for setting up an Iranian for an arms-for-opium sting during a Superbowl game.

Long ago, O'Malley had decided there was no way law enforcement could really win nowadays. But when an agent asked, then why do we bother?, he would tell him. Because society *paid* them to bother. Because *somebody* had to bother. *And because I say we are going to bother*.

Yet, despite such commitment, he knew the market for kiddie porn had reached unprecedented levels. In the United States it grossed at least $3 billion a year, in West Germany it yielded an estimated annual revenue of over DM200 million, and in Britain netted over £30 million a year. If anything, O'Malley thought the figures on the low side.

All he could be certain about was that the market was expanding. By 1990 there would be over 20 million copies of child pornographic videos sold or rented each year in the United States; the figure world-wide would exceed 250 million. Based on an average price of $25 to buy, or a couple of dollars to rent a copy, the figures made child pornography not only a multi-million-dollar industry, but part of the largest segment of movie-making in the United States. The product produced larger profits than all the TV networks, or Hollywood studios made each year. Pornographers ran the biggest film-making operation in the world. O'Malley sometimes called it 20th Century Filth.

His prime task was to trap those who used children to satisfy the cravings of an estimated five hundred thousand paedophiles in the United States. Between them they acquired almost all the kiddie porn produced. Two-thirds of the material was manufactured in West Germany, Holland, Denmark and Sweden. Its manufacturers depended largely on children from the Third World to pose and participate in the films. His gut instinct told O'Malley that Riki Sturmer could turn out to be a procurer of such children. But suspecting and proving it were, for the moment, poles apart.

He knew there were international treaties meant to stop such exploitation. The agreements had imposing titles: The International Convention for the Suppression of the White Slave Traffic (1904); the International Convention for the Suppression of Traffic in Women and Children (1921); the Slave Trade and Institutions and Practices Similar to Slavery Convention (1956). There are seven all told, hundreds of pages of protective legislation, approved by every civilized government. O'Malley could cite them all.

Then he would smile his pirate's smile, and say slavers do not pay any attention to high-minded agreements. He would add, no longer smiling, that despite all the conventions, there is still no international body, in 1989, directly and solely responsible for investigating the fate of children used in sexual exploitation.

Yet Norway's Justice Department had reported in 1988 that a million children were now annually bought or kidnapped from Third World countries. Most were disposed 'through false adoption agencies to paedophile rings, prostitution racketeers and traffickers in pornography'.

The slavers were becoming more brazen, routinely raiding villages in Burma and stealing women and children. They regularly snatched

20

young women from the streets of South Korean cities in daylight, bundling them into cars, and injecting them with drugs. Those who survived their brutal treatment were smuggled out of the country, usually to the Middle East. In Cairo, Damascus and Athens, their market value doubled. They were either put to work in local brothels or sold on to European brothel keepers. The younger and more attractive were equipped with appropriate papers – usually certificates for marriages of convenience – and sent to Canada. From there many eventually entered the high-earning sex markets of the United States. A girl kidnapped in Seoul and sold for an initial £100, could be worth ten times that figure when she reached New York, Chicago, Los Angeles and Houston – all cities into which Koreans have been smuggled. Those who bought them would expect to recoup their money in a few weeks.

In the United States, men like O'Malley fought a ruthless and relentless battle against such exploiters. The problem was there were never enough men, money or time to drive them all out of business. The art was to pick and choose – then go for it. Like he was going to go after Sturmer.

While kiddie porn remained his main concern, he had begun to look at other related areas.

The latest figures from the National Center for Adoption had caught his attention. There were two million couples in the United States waiting to adopt a child and the number increased each year. But there were only around fifty thousand children available for adoption – and the figure was dropping. The imbalance had created a growing demand for children from abroad. Over nine thousand a year were being legally brought into the United States. But legal adoption was a complicated and time-consuming affair.

Slavers had been quick to exploit the situation. They regularly stole babies in a number of Asian and South American countries and sold them to childless couples in North America and Europe. A couple would pay up to $50,000 for a child. Again, no precise figures existed, but child-care agencies suggested there could be as many as thirty thousand children a year being smuggled. The profit from such traffic could amount to $15 million a year.

O'Malley's concern was whether some of the children brought into the United States are being used for child sex rings, prostitution and pornography and now, after what Susan had said, as human sacrifices.

He remained uncertain where she would, could, or should fit into his complex plans. He wondered what sort of woman she was, and what motivated her. To check her allegations would mean his making a commitment – and that was always something he was slow to do until he was certain what was involved. Cruising through the morning traffic, he once more sent Susan off to the outer recesses of his mind, concentrating on other matters.

Spotting a gap in the flow of the Chicago morning rush-hour, he accelerated, gunning the car for a block before easing back into the stream. At moments like this, O'Malley sometimes wondered how many children had died at the hands of the men he hunted. Yet his gun with its shrouded hammer was strictly back-up. He preferred using his formidable intellect against them.

He started to think if there was, as some said, an underlying cultural trend which had led to a significant increase in child sexual exploitation. What was it that now made it so often the prerogative of the middle class? Why did they have to get off on dirty movies? What could the attraction possibly be in watching them? Sometimes he thought it was all part of a new evolution in which evil had its own metamorphic intelligence which was creeping across the world, swamping it in dirt.

By the time he had covered another block, the dispatcher had sent cars to assist a patrolman at a break-in, to deal with an EDP, an emotionally disturbed person, and to help an SCU, one of the Street Crime Units, detectives assigned to target muggers and pick-pockets.

O'Malley wondered whether the SCU team had to face the kind of bear-baiting he did from Civil Rights lawyers. They tried to pin labels on him like 'enticer' and 'entrapper'. When his evidence had put another of their clients behind bars, their attorneys looked at him coldly and asked if he really got pleasure from what he did?

He would stare at them and walk away, saying nothing, thinking he wouldn't go on if he didn't enjoy the job.

Work satisfaction had always been a prime consideration. It had driven him through school, and later to graduate near the top of the Class of '71 from North Illinois. At college he had studied journalism and still had a newsman's eye for the dramatic. He had wanted a job which allowed him to use the other dominating elements of his personality – a natural fearlessness coupled, unusually, with a caution where everything had to be proven to the last legal full stop.

He had joined the Internal Revenue Service as an investigator, and had finally quit, because the long-term prospects were not commensurate with the energy he devoted to the job. He had applied to join the FBI and the Secret Service, and came through the Federal Law Enforcement school in Georgia with one of the higher ratings in interviewing techniques, the use of firearms and surveillance. Some sixth sense told him that neither the FBI nor the Secret Service would provide the kind of return he also needed from a job – things like constant excitement, variety and fast promotion.

O'Malley drove past the first of the industrial parks filled with windowless structures that, if they resembled anything, resembled oversized tombs. The air smelled toxic. He wondered about the life expectancy of those who spent their lives inside them.

One of the attractions of his job was that he could always get out, work the street, pit his wits against those who lived off theirs. Out there was his who-dares-wins world. If he was not doing what he did, he supposed he would rather have enjoyed working for the CIA. He knew he had the right kind of covert mind.

That was why it had taken him so long to find his niche in crime-busting, until one day John Sullivan called from the Customs Service. He said he was looking for a committed investigator, someone who would not worry about the hours and was street-wise. The job paid a basic $30,000 a year, plus $6,000 to cover all overtime. There was also a government car, the right to carry a gun, and the authority of a police detective. O'Malley had chosen a handgun, taken a drop in his Federal grade and a $5,000 cut in salary. The job sounded promising enough to make those sacrifices worthwhile.

Five years later he was still there, now Head of Special Operations, the élitist unit which tackled only the most difficult and dangerous assignments. When its members showed signs of being daunted, he would encourage them with a reminder: 'David floored Goliath with a slingshot. Think what we can do with our technology.'

Though he had not yet decided to harness it for Susan's request over the Ranch, he would use that to hunt down Riki Sturmer.

THREE

The Super Cops

Inspector Prentice Earl Sanders, a homicide detective with the San Francisco police department, stood in the doorway of a trauma room in one of the city's hospitals. He knew that a younger investigator, less experienced, might have gone forward to the bedside, anxious to question the dying man who was the subject of intensive medical activity.

Sanders wondered if the same force drove doctors which motivated him. Yet that instinct also told him when to let go; that a case, for any number of good reasons, was not going to be solved.

He wondered if the rookie standing guard at the door would ever come to understand that. A few whispered questions had told him all he needed to know about the kid: twenty-two years old, six months out of the academy and still to see someone die. From the corner of his eye he could see the young officer continue to stare frozen-faced at what was happening around the bed.

To date Sanders had investigated 509 homicides, solving most within a short time. At fifty years of age he was one of the most experienced detectives on the force. Polite and gentle-mannered, he was guided by strong religious convictions. Most colleagues spoke of him with affection; a few still harboured resentment over the way he, a black, had championed his people's cause within the force. He had broken the white, ethnic Irish domination of the department with the same quiet determination he brought to his work. His calm, penetrating stare was infinitely more feared than all the bluster and loud-mouthing of some policemen. On the street, he was known as a man to be respected. The word was that he could not be bought or coerced, that he would not even accept a free coffee. From the first day he entered police academy, he was determined to be a credit to his race, an example for other blacks to follow. He saw himself as self-contained, but dependent on others, knowledgeable, but willing to know more.

24

The rookie stirred uneasily and asked if the man was really going to die. Sanders nodded and continued to watch the bedside scene.

Learning to cope emotionally with death, either actual or impending, was something the academy did not teach. It had taken him years to acquire the proper distance and respect for death. In his work, he saw it at its most violent, and an essential was to be able to deal with a body in all its gruesome reality, if needs be, sniffing at it, touching it, kneeling in its blood and juices and doing it all in a way he called intimacy without emotion. With that went the adrenalin surging at the right moment, the kind of snap judgement which often decided between success and failure out there on the streets and alleys, on a rooftop or in a basement, in all those places where the stakes were often mortal – where it was kill or be killed.

Once more the rookie broke Sanders' reverie. 'You ever see one of those cases Officer Gallant deals with? She spooked us out when she came to the academy. Some of it was real wild. Devil symbols. Voodoo signs. Human sacrifices. Real wild.'

Sanders shook his head, chuckling softly and never taking his eyes off the bed. This wasn't the time or place to tell the kid about Gallant. Like him, he was only trained in the checks and balances of law enforcement, where evidence is described and tagged, dated and cross-referenced, secured in plastic bags and signed for. Gallant was something else.

When the man on the bed finally gave up, Sanders would bag the bullets which had just been removed from his body, and dropped in a bowl. Bag his watch, wallet and neckchain. Bag anything which could be used to get a conviction.

Gallant worked in a different world. Investigator Sandra Daly Gallant said there were crimes committed where none of this was possible – ritual crimes performed by people who wore medieval-style robes and masks and offered up prayers to the Devil before they killed. Often they ate their victims. Usually those victims were babies. Generally the perpetrators didn't leave a scrap of evidence around.

Sanders knew the cynics on the force still shook their heads and growled what the hell was crime-detection coming to when the department now needed a specialist in ritual murder. Murder was murder. They had tagged her Satan's Cop – saying it was not much of a job to work out her time.

He accepted they were right about one thing: there was no precedent for Gallant's job.

But they were wrong about everything else. Gallant was no time-server, shunted-off by Chief Jordan into some esoteric corner of investigation after twenty-six years on the force. She still had her desk in Intelligence, the unit which tried to detect trends in criminal behaviour and anticipate which way the wheel-of-crime was turning.

But he suspected why some of the old-timers distrusted her. She had joined the force as a civilian, a finger-print technician. They forgot she was a graduate in criminology who had quickly switched to uniform and worked her way up the ladder to plain-clothes investigation. She was his kind of cop. She would still be the first person he would turn to with a problem.

Maybe one day, if he made being a detective, the kid would be glad to have Gallant lend him a hand. But first he would have to get used to death; simple straightforward dying, like was happening on the bed, but still a long way from the kind of death Gallant dealt with.

She worked in a world peopled by those with a hunger for the more bizarre forms of killing, including evisceration and cannibalism, one where ritual sacrifices to the gods of Voodoo vied for her attention with the rites of Hells Angels and Satanists. There were thousands of cults throughout the State of California and the natural velocity of police work, the endless moving beltway of crime, simply meant there was no easy way for her, for anyone, to keep track of all the sects, covens and 'families'.

Sanders knew only too well there was only so much police manpower available – and even that was only allowed to stretch into huge overtime payments when, what Gallant called one of the 'mysteries', alarmed the public and had them hounding the mayor.

He had never had a case like that, thank God. And this one wasn't going to blot his record. It probably wouldn't even make the local evening news. It was just another little score being settled, probably one drug pusher paying-off another. Hardly worth standing around for. Hardly worth posting the rookie as guard.

But the kid was right: Gallant could spook anybody – make even the most experienced investigator feel he was back in class.

What had happened at Bakersfield showed that. Bakersfield is a fast-growing community at the southern end of California's Central Valley, little different from any other such community. Then one morning in 1987, some of the town's children had told the local police about rituals in which they had been forced to partake. They involved knives, swords, mysterious potions, dead animals, blood, urine and faeces. Some of the children insisted they had watched live babies being cut-up and the pieces boiled and eaten.

The police dug up a field where the children said the infants' bones were buried. Nothing was found. They had dredged a lake where the children said remains were dumped. No trace of human flesh or bone was discovered. They thoroughly searched the homes of a number of suspects. No evidence emerged. The police were still looking for proof.

Gallant said the use of children as an essential part of a cult's

26

activities was still a new and unbelievable phenomenon to many of her colleagues. She had told him she understood their reaction. Policemen looked for explanations which made sense, especially to juries. For cops, it made no sense to claim that human sacrifices had taken place when there was no evidence apart from the uncorroborated testimony of small children.

Yet, there was hardly a week that went by, she had also told him, without her receiving new reports on cemetery desecrations, grave robberies, mutilations of the dead, bizarre teenage suicides, and always, devil worshippers in black robes sacrificing animals and humans – usually babies. The overwhelming source of the reports were children. Why would so many different children lie? She didn't know – and he certainly had no idea.

He glanced at the rookie. 'Won't be long now.'

The officer nodded, throat working.

Sanders chuckled. 'Betcha listening to Officer Gallant made you feel worse, uh? Got the old imagination going? Right?'

The rookie tried to smile.

Another soft chuckle, eyes missing nothing of the drama Sanders sensed was coming to its climax.

Some of his more sceptical colleagues said the allegations about ritual crimes only made sense when looked at from what was happening in society itself. Since the liberalizing Sixties, children had obtained unparalleled freedoms. Often, with that freedom came the power of being able to point fingers which sent grown-ups to jail.

Teachers who had once praised good classwork with a hug or a kiss, had learned to tell their pupils to pat themselves on the back. Fathers were careful about playing tag with kids in the local pool or on the sports field. Childless wives who had earned a few dollars baby-sitting now looked elsewhere for pin-money. Sanders knew those who asked if America was returning to the days of the Salem witch hunts found powerful voices in the media to support them. Mike Wallace said it troubled him deeply that people were being accused of diabolical crimes, where there was no proof. Phil Donohue had asked who would stop the railroading of the innocent.

Experts continued to point out that under the Constitution, worshipping the Devil was not an offence – though there were those who argued such reverence could not possibly be called religious because there was not one sacred book or liturgy which identified it with other faiths. There were others who said that Satanism was older than all forms of worship, as old as mankind itself, and that such beliefs sprang originally not from books but from the heart, and that anyone possessing a sense of wonder and imagination and who could respond to the mood of the moment, really meant no harm in worshipping the Old Gods.

27

Yet even as he stood in the doorway, wondering whether the rookie was going to throw-up, Sanders knew that in Pennsylvania, Florida, Iowa, Michigan, Texas, other police officers continued trying to unravel chillingly similar accounts of witches and devils, of rituals and chants, all described by children who said they had been forced to drink a liquid or given an injection which had made them feel strange. In Sacramento, children had insisted they had been taken to a park, made to watch animals being sacrificed and then forced to join in sexual orgies which had ended with the ritual killing of three babies. The judge dismissed the case saying he found it impossible to distinguish those parts of the children's testimony that might be true, and evidence he found impossible to accept.

It was against this background that Gallant conducted her investigations. He really respected her – as much as he did the doctors who were refusing to give up around the bed.

Two hours ago the youth had been dealing coke and smack on Third Street. Someone had walked up and pumped three shots into him and run. Sanders' partner, detective Napoleon Hendrix, had remained at the crime scene and he had come to the hospital to ask one question: did the victim have a name for his attacker? From that all else would flow. Hopefully.

He continued to watch, waiting for the senior doctor to signal him forward. At the moment the white-coated figure was bent over the bed.

The Hispanic's heartbeat moved across the monitor beside the bed; blips pulsing on the screen, recording his grasp on life which looked increasingly tenuous.

Sanders sensed the youth was aware of his presence, but probably uncertain who he was.

People often mistook him for a lawyer or a doctor. It was the suits. He had a wardrobe of greys, blues and browns, worsteds and linens. There were shirts and ties to match. And well-soled shoes, browns and blacks. His mother had often said you could tell a lot about a man by his clothes and the shine on his shoes.

Today, in the blue pinstripe, white cotton shirt, dark blue tie with polka dots and English brogues, there was nothing about him to show that he had begun life in a Texas dustbowl township, where the kids went barefooted and the men wore patches on their trousers.

Instead, with his carefully brushed hair, greying at the temples, custom-made tortoiseshell glasses and trimmed moustache, if he wasn't an attorney or physician, he could have been taken for a politician making a quick visit to one of the more troubled outposts of his ward.

Standing there, perfectly still, watching and listening, he knew he could be anybody – just as he himself knew he was far removed from the Clint Eastwood screen character of a San Francisco homicide cop. All he had in common with Dirty Harry was the choice of weapon. They both favoured a Magnum 357.

But in twenty-one years with the force, eighteen of them in Homicide, he still had not killed anyone. He hoped he would never have to. Quite apart from his own strong religious abhorrence of killing, instilled by his mother, he had always felt that if he had to shoot someone, it would be a defeat. He preferred to track killers patiently with the help of the well-tried rules of criminal procedure, and a few he had invented for himself.

He suspected that the equipment surrounding the bed, machines that clicked and pinged, provided confirmation for the medical team that all was not yet lost. They continued to take active measures to keep death at bay. Their actions grew quicker, the commands from the senior doctor more urgent as the blips on the monitor screen became erratic.

Still Sanders waited.

He had learned to suppress any rush to action or judgement. Rushing, he would chuckle to the policemen who attended his class on homicide investigation at San José State University, could be as fatal as a corpse.

The chuckle always threw them. They didn't expect it. Just as some of them had not expected to see a black at the podium. He knew that despite all his efforts racism remained alive in pockets of the department, just as he knew he would go on fighting it.

He had promised himself to do that for his mother, since that day he had sat at her bedside, blinking back tears, not knowing what to do with his hands, his powerful shoulders sagging under the knowledge that no doctor could save her. He had been sixteen years old and, until then, death held no meaning. She had entwined her fingers in his, and gently tugged his head down towards her face. She had said how tired he looked and that he would soon start to lose his hair because of the way he drove himself. Despite his sadness he'd smiled. She had gone on inspecting him carefully, before nodding in satisfaction. Then, in a whisper that he had to bend closer to hear, she said that being born black in America was still a serious disadvantage, but that she had tried to give him the best possible education to overcome it, and that she would be content to go to her Maker if he would promise to continue to make the very best of life. Too overcome to speak, he had only been able to nod.

Two days later she had died. People, he knew, still remembered her as Loretta Young's cook. He liked to think that if she was still alive she would have said she was the mother of San Francisco's first black homicide detective.

Some said he was the best on the force – possibly the best the department had ever had. He paid no attention to such praise. Humility was another of the qualities his mother had instilled in him – along with a clear understanding that, despite the colour of his skin, he was in God's eyes equal to any white man.

That was another reason why he not only respected, but liked Gallant. From the day he had joined the force – 3 February 1964, Star Number 901 – she had supported his efforts to obtain racial equality within the department. He had fought the issue all the way, forcing it up through precinct level to the Chief's office. When the going had become rough – when other cops yelled asking what the hell was he doing, understudying Martin Luther King – she had been on hand with a cool smile and words of support. He had finally asked why she was putting her own career on the line? She shrugged and said she had once dated a black, and that no one was going to tell her he was any different to a white man. She had never mentioned her private life again, and he had not probed. But it had established a bond between them, that rare one of a genuine platonic friendship between a man and a woman. He had himself been married for twenty-five years, and if there was such a thing as a perfect marriage, then his to Espanola was the one.

He thought it must be hell for those detectives who went home to an empty apartment or a nagging wife. He looked towards the bed, wondering whether the youth was married.

The doctor turned and nodded. All those around the bed instinctively drew back as Sanders stepped into the room. He walked slowly, careful to avoid the cables on the floor skirting a red-painted surgical trolley, the 'crash cart', the ultimate emergency aid in this aseptic world.

As he edged past, none of them spoke. But he sensed their frustration which long ago he recognized was associated with the reluctance of the dying to succumb. The youth, like so many others, was simply fearful of being torn from life.

'You get a name?' he murmured to the doctor.

'Johnny.'

'Nice name.' A soft chuckle.

'He's almost gone, Inspector.' The doctor had taken refuge in professional calm. Sanders suspected that deep down, they all knew they were looking at their own ultimate fate, but the stark, sterile, and brightly lit room was not the place for such thoughts.

He bent towards Johnny's face. At his shoulder the doctor stared intently at the screen. The blips seemed slower and weaker. Sanders bent lower over the bed.

'Johnny, can you hear me?'

There was no response from the figure whose life now depended totally on the sensors attached to his chest and needles inserted in each arm.

'Johnny, I'm a police officer. Who did this to you?' He kept his voice soft and clear.

Johnny's throat moved, but no sound passed his lips.

'Johnny, just a name.' He glanced at the monitor where the blips were moving more slowly.

'A name, Johnny.' He bent still closer, his voice still low, but urging. 'Just a name.' Their faces were almost touching.

'You're out of luck, Inspector,' the doctor broke the silence, 'It's over.'

Irregular blips crossed the monitor. As Sanders looked up, they were gone. A red light flashed on the machine. The doctor checked the youth's pulse. A straight unbroken line appeared on the screen. The light no longer flashed.

The doctor and Sanders both stepped back from the bed.

'Some you win,' said the doctor, still taking refuge in professionalism.

'And some we both lose,' completed Sanders. Then quietly and without fuss he detached himself from the bedside tableau, leaving the others for the moment still silently grouped around the body.

At the door he paused and patted the rookie's arm. 'You'll be fine, son. The first one's always the worst.'

Chuckling softly, Sanders went on his way.

Out in the corridor doctors and nurses nodded to him as he passed. They instinctively knew the reason for his presence. In the busy hall the dominant odour was chemical, a combination of alcohol and disinfectant. He had never become used to it.

A gurney was being rushed towards him by scrub-suited figures. He moved over to the wall. As the gurney passed he glimpsed a child's white and frightened face. He remembered then that driving into work there had been a woman on the radio who called herself a good witch, and who had insisted that the Devil had chosen California to launch his coming, and that out in the desert he had established his mission control. He chuckled and reminded himself he must ask Gallant what was a good witch.

Shortly before eight o'clock each weekday morning Susan was ready for work. On this particular day – exactly a month after she had first telephoned O'Malley – she wore a cream suit, cream blouse and light tan shoes. It was her 'lucky' outfit, one she wore when she wanted something good to happen – on this occasion for O'Malley to agree to investigate the Ranch. She had called his office twice more. The last time an agent promised O'Malley would get back to her before the day was over. That had been ten days ago.

31

Lee stood in the kitchen with her briefcase. 'Can you make lunch?'

She reached for the case. 'Not today. I'm reviewing the file on the Ranch.'

Over a year the file had grown to over an inch thick, mostly testimony from children and their parents. None surpassed the horror of Lauren Stratfield's account of what she had endured at the Ranch.

Lauren said she and other young runaways had been brought to the Ranch after being snatched off the streets of major cities by touts promising them what they needed most – food, shelter, and above all, love. Once at the Ranch, they had been forcibly drugged. The few who resisted were brutalized. Those who still refused to co-operate had, Lauren said, 'just disappeared'.

She had described how a policeman 'had a thing about wearing only his gun as he abused me. I can still recall the sound the gun made as it slapped against his thigh.'

Night after night, for over a year, Lauren insisted she had also been sexually violated by, 'doctors, lawyers and men in the highest levels of major corporations. There were also judges, politicians and entertainers.'

Susan believed those men would kill to protect their identities.

'You home for dinner?'

She shook her head. 'I've got a lecture. Another of those Concerned Community Groups. Maybe their concern will add an extra zero to their cheque if I tell them about the snuffs.'

Lee nodded, thoughtful. 'Maybe. But don't push it too hard.'

Susan smiled. 'Sometimes I think I don't push hard enough.'

At the kitchen door Lee hugged her one more time. Then she walked quickly to her car, toting her bag filled with secrets.

Susan drove out of the suburb of family houses and ageing cars, and into the Singles Only world of apartments and condos, of new Porches and BMWs. Those cars were parked among the same kind of plants in the same terracotta containers: coconut palms, ferns and rubber trees, as carefully placed as the grass was barbered, the stucco walls painted bright white to show off the red and green roof tiles. Shiny black wrought-iron on the windows and balconies added to the impression of affluence.

There wasn't a child to be seen. The other day, addressing another group about the Center's work, she had tried to stir a reaction by saying an increasing number of those who settled in Southern California looked with disfavour on either the young or the old. 'They don't want to be reminded of what they were and what they are going to become. They think this kind of denial puts off mortality.' The audience had smiled its silent collective icy smile.

32

She wouldn't make that mistake again.

But she would begin tonight's talk the way she always did, by saying it was almost always untrue to say that children lied about being molested, when they had not. It was even less true to say a molester was a dirty old pervert with a bag of candy. Almost two-thirds of all molestations were carried out by someone the child knew, either within the family, or a friend, neighbour, teacher, sports coach or religious counsellor.

She would tell them about the 'fadeaway children'. They were the minors who either ran away from home or slipped through the ever-widening cracks in the juvenile protection and social services systems. The fadeaways remain prime targets for exploitation.

During the late 1980s, two markets have rapidly developed where the fadeaways are further exploited. The first are 'the circuits'. Each circuit consists of a dozen or more tightly-controlled sites scattered throughout several states. Each site is controlled by traffickers who manage hundreds of boys and girls, often in their pre-teens. In return for being supplied with drugs, the children work long days selling their bodies, some earn their 'keepers' over $100,000 a year and some keepers have a dozen children working a site. Few children last more than two years before succumbing to venereal disease and, increasingly, AIDS.

She would tell them about the second market – teenagers recruited specifically for the trucking industry. Traffickers positioned the girls – there was almost no market among the drivers for boys – at truck stops across the country. The great majority are pre-teens, some not even ten years old. The children move from one trucker to another. A child could work thirty cabs a night with each visit earning between $20 and $50 for her procurer. Some pimps have up to twenty girls working a trucking site. In a year they could earn him close to $5 million.

There would always be a collective gasp at that. She would pause, as she had learned to do.

'Never rush,' Lee had said when she had begun to give these talks. 'A lot of the story you tell has been around a long time. It's how *you* tell it that counts.' She could not have had a better mentor than Lee in the art of public speaking.

As she always did at this point, she would hurl the words at the audience.

'Pay-off!'

Then her voice once more calm and collected she would go on to explain how part of these vast profits are used to pay-off police and other officials while child hustlers are transported around the country. Pimps often used truckers to convey the hookers across state lines, or between Canada and the United States, or to and

33

from Mexico. Many of the older-looking children travelled on false identification papers, including birth certificates and social security cards, all paid for out of those profits.

That was usually enough to guarantee a good-sized cheque for the Center.

But tonight she would go further. She would speak about the snuffs – the ultimate horror in video movies.

Susan was two-thirds through her lecture. She had them. Even as they sat there in their conservative suits and dresses, hands folded or clasped in their laps, she knew she had them. She could see it in their eyes – that not-wanting-to-believe-yet-knowing-it-was-all-true look.

She had led them, increasingly horrified and captive, to where she wanted them.

Now that she had reached that point, she paused, eyes searching the packed hall, settling briefly on one rapt face after another. She thought how well she had heeded Lee's injunction. 'Build them up. Just keep them waiting. Never rush.'

She resumed with a question. 'How many of you know what a snuff movie is?'

They looked back at her, expectant, a few uneasily, but all wanting to know.

She began to tell them. She explained how the term had been coined in 1976 by a *New York Times* writer to try and describe reports of murders occurring during sexual activities during which the victims were filmed.

A Canadian researcher had created a definition which became accepted by the few police officers prepared to keep an open mind. Snuff movies involved, 'murder, captured on film without special effects; the victims may be either willing or duped into taking part by unscrupulous directors or producers; the murder must be planned in advance and be part of the production – not accidental, coincidental or unrelated to the production'.

The lips of a woman in the front row had begun to tremble. A man a few seats away who until now had been staring fixedly at Susan, shifted his gaze.

She moved to her next point.

At first it was claimed the movies were produced in Argentina, Chile and Bolivia and then smuggled into the United States. There they developed a cult following among the rich and powerful with stomachs strong enough to view such murders in the sanctuary of their homes. Snuff movies were not cheap

34

to rent. It was said, they cost up to $750 per rental, and up to $10,000 each to purchase. No one knows how many imports exist. Estimates vary from under a hundred to over a thousand. In each one a life was sacrificed – usually a woman or child. Unable to locate the films or identify their victims, most police officers still say they either do not exist – or are clever fakes.

She looked into their faces. No one even half-laughed, even out of nervousness. There was not even a smile. She moved on, sweeping them along with the fluency of her arguments.

Perhaps inevitably, given the state's close links with film-making, California soon became the focus of allegations that this form of ritual murder was being performed on American soil; that movie makers who have learned their trade in Hollywood are subverting their talents to record actual killings.

Once more she paused, preparing them for the next point. A year after the *New York Times* report, police in Orange County, California, arrested two men, Fred Douglass and Richard Hernandez, alleging they had planned to 'snuff' two undercover women police officers at a place subsequently only referred to as the 'Ranch', out in the desert beyond the fertile fields of Orange itself. Because no actual crime had been committed, both men were put on probation.

With a quick handwave, she stifled the start of shocked murmurs.

On 13 August 1982, the men persuaded two other young women, both with acting aspirations, to accompany them out to that mysterious Ranch. The girls, one aged nineteen and the other turned just sixteen, were told that they would take part in a film which would launch their careers. Six months later their skeletons were discovered in the desert. Forensic examination revealed they had been sexually tortured, choked and battered with rifle butts.

This time the silence was total.

Friends of Douglass told police that he had spoken openly of his plan to make his fortune by luring girls out to the desert and killing them on camera – and then selling the film for substantial sums. He claimed to have a list of wealthy clients who would buy them. Hernandez testified against Douglass

35

in return for immunity. With their case secured, the police made no attempt to investigate the Ranch. In December 1984, Douglass was sentenced to death. On Death Row he boasted of his wealthy and powerful connections. He told prison officials he knew who other snuffers were. No one checked whether he was telling the truth.

A chorus of 'oh, my God', and 'how dreadful' swept the hall. She allowed it to continue for a moment, then again waved for silence.

She next described how, after Douglass's conviction, police in the quiet township of Atascadero in Southern California, raided the home of Rodney Phelps and his wife, Linda. The couple had fled shortly before the police arrived to question them about fifteen children who were said to be Mexican or other foreigners.

The couple were alleged to have sexually abused and then murdered the kiddies, again reportedly filming the killings. The police found film-making equipment, but no snuff movies. They assumed the Phelps had either destroyed any such films, or taken them when they fled. Given the number of movies they were said to have made, the Phelps would have been able to unload them for substantial sums.

This time when she paused the silence was once more unbroken. The woman in the front row was biting her lips. The man had closed his eyes.

Acting on statements made by several local children, the police combed the area around the Phelps' home for signs of graves. They found none. Some of the children then alleged they saw the Phelps drive off into the desert with foreign-looking children. Increasingly sceptical of what they heard, the police did not pursue that line of enquiry.

Surely and with quiet confidence, she continued impaling them with her revelations.

Since then there have been other reports of snuff movies made in the California deserts. Some are said to feature foreign women and children smuggled into the United States from Asia and Latin America, specifically to be killed. In January 1986, Linda Lovelace, the star of the soft-porn movie *Deep Throat* testified to the US Attorney General's Commission on Organized Crime that women were either being murdered

36

on camera, or after filming, when the pornographers had no further use for them. Of course, because it was Linda Lovelace, no one listened.

She allowed a brief burst of laughter, knowing it was involuntary, a tension-breaker, a very necessary relief for what she was going to say next.

When the silence was once more complete Susan resumed by saying Fan had been just twelve years of age and beautiful, with long black hair and high cheek bones. One day she ran away from home, taking a train to a strange city. There she had been befriended by a woman who offered Fan work as a housemaid at the home of a movie director. Fan accepted.

Trying to reconstruct what probably happened, Susan said Fan was very likely astonished, and then delighted, at being told by her new employer that she was too attractive to be a maid. Instead, he offered Fan a more exciting role – that of a film star. To the naïve girl, who only twenty-four hours before had been living in a remote country village, the prospect must have been dazzling.

The woman in the front row was nodding in nervous agreement. The man was once more staring fixedly at the podium.

> The director led Fan to a room he had converted into a small film studio, equipped with video, camera and lights. The centre-piece of the set was a bed. He almost certainly told Fan that before he could offer her the part she must take a screen test – and that, just like any Hollywood hopeful, she must play a love scene.

No doubt still overcome at the change in her fortune, Susan continued, Fan probably had not hesitated.

Several women in the body of the hall had thrust their hands or handkerchiefs over their mouths.

> The man started the film, asking Fan to answer his questions on camera. After giving her name and age, the little girl was invited to sit on the bed and answer more questions. Was she a virgin? Her blushing confirmation was videoed, as was her next response. Had she ever imagined what it would be like to have sex? Fan shook her head, the unease on her face plain. Would she like to have sex with an older man? Fan had looked suddenly frightened. All these reactions were caught on camera.

Susan did not pause, gave them no chance to react. Not now.

Fan's look of sheer horror was also filmed as a man suddenly walked into shot towards the bed. He was naked and masked. The camera recorded Fan's struggles as she was brutally raped. The cameraman took care to concentrate on the terror on Fan's face. After she had been assaulted, her attacker had casually reached for a pillow and smothered the child to death.

She stopped, staring at them, her silence willing them to accept the truth. Then, when she judged the moment to be right, she added one sentence.

'That incident took place in Bangkok. And, as we all know, Bangkok is a long way from here.'

The woman in the front row was now nodding vigorously. Throughout the hall, people were doing the same thing. Bangkok. A long way away. Terrible and horrible. But a long, long way away.

'But not *that* far away!'

She hurled the words into the audience, startling it into silence once more.

Then, in a series of hammer-blow sentences, she told them that within hours of Fan's murder, the tape had been hand-couriered to Amsterdam, one of the European cities where slavery's film specialists work.

'When they had done their editing, copies were made, and Fan's death was distributed worldwide on the snuff network. It services the growing number of men and women who actually enjoy watching real-life sex-murder videos.'

Susan delivered her final thrust.

'The demand for snuff movies comes mostly from the United States – and especially from California.'

She stepped back from the lectern, knowing that in Fan's story she had managed to convey something of the worldwide activities of today's slavers.

FOUR

Converging Skills

O'Malley drove away from Oakley Park post office in the Chicago suburbs. For the eleventh weekday morning in a row the rented box was empty. Riki Sturmer still had not responded to him.

In the weeks since the German's name first came to his attention, the technology which O'Malley liked to remind his agents about once more had served him well. After that initial alert, when O'Malley had spotted Sturmer's name coming up as a supplier of child pornography in the course of a number of successful operations his men had ran against American paedophiles, he had moved quickly but carefully.

Police and other law-enforcement agency computers across the world, to which he had routine access, were programmed to search for every reference and cross-reference to Sturmer.

Information had come from as far apart as Manila, Bangkok, Karachi, Dubai and Frankfurt. These were some of the staging points in Sturmer's operation. Not only was he clearly a pornographer of substantial proportions, but O'Malley's suspicions deepened to the point that he thought that Sturmer could be an actual trafficker, buying and selling Asian children for other pornographers.

From the information, O'Malley had created a psycho-profile of Sturmer. He was twenty-nine-years-old, single, with a comfortable lifestyle in a village in the Black Forest area of West Germany. His bank accounts revealed substantial deposits and he travelled extensively, usually with a different young woman on each trip. His sexual appetite seemed voracious – judging by the regular visits he made to brothels in places such as Munich and Frankfurt.

This snippet of information formed the key to the sting O'Malley had launched to persuade Sturmer to come to America. O'Malley had begun to trade on the German's constant need for new sexual experiences.

Once he singles out a target, O'Malley uses a range of weapons to catch them: passports with forged names, fake travel documents, credit cards made out to non-existent persons, and bogus companies trading in the very pornographic goods he and his men seized. But above all, he likes creating an alias.

For Sturmer O'Malley had invented a woman called Sheila. In his first letter asking for samples of the pornographer's 'product', he simply signed her name. Sturmer responded by return with brochures featuring Asian children in pornographic poses, usually with white, middle-aged men. But it was the cover letter which brought the pirate's smile to O'Malley's lips. Sturmer asked whether Sheila was 'one of those sexy American women European men long to meet'.

O'Malley cautiously responded she could be, adding she was 'young and wealthy and the owner of an erotic book shop'.

Into the mail box drop had come another packet of filth, even more explicit and damning, but only if O'Malley could manoeuvre Sturmer into US jurisdiction.

In his letter thanking him for the packet, O'Malley, in Sheila's name, said she was 'curious to know was it true what they say about the sexual capacity of German men'.

Sturmer immediately replied that in his case it was, giving specific details of his sexual activities and preferences. With the letter came more child pornography.

O'Malley knew the trap was baited and waiting to be sprung.

Then the supply of damning evidence had stopped.

Driving through the Chicago suburbs, O'Malley reminded himself that it had taken almost a year to bag the Dutchman who ran a securities scam and used the profits to import Thai girls through San Diego. It had needed even longer to nail an Italian, after his first call had been intercepted and traced, during a routine tap on a procurer's phone in Los Angeles. O'Malley still remembered his disgust after reading the transcript. The Italian had asked for a little girl 'in the five-to-eight age group for hard sex'. He had said he also wanted to whip the child before being allowed to kill her.

Sensing a trap, the procurer hung-up. A Federal agent had called Milan, posing as the procurer's associate, offering to provide a child – if the Italian would come to the United States. But it had needed a further year of careful telephone playing before the man was arrested as he stepped off the Rome flight at LA. The lawyers were still arguing about the specific details of the charges; it could be two more years before the case came to trial. Meanwhile, the man was back in Italy on a $1 million bailbond. O'Malley wondered whether he would ever see the inside of an American court room.

It brought him back to thinking about Sturmer. Should he write to him again? If he did, should he again sprinkle the paper with Opium perfume? Choosing the scent had absorbed O'Malley. He visited several shops pretending to buy a birthday gift. Counter clerks sprayed the back of his hand with a range of perfumes. None somehow seemed right. He wanted the scent to be compatible with Sheila's persona – that of a degenerate woman seeking sexual gratification through voyeurism.

Finally, he had mentioned the matter to Judy. She recommended Opium. Its smoky fragrance would conjure up further fantasies in Sturmer's mind. O'Malley bought a bottle, charging it to the special fund he had for props used in his stings. He bought a second perfume – Chanel – for Judy out of his pay cheque.

Judy had been his wife for fourteen years and was the mother of their three children. Last Christmas, after he put up the tree, he told her he could not do his job properly without her support. She had squeezed his hand, and promised he could count on her always being there. Like his faith, this was a great comfort.

If she sometimes felt fear, she never showed it, not even when the bedside phone rang in the small hours, and he would grab it quickly so as not to disturb the children in their rooms. Judy would lie there, pretending to be asleep, listening to him listening. She never asked who had called. She never showed fear even when he came home at dawn or disappeared for weeks. Not even when he had gone to Bangkok, travelling on a false passport the CIA had provided, and with a made-up name on his Diners Club card. He had meant it: he just could not function so effectively without Judy being the kind of wife she was.

Over the car radio came the voice of the police dispatcher broadcasting an all-units call that shots had been fired in the Loop. As cars began to respond, sirens blared in the background of their acknowledgement transmissions. O'Malley turned-up the volume a fraction.

Once, the prospect of impending action would have tempted him. But no longer. Part of this came from the job itself. The years of living with that inborn steelwalker's balance had taught him not to chase other people's problems.

The flat voice of the dispatcher told a police car to report its location.

O'Malley smiled. She probably knew the car was parked outside a deli, its crew inside having coffee. He sympathized; he could not start the day without breakfast with Judy in the kitchen. It was as much a part of his life as going to Mass, saying the rosary, or being a good Catholic. Some people said Christianity had lost its soul and that religion had become another marketed product. But not his old-fashioned faith which had been imbued in him by his mother, whose grandmother had brought it from Ireland; he rejoiced in belonging to a strong Church led by a charismatic Pope.

41

He wondered if Susan was a Catholic. She had the kind of missionary zeal he admired, but did not altogether trust.

Maintaining a steady speed O'Malley headed across the city, listening to the dispatcher pulling more cars into the Loop. The immediate panic was under control. He lowered the radio volume and thought more about Riki Sturmer.

The German traded in hard-core videos and photographs, the kind which rarely surfaced outside the closed world of collectors of more extreme child pornography. He was the sort of man who could be involved in smuggling an unusually attractive Asian child to Europe, where in Paris, Rome, Frankfurt, and sometimes nowadays London, that child would be sold to a North American ring.

More than one woman was ready to risk prison for the fee she received in smuggling such a child into the United States: her paperwork would be impeccable down to the last official stamp, showing she had adopted the child. Once in the country, she handed over the child and received the balance of her money. No woman was used a second time. The number willing to do this kind of work was probably only surpassed by the number of children procured.

By the time O'Malley reached the freeway exit, he had decided to continue until the end of the week checking the mail box twice a day, morning and evening, to and from work. If there was still no letter from Sturmer by that time, he would decide on the next move.

O'Malley drove past stockyards and rail-freight sheds, grimy warehouses and delivery lots filled with new cars. People said there was a recession. He couldn't see it. People were willing to pay anything for pornography. That was one of the points he had made at the last staff meeting, when he had reviewed Sturmer's links across the world.

They extended from Frankfurt to Dubai, where the German had recently established contact with Mohammed Saleem. Defence for Children International, and other child-care agencies were kicking up a sandstorm of protest about the camel-boy traffic, and the diplomat who acted as Dubai catch-all for US Customs, had told Washington that Saleem could soon be looking for new markets.

O'Malley wondered how long it would be before his colleagues in Germany told him still more children from Karachi were being smuggled to stock the Federal Republic's sex rings.

What was it about German paedophiles, he mused, or, for that matter, their counterparts in France and Britain, which made them crave small children from the Third World? Was it something to do with the residue of lost empires? Was it some kind of subliminal racism? No doubt, if he had asked psychologists at the department of Justice they would have come up with an answer. He had not asked. Instead Saleem had been placed on the computer, cross-indexed to Sturmer.

Making the seemingly unconnectable connect was, O'Malley always thought, that much easier with the help of IBM.

A little before nine, O'Malley swung into Canal Street. The Customs House is built like a fortress nine stories high and, from whichever way you approach it, presents a daunting durability. The world could come and go, but this substantial building would remain as a monument to an architectural style all but vanished elsewhere. It was a thought which stirred something deep in O'Malley's Irish soul.

He could speak about his work with passion, and indeed, he had prepared a formal speech which he regularly delivered. Creating public awareness was one of the tools which allowed him to go on fighting his secret wars on the other side of the world. He knew he was equally skilled at both the image building and warring against slavers.

If O'Malley said it once, he had said it a hundred times to all those organizations who invited him to speak:

> We must beat their technology. Satellites make it possible to beam down the filth from outer space. A ground station can be in Central or South America, and the screens in Boston or Detroit. Electronic publishing makes it possible to make an operation virtually undetectable. Hard porn photographs are taken in Paris or Stockholm, the negatives are processed in Frankfurt or Amsterdam, because they have the top labs. They are printed in Barcelona or Madrid, because quality-wise, they are the cheapest for the best. The prints are faxed to Los Angeles or any other American city. The final package is put together in some suburban house and marketed through the usual channels across this country. Pornography is a thriving international free market for all those involved, except the victims. Always: *except* for the women and children.

He came off at 610 Canal, easing the car into the parking lot at the rear of the Customs House. Switching off the radio he locked the car, and loped the thirty yards to the building. His eyes continued to take in the street, people, dogs, anything he saw move. A few weeks ago in broad daylight, just before people had started for home from the building somebody had killed a man, knifing him on the sidewalk and severing his carotid, and then ran off with his wallet. Next day's *Tribune* gave the incident a paragraph: 'Hunt for $10 killer'.

In the bright morning sunlight, O'Malley's eyes were startlingly intense and rimmed with red, topped by shaggy eyebrows and a Kennedyesque shock of thick red hair. His nose is large and high-bridged. People invariably said he could only be from Irish stock. That, too, he liked.

This morning, O'Malley wore a Brooks Brothers look: dark blue suit, white shirt with a button-down collar, blue and gold striped tie, black loafers. The total effect was not so much preppy but timeless. It also made him look younger than the thirty-eight he was.

He kept the government-issue briefcase close to his body. It was stuffed with the latest reports on men and women with the morals of alley cats and the killing instincts of cobras. They include aged Germans who had learned their skills as slavers in the Third Reich and Frenchmen who had escaped arrest when the Marseilles Connection was broken up, and who now service the porn industry with bodies. Asian middle-men with shadowy ties to the Korean CIA, who help them transport cargoes of women and children around the world, and Hong Kong financiers who bank the profits from the deals. There were reports on international entrepreneurs stationed from Sydney to Stockholm, from Tokyo to the Lebanese port of Tripoli. No fact however small, or rumour however improbable, was left unchecked in his pursuit of those he hunted.

O'Malley saw them all as flies attracted to carrion, feeding off the misery of the enslaved. He could not know enough about any of them; whenever he had a spare hour, he dipped into his files, searching for further clues to a person's weaknesses. Experience had taught him that everybody possessed at least one.

Reaching the building he quickly crossed its featureless lobby to the elevator. An instructor at training school had said that more agents were killed in lobbies than gunned down in the streets. That made a lasting impression on O'Malley.

He remained wary of his surrounds – almost as much as he was of predicting the outcome of a sting. That was why he continued to hesitate about Susan Davidson's request. He did not want to get into something and then have to back-off. The Ranch sounded iffy: *if* he could think of a way of getting in; *if* he could get the evidence; *if* he could prove all the things he would need to prove to bring the case to court. It was all very *iffy*. A sting that failed could cast gloom over everyone on the eighth floor.

But given the usual breaks, often no more than making the most of his luck and sixth sense, O'Malley felt Sturmer could still be taken. Riding up to the eighth floor he began to conjure up new ways to achieve this.

Almost a month had passed since Susan had worn her lucky cream suit, August turning into September, and still O'Malley had not phoned. Lee advised patience, perhaps the agent was still putting together a plan of action.

44

This morning she was dressed in light grey. The weather for this time of year, was unseasonably cool. By the time she reached the first of several freeways she negotiated every day, the traffic was starting to slow.

Johnny – even among her staff Susan preferred not to use a surname, so protective was she of the children – had travelled this way with an United Church of Christ minister, and chairperson of his local concerned citizens group. Johnny had always been a troubled child. The eleven-year-old could not get along with his father – his parents were divorced – and had difficulty in adjusting to his stepfather.

When the minister hired the boy to help with church repairs, Johnny's mother was delighted, thinking the clergyman would be a good influence on her son. Two months into the weekend job, she became suspicious of the gifts and money that Johnny had received from him. She questioned her son, who eventually admitted he had been persuaded by the minister that taking part in homosexual acts was no more than an easy way to earn pocket money. Johnny's mother had confronted the clergyman, who denied the whole matter. She went to the police. By the time they questioned Johnny some days later and went to call on the minister, the man had fled. His name was routinely circulated, but nobody in the police department expected anything to come of it.

Indifference, Susan told the investigating detective, was precisely what the abusers counted upon. She had gone on to say that official disbelief, fear and ignorance, and even downright rejection, all made it that much easier for the empire of slaves to function.

He had interrupted. 'The empire of – *what*?'

'Slaves, officer. Sexual slaves.'

He had stared for a long moment at her. 'Slaves? Here in California. You mean, slaves as in a movie?'

His reaction did not surprise her. 'No, officer. Real slaves. Children being made to do all sorts of terrible things. By their parents. By cults.'

He had walked out of her office. 'Lady, I'm a cop. If you wanna talk about slaves then go talk to the DA's office. Okay?'

Susan had seen no point in telling him she had done so already. When she had first heard about the Ranch, an assistant district attorney had listened politely and promised to look into the matter. A year later she had not heard a word from him. Her calls were never returned. She had since discovered he was a member of a cult whose dark ceremonies included ritual slaughter of animals.

Her files contained the names of a growing number of similarly involved professionals. Many she now linked to the Ranch. They include members of the René Guyon Society in Los Angeles. It claims five thousand members; men and women in respected and influential positions, who believe that young children should experience sex. With its slogan of '*Sex By Age Eight – Or It's Too Late*', the group uses child porn to stimulate youngsters. Others are enrolled with the North American Man-Boy Love Association, NAMBLA, a homosexual group with chapters around the country, an emergency defence fund for members accused of molestation, a prisoner support committee and a lending library of what NAMBLA calls 'Boy love literature'.

These are only some of the powerful enemies Susan faces with little more than God's commandments to help her.

At the last staff meeting, she had told her small team that fighting evil has never been easy; it is getting harder. The enemy is becoming more skilful at covering its tracks; it knows how to use the media to mock and discredit; it has reached into the very heart of law-enforcement to protect itself. Nowhere is this more evident than in its ability to destroy the credibility of young children. That is why children make such perfect victims.

Sunny was a good example. The girl had come to her attention through a poster from a mid-West police department's child-porn unit. There were several photos on the xeroxed sheet. One showed Sunny at the age of six, a tow-headed child with a toothy grin and wide and still innocent blue eyes. Susan guessed the family had provided the picture. The next was of Sunny, probably two years later. The smile was now a half-smirk, as Sunny engaged in oral sex with a man. The caption explained the photo had been clipped from a porn magazine. The last picture showed Sunny in her early teens engaged in a savage act of sado-masochism, the photo was taken from another porn magazine. The police flier, which had come in 1988, ended with the alert that Sunny could now be in Southern California. Susan knew that if Sunny's life parallelled statistics, she would now, barely thirteen, have been discarded for a younger girl by whoever was running her. Sunny would then work the streets – and become a likely candidate for the Ranch.

As well as Lauren Stratford's allegation, Susan's file contained new allegations that behind its close-mesh fence children, youths and young women were forced to submit to gross sexual abuse, and that a continuous supply of human beings were shipped across the country in semi-trailers before disappearing into the Ranch. There were too many reports telling the same story for Susan not to believe them. But the kind of proof the police would insist upon was still missing.

Susan also recognized the difficulty she faced between going public and protecting her sources. She knew she could pick up a telephone and summon the networks to create a media hoopla. She never liked doing that. She just hoped that one day she would find sufficient evidence to convince the police they must investigate.

She often thought how the traffic in children had developed its own nefarious support system. Films like *Pretty Baby* and *Taxi Driver*, in which Brooke Shields and Jodie Foster played pre-teen prostitutes, may have woken up some people to what was happening in real life, but the movies give prostitution a spurious glamour. Susan wondered how many children had been enticed into imitations of Foster's and Shields' screen roles?

She also believed that Dark Rock – music with sexually explicit messages in the lyrics – promoted violence. Among the papers in her briefcase was a report by Dr David Guttman, Professor of Psychiatry at Northwestern University, in which this recognized authority on adolescent behaviour argued that Dark Rock helped to create a desensitizing which, in turn, had led to another musical phenomenon, Black Metal – rock music with a distinctive satanic influence. Such thoughts brought her back to thinking about the Ranch.

On Route 405, the San Diego freeway, Pamela Harris, Susan's deputy, gripped the wheel of her station wagon and thought, not for the first time, that she wished she could have reached her present age of thirty-two without having had to come to know a great deal more than most women did about fear, loss and evil. Then, she reminded herself, she should not really have expected anything else, given they were the basic elements she dealt with in her work. She confronted them with quiet confidence, keen awareness and infinite patience. These are some of the skills she uses in counselling; part of her training was to probe the past, make the present livable and the future hopeful.

Pamela saw herself as a kind of detective, moving quietly through the pathways of the unconscious mind, searching for clues to help child victims and their families. Her work brought her into daily contact with California-based law-enforcement agencies and the judiciary, so much so that she joked about knowing more police chiefs and judges than the State Governor.

Her contacts expanded to police forces further afield. Pamela still remembered the time she enlisted Scotland Yard's help in tracing a missing child; she imagined the desk sergeant in London who had taken her call to be sitting in a cubbyhole near the Thames, and the river air smelling like a damp flannel.

The Dickensian image fitted what she discovered was the reality about tracing missing children in Britain in 1989. In a country where computers can query a credit card purchase in seconds, there was still no agency, such as the Home Office, which keeps a continuously updated central record of missing children. In the United States every parent has the right for details of their missing child to be entered in the FBI computers in Washington, to which every police officer in the country has access.

Pamela had finally found her runaway after a private detective had intercepted the girl's telephone calls to a friend in California. Pamela called the London number and persuaded the teenager to return home.

Some also said she was among the best in Southern California at the difficult business of persuading children to talk about what had been done to them. A lot of her time was spent on the floor with the children, getting down to their level and helping them overcome their fear of speaking to an adult.

Pamela is five-six, but her immense poise makes her seem taller. Her hair is a thick reddish-brown, with red highlights, worn back-combed and long, so that it frames her face. When she is angry, her eyes narrow and turn a darker brown. Mostly they remain wide open and appraising. She looks like a model, not the mother of three daughters.

Now, alone in her car, its doors locked and the tape playing, she was isolated from domestic demands, the telephone, and the other interruptions which break up her day. The drive to work was when she concentrated on especially difficult cases, like Charlie.

Charlie's therapist had diagnosed the ten-year-old as suffering from post-traumatic stress, a still little understood clinical condition. It is more usually seen in survivors of disasters, or in people who have been kidnapped or held hostage. Like Charlie, those victims are often unable to speak fully about their experiences, and display similar disturbing behaviour: tearful outbursts, insomnia and rage. The usual treatment is intensive psychotherapy and good, old-fashioned tender loving care. Charlie had been given plenty of both.

Pamela knew the child's therapist was a careful and caring clinical psychologist. So were the other physicians who had treated the boy. But their combined skills had done little to relieve, let alone cure, Charlie's severe psychological and physical symptoms. He was still prone to alarming hyperactivity, rhythmic body twitching, sudden periods of lethargy and sleepy spells, alternating with violent outbursts during which he would threaten to kill his bewildered family and himself.

Some of the doctors had concluded that as well as post-traumatic stress, Charlie had begun to display symptoms of more serious mental illness. They had spoken about the way he had begun to show *depersonalization*, what they termed 'a loss of the sense of existing as a person', and further, they suggested his strange grimacing and twitching were perhaps really indications of the onset of catatonic schizophrenia.

Catatonia is usually marked by sudden outbursts of agitation and explosive psychotic excitement, often as inexplicable as a patient's incoherent utterings. They agreed that Charlie was unusually young to be experiencing the illness. But the symptoms fitted. One doctor concluded that, in Charlie's case, 'his internal experiences are disturbed by his thought disorders, and his emotions by his hallucinations and delusions'.

At that stage his even more worried parents had decided to bring Charlie to the Center for a further assessment.

Some of Charlie's doctors doubted if much more could be done for the boy. His fantasies were unusually bizarre, particularly Charlie's repeated claim that his family and home would soon be destroyed because he had not kept 'the secret'. He had told no one what it was and the doctors thought it was probably another manifestation of his personality disorder.

At the Center, Charlie's psycho-diagnostic evaluation had been conducted by Pamela. She concurred with the broad medical picture of abnormal fear in the boy. At times he looked and acted as if some inner force was taking complete control of his mind and body. But, after months of counselling, she was convinced Charlie was not hallucinating. Pamela was certain the cause of his angry outbursts, and a 'general free-floating state of anxiety', was the result of what had happened to him – and was locked in his mind.

Against all medical opinion, Pamela concluded that Charlie, in the true Biblical sense of the word, was possessed by the Devil.

The previous night she had spent several hours reviewing Charlie's clinical notes with the Reverend Ed Sempstrott. He was a minister who had carried out acts of 'spiritual reversal' – exorcisms – on some of her other little patients. When all else failed, she sometimes recommended exorcisms to parents as a way to free a child from possession. She knew that many churchmen dismissed demonic forces as aberrations, just as doctors often attributed them to an altered state of consciousness. But when she questioned them, they admitted their own perception of exorcism was influenced by lurid stories in newspapers or on television. Some insisted however it was still simply naïve to regard the Devil as a literal personal force for evil.

Pamela believed otherwise. She cited in support not only the words of Jesus in the Gospel of St Matthew for Satan to get behind Him, but also how the Bible gave numerous examples of demons invading and possessing bodies. When she quoted Scripture, doctors and sometimes clergymen looked kindly at her. She smiled back. She felt comfortable with her belief. It had sustained her as she had begun to unravel Charlie's trauma.

49

Sometimes he had sat, head bowed, refusing to go on. Other times his face became animated and his voice grew thin and quivering, a trembling broken sound like the wind rustling through fallen leaves. He had sucked his thumb for an entire session, rocking back and forth. Another time she sat on the floor of the interview room with him, cuddling him until his trembling stopped. Once, he had run from the room, crying.

She had known, then, he was coming close to talking about the secret. And he finally had – or at least told Pamela enough to know she was dealing with full blown horror. She had discovered that the elemental forces which possessed Charlie – possession was still the only word Pamela felt was appropriate – had chosen to do so at a moment when the boy was making his first religious contact.

Charlie had started attending Sunday school. Afterwards the pastor had invited Charlie, and a number of other boys, to remain behind. Charlie was thrilled to be asked, and had followed the others into a back room. There, the pastor had taken him aside and said he had something 'secret and special' to show Charlie. Watched by the other children, Charlie had followed the clergyman.

What happened then was so horrific that the boy still could not fully describe it. He had whispered to Pamela about being taken to a small room by the pastor, who had shown him a human skeleton and the freshly dismembered remains of a cat. The animal's head was on an altar plate, the legs on another, the torso on a third. Its blood was in a silver cup. Pamela was certain the room was the sacristy, next to the altar the most holy place in a church. The pastor drank the blood in front of the terrified boy.

Pamela had waited for Charlie to continue, already fearful and sickened over what had been shown to the boy. But all Charlie had been able to do was to open and close his mouth in abject terror. Finally, he managed to whisper how the pastor had produced a handgun, and said Charlie would die if he ever told anyone what he had seen.

Under Pamela's careful questioning, the boy explained how the pastor took him to a waiting van, already filled with the other children. The pastor's wife sat among them, she had insisted that Charlie should take a drink of lemonade and too terrified to refuse, he had done so. He had felt sleepy on the drive out into the desert.

Charlie was still too traumatized to describe what followed. But when Pamela asked if he would like to draw what he remembered, Charlie had, after a great deal of hesitation, produced several pictures of monster-headed figures grossly abusing children, while other monsters watched. Around the scene Charlie had drawn a high fence.

Pamela was certain he had been taken to the Ranch.

Separately from Susan, Pamela had produced her own description

50

of the Ranch. She located it to the north-east of Orange, out beyond Edwards Air Force Base, and reached by a turn-off on Interstate 395, beyond the town of Barstow. Some of the side roads leading from the highway are open only to the military, men with business at the China Lake Naval Weapons Center and other defence installations in the area.

Pamela believed that some of those who visited the restricted areas also patronized the Ranch, and that some of its employees lived in Barstow, Lancaster and Bakersfield, where those twenty-nine babies are said to have been sacrificed. All three towns are in comfortable drivable distance from the Ranch, though it is some way from the miles of tilled land of Orange County, with its drills of tomatoes, strawberries, peppers and root vegetables, tended by migrant labourers from Mexico, known as wetbacks.

She knew that, from time to time, children disappeared from those rich dark fields. Then, the Highway Patrol set up road blocks and peered into each vehicle, pulling over a few for a closer scrutiny and sometimes catching another handful of wetbacks. Each time, after a day or so, the hunt would peter out. A bored patrol officer had once told her they were only Mexican kids, and everybody knew wetbacks were always skipping some place or other to live on welfare when they got tired of picking berries.

A distance out in the empty scrub, at a point where the Granite mountains were visible, Pamela knew was the turning off the highway which led into the wilderness where the Ranch was situated.

Even in the burning noon sun it is a sinister and forbidding area, untouched by the closing decade of the twentieth century. There are still mountain lions roaming the gullies and canyons; snakes – rattlers, garters and kings – make the bridle paths dangerous. People went out there and never returned. No one knew where to start looking for them.

Pamela could not think of a more perfect place for the Ranch. What went on inside the chain-mesh fence she had culled from a number of sources. Who they were, and how they had managed to enter the Ranch and find their way back through the wilderness, redeemed from what she called 'hell on earth', are among her most closely-guarded secrets.

She had not shared her sources with the Reverend Sempstrott.

All she had told him was that she immediately recognized the Ranch from Charlie's drawings. 'It is a compound-like structure surrounded by a chain-link fence topped with barbed wire. The fence is regularly patrolled by armed guards in trucks. They also use a helicopter.'

Drawing upon the testimony of her undisclosed sources, Pamela added:

51

The place is used by high-ranking government, military and civilian officials who want to have their way with the children. Anything they want to do to a child, they can do out there. Children are killed there – murdered for the sexual gratification of the onlookers. This is a place where children are held as slaves, where they are abused and put through every form of pornography. They are filmed, tortured and finally murdered.

When the Reverend Sempstrott asked if she had gone to the police, Pamela had explained that, like Susan, she also had encountered 'real difficulties' in persuading the police and FBI.

I have given law-enforcement the information they needed to focus on this place. I chose my people carefully, at least so I thought. I left them alone to follow it as they wanted to. No pressure, no phone calls, nothing like that. I wanted a couple of months to check-in with them. When I did, if I even got through, it was a double-nothing. Nothing had been done. Nothing was going to be done. It is as if someone with the power to do so had sent down the word that the Ranch is not to be investigated.

Yet, she told the minister, she remained as certain about the existence of the Ranch as she was of the meaning of Charlie's drawings.

After studying them, Reverend Sempstrott asked whether Charlie's doctors considered if the boy suffered from the multiple personality disorder, MPD. The most famous case was that of Sybil Isabel Dorsett, whose numerous 'selves' made the public first aware of one of the most complex and most bizarre conditions known to psychiatry. Since Sybil, there have been a growing number of other cases reported in the clinical literature.

Some doctors think there could be thousands of MPDs, living with one or more personalities within their bodies, each personality possessing a different set of values and behaviour systems. MPD is now distinguished by the way the personalities not only maintain a separate existence, but remain unaware of each other. The home life of those who have the disorder is often characterized by severe family discord, or by obvious psycho-pathology in one or both parents. Since Sybil's case, doctors have discovered that the disorder is caused by sudden, severe physical sexual and emotional abuse as a child. Typically, the first personality split occurs before the age of ten.

The Reverend Sempstrott had explained that if Charlie was MPD, the chance of a successful spiritual reversal would be greatly diminished. The demonic forces would try and transfer from one personality to another, causing further severe mental conflict in the boy.

Pamela had said she was certain, despite all that Charlie had endured, he was not MPD. Charlie's parents were a couple who cared deeply for each other and their son. She added that they totally supported her conviction that only exorcism could finally free Charlie, and perhaps allow him to reveal everything he knew about the Ranch.

The minister had promised to consider performing an act of spiritual reversal. But first he would need to speak to the boy.

During the drive to work Pamela pondered Reverend Sempstrott's parting question, that if Charlie told all he knew about the Ranch, what would she do with the information? Pamela still did not know – except that she would not immediately go to the police. Charlie had made her promise not to do that. He had said the pastor had warned him that if he ever told the police, he would have him murdered – by other policemen.

FIVE

The Cross Bearers

Half-a-block beyond the police crime-scene ribbon, Sanders flipped open a notepad and wrote down the time and date. He kept a packet of pads in a desk drawer, a fresh one for each case. Sometimes he needed to fill only half a pad before solving a crime. The drug-pusher killing had been one of those. The case had been wrapped-up inside a day, the suspect cautioned and booked. Business as usual, Nap had said. Now, two days later, there was a new homicide for them to investigate.

Sanders had already seen enough to think he might need to use several pads for Incident Report 4492. His jottings would later be formalized into Exhibit A in the death of John Doe Sixty. John Doe, because as yet, Sanders had no idea of the body's identity, or how it came to be wrapped in a yellow blanket and covered by a large plastic trash bag wedged between the kerb and the right support of a semi-trailer, parked on the 1200 block of Sixth street in San Francisco. Number Sixty because this was the sixtieth unidentified corpse the Homicide Detail had on its active file.

Sanders still sighed wearily over the way the public expressed surprise at the number of John and Jane Does there were in this age of sophisticated record keeping. The truth, he would say, was that no system had yet been devised to keep track of all the people all of the time. Even the Welfare computers were not infallible, as all those who moved around the country bilking the system proved. Anyone who wanted to, could change their identity and simply disappear. Those of them who turned up dead usually left nothing with which to begin to run a trace; a check with the FBI computers for fingerprints, or a photo circulated along with a print of dental casts, seldom produced a name.

The Does kept turning up, a John here, a Jane some other place. They had to come from somewhere. But he didn't know a single police officer who had found a sure-fire way of quickly finding out from where.

Sanders continued to do what he always did at the start of any investigation. He allowed the scene to go flat, so that he could find a place in his mind for the all-important first impressions. Standing perfectly still, breathing slowly and evenly, he absorbed information with his eyes and nose. He took in the familiar movements beyond the ribbon; the arrival of more police cars, trucks and an ambulance; the breeze coming off the shore; people coming out of buildings to stand in small groups, silent and watchful. He could smell the odours from those who had edged close to him, the smell of people who lived without air conditioning along hallways and stairwells where the sea breeze never reached, and the daybeds remained damp from last night's sweat. He knew they looked at him, not knowing who exactly he was, but resenting him as another outsider.

Inside the ribbon, a methodical grid search of the scene-of-crime continued. He didn't expect it to turn up the weapon which had been used on John Doe Sixty, but the search was part of Criminal Procedure.

He saw, with satisfaction, that everybody took care not to go too close to the body. If there were clues, they would be there, within a few feet of the strangely boneless disarray in the lee of the semi-trailer.

He watched an officer write down its registration number and walk to one of the cars. He was calling Operations, to pass on the details. All that probably needed to be known for the moment about the trailer's ownership would be radioed back. There would be more questions later. Who had parked the trailer and why? How long had it been there? The entire history of the trailer and all those who had used it would, if necessary, be written out on interview forms. There were forms for every aspect of an investigation, even a relatively straightforward investigation used dozens of forms. John Doe Sixty, he sensed, could run to the size of a Russian novel as checks led to more checks, and all the answers were cross-referenced against each other.

But that would all happen in good time. Right now, he just wanted to absorb, to wait for that first hint that something had started to make someone's nerves begin to resonate. He prided himself on being able to hear the vibes before most people.

But not this time.

Driving to Sixth Street, Sanders had told his partner he had a feeling their record of swift solutions was about to end. Hendrix had said the only certainty was that the stiff would still be dead, whether it took a week or forever to find out who had done it.

'Not forever,' Sanders had chuckled. 'Not with our budget. They'd like us to solve it like they do in the movies. Sixty minutes, less the commercials. No longer, Nap.'

Sanders watched Hendrix circling the trailer, moving slowly, a tall figure in a three-piece suit and polished shoes. There wasn't a female traffic cop who hadn't had her moments wondering what the soft-voiced, well-mannered Hendrix was really like. He kept them all guessing with easy banter.

Ignoring the activity inside the ribboned-off area, Sanders studied the street. The houses had all gone up in the twenties, the tail-end of the rebuilding after the '06 'Quake. He always chuckled at the way native San Franciscans only spoke of the fire which had devoured the city and almost never of the massive tremor which had already left it in ruins. The houses on Sixth had been allowed to fall into disrepair over the years, and the street itself was another where pitched battles are regularly fought over who has the right to throw bricks and bottles. He imagined Beirut must have looked like this before matters there became serious.

There were gaps between the houses, vacant lots filled with weeds and rubble and protected, for some reason, with strong mesh fencing, as if there was a problem with people stealing weeds and rubble. Graffiti was everywhere, rising from sidewalk to stretched-hand level. The man who invented the aerosol can, he chuckled again, could have retired on the profits sprayed around this street.

He ignored the looks people gave him. He continued to remain insulated from them. Later, he would get to know some of them, when he would look into their faces, into those taxidermic eyes following his progress.

Beyond the ribbon he heard Nap's voice raised in sudden exasperation.

'Whaddy mean, are we gonna chalk the site? This isn't TV, boy. This is real. I don't chalk outdoor sites. Just as I don't do barmitzvahs or kids' parties. It'd be a waste of time. You know what'd happen if I do that? The whole thing'd be spray-canned before John Doe's on the table. Chalk the site? Is that what they teach now at the academy?'

Hendrix turned away, disgusted, from the young uniformed cop.

Sanders gave another chuckle. The early part of an investigation often produces over-eagerness from those in uniform who want to transfer into plain clothes, and meantime spend their free time reading the Detective Guide.

He continued studying the buildings on either side of the street. Despite what they had endured, many stood proud and defiant. Craftsmen had given them a symmetry that no amount of vandalism could undo, a quality which he did not see in the new high-rises. Here, there was a wholeness to the design and execution: everything seemed in proportion, as if the architect had actually watched over the builder.

He had grown up in a house like that: a solid, family house, one which protected its occupants from the world outside, allowing them to develop relationships within. He always believed that the reason why he had done so well at school and college, and later in the Army – he was still a Major on the Reserve – and finally in the force, was because his mother had made their home such a bastion. Espanola did the same. That was why the children, Marcus and Margarita, though grown-up, had never grown away from home. That was why he had been able to find the time to acquire two Masters at the city's Golden State University, one in Public Administration, the other in the Administration of Justice; why he was going for a third, a degree in Business Administration. He could do it all because of the kind of loving home background he was sure John Doe Sixty had most certainly not enjoyed.

Sanders paused before the houses, looking each one over carefully. Behind their battered fronts were probably still a few of the kind of solid citizens his parents had been. He could still remember his dad going off from a house like one of these, to work at the aircraft plant, and his mother to tempt the palate of Miss Young and other movie stars.

He started to walk slowly towards the ribboned area, still ignoring the people standing in the doorways and leaning out of windows.

The ribbon was guarded by one of the two uniformed officers who had been first on the scene. They had parked their car across from the trailer, and between them they had removed the trash bag and unrolled the blanket to reveal the naked body of a young male. He had been so severely mutilated that one of the officers had thrown-up. His companion had radioed for detectives and the Coroner's Officer, and then taped-off the area.

When Sanders and Hendrix had arrived, the ribbon was stretched across the street on either side of the crime scene, creating an island of about sixty feet long. Pringle, from the Coroner's office, had, in the absence of any identity, designated the body that of John Doe Sixty.

Ignoring the uniformed kid who looked pasty and smelled of vomit, Sanders had questioned the other patrolman, noting down his responses: the officers' names, ranks and star numbers, their car's exact time of arrival, the precise location of the body, what steps had been taken to ascertain it was a confirmed DAS, Dead at Scene, who had been called, what time he had noted the arrival of the Coroner's Officer, the weather and street conditions. He remembered the kid had stood guard at the trauma room door. He was shaping up.

When the rookie finished, Sanders walked over and briefly

inspected the body. Pringle formally pronounced John Doe Sixty to be dead.

'If he isn't, he's sure playing possum,' Sanders had chuckled. 'He surely is.' *Sur——lee.*

Now, his stroll along the street complete, Sanders reached the ribbon and ducked underneath, a quick and economical movement which belied his years. He was physically fit, with no sign of the asthma which had plagued his childhood.

He looked at the rookie. 'You complete your entries?' *Ent-rees?*

'Yes, sir.'

The officer reached for his note book. 'You want to check, sir.'

Sanders flipped open his pad. The chain of evidence always began from the moment the first officer arrived at the crime scene. A case could be lost if the evidential chain is not properly anchored, and just one entry time is wrong or out of sequence.

He glanced towards the body. 'So read on, son.'

Sanders listened intently, referring to his own note pad several times while the officer read back his entries. They were complete and accurate, and he told him so.

'Thank you, sir.'

A thought struck Sanders. 'What'd you do when you left the SOC?'

'Sir?'

'Somebody brought him here. And that somebody, unless he lowered our John Doe by helicopter, could have left footprints. Did you think of that?'

The officer nodded earnestly. 'Yes, sir. I backed off in my own prints.'

Sanders nodded approvingly. 'What about the other officer?'

'I made him do the same.'

Sanders hoped that would get the kid a pat on the back when his report made its way through the system.

'Okay. You keep everybody out who has no business.'

Sanders glanced towards the other officer, leaning against the door of the patrol car. 'His first body?'

'Yes, sir.'

'And you?'

'Fourth now, sir.'

'Veteran, huh?'

The rookie smiled.

Sanders turned away to watch the arrival of the Crime Scene Unit truck. It parked outside the ribbon. A photographer emerged with his camera, followed by two men with tote bags. They nodded towards Sanders. He waved them towards the body.

Moving to within a few feet of John Doe Sixty, the photographer began to take his shots, and the technicians started to bag whatever samples or specimens or detritus they needed, or Hendrix asked them to collect.

Ignoring them, Sanders moved to stand directly over John Doe Sixty, noting the ground was too hard to have left any footprints. The corpse was lying face up. There was a small cut on his upper lip, a pentagram carved into the skin over the chest, the scrotum had been cut open and the right testicle removed. Those wounds sent him to the nearest telephone.

In her home in Pacifica, down the coast from San Francisco, Gallant sat at her kitchen table writing up the copious notes she had made at yet another conference on the use of children in Satanic ritual. A speaker from a Washington-based child-care agency had attracted most of the media coverage with his claim that fifty thousand children went missing every year in the United States.

She wondered how many were missing in the police sense of the word. Those never traced – at least alive? How many were runaways who had gone for a few days before turning up again? How many had run away more than once?

But then, she thought, if she cut the speaker's figure in half, it was still a very large one.

She nagged at the question. If there were twenty-five thousand – where had they all gone? She doubted if they could all have been absorbed into cults; the number was the size of a Californian town. But supposing she cut the figure in half. Twelve thousand. That was more than all the kids in Pacifica, that was still a lot of kids.

Reviewing her notes, she felt the situation had worsened. At one of the conference workshops, where agents from different organizations pooled information, one had told the story of José. The nine-year-old had been bought from his impoverished family in Acapulco by a New York school teacher and the man had told the boy he now owned him. They had walked past Immigration at Kennedy Airport without trouble. For a year, José had been sodomised every day by the teacher before physically collapsing. When the boy had recovered in hospital, the Immigration service promptly deported him, forcing the police to drop their case against the teacher. The agent from Immigration had explained, as it now stood, that was the law: the prime consideration was to return a child to its parents.

Gallant wondered if a teacher could so easily smuggle in a child to the United States, how many more were being brought in by professional traffickers?

She was on her second coffee when the phone rang. When she and Bob had first lived together, and she had not wanted to disturb him with her early morning calls, she had learned to pick it up on the second ring. Those had been the mornings when she had later gone back to the bedroom with a mug of hot black coffee and placed it on his bedside table and then shaken him on the shoulder. She would perch on the edge of the bed, watching him drink, his face veiled in steam. Then, she had loved him more than ever. Now she felt nothing for him, not even anger. Only that deep-seated pain that she wanted to share with no one. It was hers, and hers to bear alone.

When she had met Bob, it had been like an Indian summer, and though it had come late, it had come. She had thought, then, that she had not waited to no purpose, or kept faith with herself for nothing. On the day they had married, she had told herself that this was the start of a new dawn, with its own special sound and colour of pure joy. She had truly believed it. That was why it especially hurt. The pain was all that remained from four years of marriage, the terrible, empty pain.

The phone continued to ring.

In that first year, after she finished her shift, she tried to leave her work behind at headquarters. She had realized it was important to separate her professional and private life when she had married. It had made no difference.

She let the phone ring. Few people had her unlisted number. By the second year of marriage she had been glad work continued to intrude.

She finally reached for the phone.

'Sandi?' *San—dee*.

'Yes?'

'Sandi, I wake you? This is Earl.' *Ea—r—ll*.

'No. Been up a little while.' She cleared her throat. 'Just on my way in.'

She realized her voice still sounded tired.

'Yeah?' Sanders always sounded so cheerful. 'You do a heck of a good imitation of someone just waking up.'

She laughed, thinking he was probably the only person who could make her laugh so early in the day.

'You're up early.'

The voice in her ear chuckled again. 'Who wouldn't be with what I've got? A John Doe with funny marks all over him. And most of his blood gone.'

She gathered herself. 'What sort of marks?'

Sanders was suddenly serious. 'The kind you understand. Inverted star. The one you call a pentagram . . .'

'Where?'

Sanders replied in his best evidence-giving voice. 'His chest. I haven't got the ME's report. But I'd say probably done with some sort of knife . . .'

She interrupted. 'Where are you?'

The chuckle was back. 'When I finish up here on the way to the back room.'

She groaned. 'You want me to come?'

The chuckle deepened. 'Can't get started without you.'

She hated going to the morgue.

Sanders continued to take his time at the crime scene.

One of the points he stressed to students was always to take a good look at a body and its immediate surrounds. A detective should take so long that, a year later, despite what had come-up in between, he could recall every detail. No matter how good an investigator, once he walked away from a body without that leisurely look, there was no way to get the scene properly fixed in his mind.

Sanders hitched up the legs of his well-cut trousers and squatted beside John Doe Sixty, eyeing him carefully from the top of his lank hair to his uncut toenails. Everything else beyond the body seemed to recede as he continued to stare and listen. He always had to explain about listening. No matter how many bodies he looked at, the feeling always came at a certain moment – that the body wasn't a body. That if he looked and listened long enough he would see the chest rise and fall and finally he would hear a heart beat. He knew what caused that expectation. It had to do with focussing. The feeling passed as soon as he released his first long and slow breath over the body.

His eyes returned to the crude five-pointed star carved on John Doe Sixty's chest. One point extended from the navel diagonally to the right nipple. Another began at the waist and ran, ever widening, across the body, a jagged V-cut which encompassed the entire left breast. The remaining three points of the star had been scratched from the bottom of the breastbone almost up to the neck.

In one of her lectures, Gallant had described how cultists regarded a pentagram as representing the Four Elements of Life plus something called the Great Unseen, a place, Gallant had explained, they believed was the source of all supernatural power.

He'd come away from that lecture thinking the world was a crazier place than even he had imagined. But then, he reminded himself now, he hadn't seen a mark like this. Whoever had done this to John Doe Sixty was a homicidal maniac. He continued to stare at the tracing on the skin, trying to decide if it had any human form, whether the shape was meant to represent outstretched arms and legs. Gallant had spoken about the Star of Microcosm, in which, to occultists, a pentagram represented the five senses of man. Maybe whoever had done this actually believed he would acquire John Doe Sixty's senses by doing so? He shook his head. The world really was a sick place.

He peered harder at the livid flesh wounds. Maybe the two upper points were the Horned God Gallant had spoken of – the earthly representation of the Devil for cultists? But did Satanists remove testicles? Gallant had given a talk on phallic worship, but he couldn't recall now whether she had actually mentioned the matter.

Sanders breathed out slowly, this time into the jagged hole in John Doe Sixty's very cold neck. The hole had not been visible until he had come down to this level. As soon as he breathed in, he wrinkled his nose at the distinct fungus-on-a-rotting-wall smell. Other bodies he had crouched over had the same stench.

Sanders began to write down his first detailed observations of John Doe Sixty: that he was white, poorly nourished, in his mid-twenties, probably somewhere between five-three and five-five and weighing somewhere around 130 pounds. The skin was a waxy colour. There was no blood at any of the entry wound points. The belly had patches of reddish-brown stain. The torso was covered in loose hairs.

He stared at the discolouring for some while. The staining was from PML, post-mortem lividity, the effect of gravity on blood after the heart stopped pumping, and the blood settled into the lower parts of the body. The PML staining should have been on John Doe Sixty's buttocks and his back, between his shoulder blades, not on his stomach. He made a note of the discrepancy.

Hendrix came and stood over the body. 'There are drag marks from in front of the trailer to here. About ten feet. And fresh tread marks. I'm having them cast.'

Sanders nodded, not taking his eyes off the body, but still not touching it. He asked Hendrix a question. 'Any witnesses?'

Hendrix squatted down on the other side of John Doe Sixty. 'A guy who says he saw an old blue van with windows all round parked beside the trailer. There were two guys. The trailer was open and they were doing something inside. Our guy didn't see what.'

'Did he get a make on them?'

'Latin types. One young. One older. Could be father and son.' Hendrix nodded at the body. 'This one don't look like a quickie. More like a forever.'

'Let's try and get a make on the van. And anything more on the Latins. They sound promising. Could be Cubans. Or from Haiti or somewhere down there. They could be the sort of guys we're looking for.'

Sanders shifted slightly so that he could look under the body. It was slightly raised from the blanket because John Doe Sixty's hands had been tied at the wrists behind his back.

'Gotta real messy one here, Earl. More like a forever, forever.'

For a while they studied the body in silence. Then Sanders lowered his face to within a few inches of John Doe Sixty's, peering intently at his eyes. He sighed as he straightened, nodding as he spoke. 'They dripped wax into his right eye and some on his hair.'

Hendrix peered hard into John Doe Sixty's face. 'Think this is more Santeria stuff, Earl?'

'Looks like it, Nap. But let's wait for Gallant to tell us.'

Their silence once more stretched over John Doe Sixty. Sanders wondered what removing John Doe Sixty's right testicle had to do with pouring wax in his right eye? He noted the three separate stab wounds, two in the neck, one in the chest, and wondered which one had proven to be fatal.

'What they do with the blood?' Hendrix finally asked.

'Probably drank it.'

After a while Sanders got up slowly and stepped backward out of the crime scene, digesting what he had seen. Hendrix remained crouched beside the body. The sun caught the gold frame of his spectacles, setting a beam of light playing across John Doe Sixty's face. After a while Hendrix came up off the ground in one quick movement which continued until he backed away from the body. They stood looking at the ground. Then, nodding to each other, they once more stepped forward carefully and resumed crouching on either side of John Doe Sixty. They continued to enter observations into their note pads. They exchanged no word during all of this.

Sanders noted that John Doe Sixty's eyes were half-open, giving him an Oriental look. The corneas were milky. His mouth was slack, showing a row of poorly kept teeth.

'Take a look at this, Nap.' Sanders pointed to the deep wound in the left-hand side of the neck. It had exposed the cartilage and neck muscle. The severed stump of an artery was clearly visible inside the entry hole. The wound had pulled open at the edges under the tension placed upon the surface layers of skin by the underlying muscle.

'Think Dracula's got to him?' asked Hendrix conversationally.

Sanders chuckled. 'Maybe son of Dracula. The hole could have been used to suck the blood out of his body.'

Hendrix sighed. 'Oh boy. This is one forever, forever, forever.'

Sanders asked one of the CSU technicians for gloves. Hendrix put on the thin plastic and gingerly lifted away some loose hairs from John Doe Sixty's chest. He handed them to one of the technicians. The man bagged and labelled them, writing, under Hendrix's instruction: 'Hairs animal(?), removed from victim's torso.'

Next Hendrix removed similar hairs from the blanket. These were also bagged and labelled.

'Think he was sleeping with an animal? Like a dog? Or maybe some circus animal? Think an animal did this to him, Earl?'

Sanders shrugged, 'Maybe an animal was involved. Maybe the

blanket could have come from an animal's bed. They just wrapped him in it because it was handy.'

Hendrix nodded. 'Makes sense.'

Sanders chuckled. 'Nothing makes sense, Nap. You know that. We're just fishing.'

Hendrix grinned. 'Wish I was, Earl. Sure wish right now I was off fishing.'

Around them the CSU men continued to bag soil samples, a snipped-off piece of blanket, some skin scales on the blanket. Sanders pointed to the neck wound. 'You don't usually go digging in the carotid area unless you know what you're doing. And the cut on the lip looks almost surgical to me.'

'Maybe a doctor or paramedic did this?'

Sanders chuckled again. 'That's for us to find out.'

Hendrix asked another question. 'Shall we turn him?'

Sanders shook his head. 'Let's get him to the back room.'

He rose to his feet and turned to the Coroner's officer. 'All yours.'

Pringle beckoned his assistant to wheel forward the gurney from the ambulance parked beside the CSU truck. Between them the two attendants once more wrapped-up John Doe Sixty in the blanket and trash bag. Then they tucked him into a body bag. Pringle zipped it up. They lifted the bag on to the gurney and strapped it securely. At a trot they wheeled the gurney towards the ambulance.

Sanders called after them. 'Tell Dr Ferrar to wait for me, and that Officer Gallant's coming.'

Neither of the Coroner's men responded.

'They take the city's money. They think they own it,' grumbled Hendrix.

Sanders watched the ambulance drive away through the crowd of silent closed faces.

Hendrix nodded towards the onlookers. 'Think the perps are here?'

Sanders glanced towards the crowd in an off-hand manner. He said softly, casually, 'Could be.'

'I'll get the CSU pixman to take shots? Sort of, by the way? No big deal.'

Sanders considered. 'Okay. But tell him not to make a thing out of it.'

Hendrix went to instruct the police photographer. The man continued to take photographs of the trailer. Then, after a few moments, he positioned himself so that he could take pictures of faces in the crowd. Later they would be used as part of door-to-door inquiries: who had seen who, where and at what time?

Hendrix returned to Sanders. 'How about an ACU to mingle?'

An ACU is an Anti-Crime Unit, plain-clothes officers who work the street to combat low-level crime.

Sanders nodded equably. 'Go ahead.'

Hendrix walked to the car to use the radio. Sanders went to the CSU team and began the painstaking job of isolating every item which would help his investigation.

The work requires an intuitive sense of the crime scene based on the leisurely study of the body. This is where judgement comes into play: where the hard-won experience which separates a good homicide detective from the rest of mankind, pays off. The art is to focus the search for clues without appearing to do the CSU's job.

That meant, in this case, Sanders walking around the trailer, then expanding the search in ever widening circles, until he had reached the ribbon on either side of the crime scene.

While the CSU team continued about its business, Sanders joined Hendrix in their car, still watching the technicians collecting, sketching, measuring, relating everything they did to the central compass point of where the body had been found.

After a while Hendrix volunteered his first theory of the investigation. 'Whoever killed our John Doe took a risk dragging him here.'

'Think they panicked?'

'Maybe.'

Sanders shook his head, offering a judgement. 'Someone who can do this to our John Doe isn't the panicking sort. My guess is that they had a very good reason to bring him here. Lying him out in the open was the final part of some ritual.'

Hendrix groaned. 'A case like this could shoot our record.'

Sanders looked at him seriously. 'It could do more. I don't know about you, Nap. But from now on I'm going to carry a New Testament as back-up for my gun.'

He got out of the car and walked slowly back to the CSU team. He ignored the hostile eyes beyond the ribbon. But he had already seen the ACU team had arrived and begun to mingle.

As she entered the building of tan brick and glass, Susan's thoughts focussed on the day ahead.

Her first consultation was with Bonnie-Q. The woman had been coming to the Center for the past six months after her little girl had been sexually abused and killed by Bonnie's live-in. In 1989, in the United States, two thousand other children would die from abuse. Bonnie had convinced the court of her innocence; her lover had drawn a thirty-two year sentence for second degree murder and aggravated child abuse. When she reviewed the trial papers, Susan saw he, too, had been a victim: the man had been sexually abused at the same age he had first assaulted Bonnie's little girl.

Over 90 per cent of the US prison population are now victims of child abuse. Most other Western industrial nations report similar percentage figures.

This morning she planned to explore with Bonnie something the woman said at the end of her last visit. 'He wanted my little girl for himself. As a possession. He used to say she was his doll.'

Susan sensed Bonnie's words offered a key to unlock the woman's trauma. Possession is a strong motivation theme running through much abuse, especially that which culminates in killing. In these cases *death* itself, not sex, is the prime satisfaction, the ultimate power to possess by killing.

In his pre-trial psychiatric examination, Bonnie's lover admitted to killing a cat and birds when he was a child to make them 'his'. Susan knew that if she could convey to Bonnie that the same motivation had also driven him to kill her little girl, then the woman might begin to allow to the surface the guilt and rage which made her so hostile. Once that was out in the open, Bonnie would be easier to counsel.

Susan left the elevator on the third floor and walked down the corridor towards Suite 3100. On the left-hand side of its door was a notice: ADAM WALSH CHILD RESOURCE CENTER. Though no one could tell, the door was surprisingly strong, with a steel frame, bracing batons and heavy wood beneath the veneer. It was fire-resistant. As a further protection, the estate agent had pointed out, the door was secured by a mortised dead-lock. Its security was one of the attractions of the suite for Susan. Only she and senior staff had keys to the door. Approaching it, she had a sudden feeling something was wrong.

PERFECT VICTIMS

In the mail the other day was a poem that says it all. I've read it so many times I can quote it by heart. Here, listen. '*A victim must be found – must be found. I've got a little list of society offenders who might well be underground. And who never would be missed – who never would be missed.*' The person who wrote that is a relative of someone killed by David Borkowitz, who did all those 'Son of Sam' killings. What that relative wants us to know is that there are other 'Sons of Sam' out there, and God help the world. We know he's right but nobody wants to believe it. That's why there are so many perfect victims . . .

Excerpt from author's interview with Allen Simmons, then Community Resource Director, Adam Walsh Child Resource Center, Orange, California; 14 July 1988.

SIX

Satan's Underworld

Susan reached the door, put in her key and turned the lock.

She entered the Center and switched on the lights. Parents were often surprised and children always delighted, at the bright decor. There were posters on the walls, and toys scattered everywhere. There wasn't a diploma in sight. Susan had deliberately gone for a style far removed from the usual clinical atmosphere. Kids who came here often had had more than their fill of such places, where they had been pumped full of shots and pills, the so-called 'sweetheart drugs', supposed to make it easier for them to cope with bad memories.

Susan had once attended a lecture by a renowned psychiatrist who had spoken about the need to 'balance the side-effects of anxiety-created insomnia' against the 'undoubted soporific result from the super-amphetamines.' He had concluded his homily to the pharmaceutical industry by saying 'the art is getting the optimal dosage right without being overly concerned about a child's long-term biochemical system.'

Standing in the doorway, the tightness remained in her chest. A homicide detective had told her sudden fear is caused by the brain releasing a chemical.

Forcing herself to remain calm she surveyed the reception area. The jar of candy on the receptionist's desk needed refilling. There had been no calls during the night on the hot line which children or their parents could use toll-free when the Center was closed. Susan switched on the day phone.

The feeling was still there. Something was not right. Should she wait here for Pamela? She shook her head, almost angry with herself, trying to shake off the feeling. She made a right turn into the short passageway which led to her office at the rear of the suite.

The door to the children's interview room was closed, where the previous evening she sat for almost an hour trying to coax Danny to tell more of his experiences. She had put a lot of thought into the

69

room, equipping it with audio-taping equipment, while furnishing it with toys, games and books to offer a child a sense of security.

She stopped by the door. The harder she tried, the more the feeling persisted and grew. Something was terribly, terribly wrong. She slowly opened the door and peered in. The room was exactly as she had left it. She wondered if this feeling was somehow a delayed reaction to Danny's revelations.

After weeks of counselling, the pent-up fear, anxiety and anger had finally exploded with one shocking statement from Danny. 'They took photos of us naked, and then made us watch them eat the baby. They took more pictures while we had to eat what was left.'

She had begun piecing together a horrifying story of devil worship, cannibalism, eating faeces, drinking blood and urine, torture and perverted sex.

Danny was so severely traumatised she guessed it would be many months before he would feel able to speak fully about his experiences to outsiders – let alone face the tough questioning of policemen. But by the end of last evening's session, Susan was convinced the boy had told the truth, especially about what he had called a 'very secret place' in the desert. From all he had said it had to be the Ranch.

As she walked down the corridor, there was a smell in the air which brought prickles to the nape of her neck. Something had happened here last night.

In the alcove at the end of the passage the reference books were neatly arranged on the shelves. It annoyed her when anyone took a book and did not replace it in its proper place – volumes about Satanism were on the top shelves, textbooks on child abuse below, and the bottom shelves filled with the works of psychologists and psychiatrists.

Her sense of unease increased, at the way everything was as usual, and yet feeling it was not.

The door to Pamela's office was closed. Pamela always made sure to do so even when she went to the toilet. Only Susan knew all the secrets in her deputy's filing cabinet and those stored on Pamela's computer terminal.

The smell was stronger. Susan dug her nails into her palms, silently and fiercely telling herself she was behaving like a fool.

She turned towards the closed door of her own office. It was across the corridor from the conference room. At that moment she knew it was not her imagination.

The door to the conference room was ajar.

The night before she had closed it. Susan knew she had not forgotten to do so.

It is another of her habits, part of the routine before going home of making sure the photocopier is turned off, the lights out, the air conditioner at its overnight setting, ensuring the garbage bags are absolutely full before being sent out. Such checks save a nickel here, a dime there. She set an example with her own $20,000 a year salary. It is half what she earned in her previous post with the Orange County District Attorney's office.

Susan stood, no longer uneasy, now almost petrified with fear. The smell came from the conference room. A sour and unmistakable human smell.

She forced herself to push the door open wider. The video tapes she played to new staff or visitors, so that they could understand the Center's work better, were scattered over the veneered mahogany table filling most of the room. The night before, its surface had been bare. Now, it was also dotted with styrofoam cups.

The smell came from them. Steeling herself to walk over to the table, she picked up one of the cups and sniffed. The unmistakable smell of stale urine made her feel physically ill. She put down the cup, trying, despite the tremble in her hand, not to spill the contents. The other cups contained the same amber liquid. One or two had cigarette butts floating in them. Whoever had sat round the table during the night watching the videos must have been Satanists. She backed away from the table. Only Satanists could have done this. She was certain of that.

She reminded herself that twenty years of working with assistant district attorneys, judges and police agencies, had taught her to think quickly and clearly. She knew this was the moment to take control. She should pray. She silently recited the Lord's Prayer. She felt calmer. The smell was not as sickening as before. She counted the cups. Six. Six persons. Six Satanists. Why? Why had they broken in? There was nothing on the videos they probably already did not know.

Susan turned, crossed the corridor and opened the door to her office. They had been here too, and even before she walked over to her desk she finally knew why they had come – to search out her precious file on the Ranch. She had left it on her desk, buried in a pile of papers. A detective had told her this was one of the best ways to hide important evidence. The pile of papers was scattered over the desk. The light-brown folder was on the floor. It was empty.

Susan prayed again for God to protect her and give her strength. She stood by the desk, feeling her resolve grow. She would not be frightened off. No one could frighten her. Not with God protecting her.

She walked determinedly to Pamela's office and opened its door. Pamela's desk was mahogany veneer and battered. Its top overflowed with files, journals and mail. There was a plant pot with a fern in it. The desk chair and the easy chair were equally worn. A filing cabinet

71

stood against one wall. It was a cosy and comfortable room, one in which children could be happy and their parents find relaxing.

The screen of the computer terminal was aglow and covered with strange words. She stood before the terminal, knowing whose language it was. She began to recite aloud the Lord's Prayer, her eyes scanning the screen.

'*Micara! golo Pe IAD! zodir com-zelshe azodien biabe oz-londohe. Noezodachasia Otahila Gigipahe; vaunud-el-cahisa ta-pu-ime qo-mos-pelehe telocahe.*'

From the doorway a voice began to translate. 'Behold! saith Satan. I am a circle on whose hands stand the Twelve Kingdoms. Six are the seats of living death; the rest are as sharp sickles, or the Horns of Death . . .'

Susan turned and stared at Pamela.

'It's part of the Enochian Keys. The Third. The one they use to summon up their magicians to protect their secrets.' Pamela continued studying the screen.

'Not the way I would have chosen to start the day,' said Susan. After the words came a wide and utterly mirthless grin. It was her way of showing anger.

'How did they get a key, Susan?'

Susan sighed. 'It's someone connected to the Ranch. It has to be.' She told Pamela what had happened.

Pamela walked to the desk, removed a key from a drawer and went to the cabinet. She put the key in the lock and turned it. A drawer slid open. She stood for a moment staring at the rack of files. Then she started rummaging through them, searching, her eyes beginning to narrow and darken. Finally, she pulled out a folder. She turned to Susan, holding the file by its metal spine so that it flapped open. The lightly-tanned skin stretched taut over Pamela's high cheekbones. The file was empty.

Susan's mirthless grin returned. The file contained allegations every bit as shocking as those about the Ranch.

For two years Susan had been collecting information that Third World children were being bought or stolen, and were being medically killed so that their eyes, kidneys, hearts and livers could be removed and transplanted into the bodies of patients with sufficient money to avoid the ever-lengthening official waiting lists.

The claims that children were used for such purposes had, from time to time, been linked to snuff movies. There was talk that organs from the victims were sold for transplants. But, as with the films themselves, the police were unable to find any proof.

The one absolute certainty about the allegations is that the demand for transplants far exceeds the available supply of organs available by legal means.

On any given day in 1989, fifteen thousand Americans waited for replacement organs. Kidney-failure patients topped the lists. They could be kept alive by dialysis, a twice-weekly cleansing of their blood. But it cost more than $30,000 a year to keep someone on an artificial kidney. In the past decade, new drugs which prevent the body from rejecting foreign tissue, improved tissue-matching techniques and more sophisticated patient care, have made kidney transplants less a risky experiment and more a standard therapy.

Nevertheless, patients needing new kidneys often have to wait for an anonymous death – and for men like Bill Cantirino.

Cantirino is a professional organ hunter for the Gift of Life Organ Procurement Organization, based in New York. His task is to convince parents or children, husbands or wives, all in the depths of immediate grief, to donate organs from their just-deceased loved ones. Cantirino is in constant radio contact with New York's emergency departments, seeking victims of car accidents, shootings or suicides, ready to use his skills to persuade relatives to part with those organs which have escaped injury. What he does is perfectly legal.

Most major American cities now have similar organ hunters. They are men who keep a low profile, never speak of money or their clients, and who work in the midst of trauma. Yet, despite all their efforts, the gap between demand and supply is widening.

Kidneys removed from a donor remain transplantable up to forty-eight hours afterwards, and the operation carries a 95 per cent success guarantee. Hearts are generally useable for up to five hours after they have been excised; livers can survive twice that length, eyes for half the time. In the US a kidney transplant costs around $40,000; a new heart, twice that amount; a liver graft can cost up to $500,000. As well as the ability to pay, doctors often exercise other considerations. Unlike Canada, the majority of American transplant centres will not authorize a new organ for anyone over the age of fifty-five. Homosexuals and the mentally handicapped are often also excluded.

Susan realized the potential for a black market was very real.

A number of Brazil's three million children of the streets – its legions of tiny beggars, pickpockets, thieves and prostitutes who work and live on the pavements in the country's major cities – who became the victims of road or other accidents, are said to be taken by ambulance men to private hospitals and clinics in Saõ Paulo and other cities. The men receive a kickback for every child they bring in. The doctors place the children on a monitoring system until brain death can be clinically confirmed. They then remove all the healthy organs from the

73

corpses. In hours they are transplanted into the bodies of those able to pay.

The particularly gruesome aspect of such activities was highlighted in January 1987, by Eduardo Bermundez, the secretary-general of Honduras' main government-run child-welfare agency, Junta de Benestra Social, JBS. The agency has a reputation throughout Central America as a respected organization. It works closely with Defence for Children International, the Commission for Human Rights in Central America, the International Federation of Human Rights and the International Association of Democratic Jurists.

Bermundez alleged that thirteen babies discovered in a house out-side the Honduran capital, were waiting to be taken to a private clinic where 'they would be medically killed and their vital organs extracted and flown to the United States'.

The day after making the claim, Bermundez retracted it, resigned his post and disappeared from public life. Reports from Honduras said Bermundez was silenced by high government officials. Others said the pressure to remove him came from the United States.

Theoretically, no US surgeon would dare transplant such a stolen organ. The American Council of Transplantation had introduced strict new regulations to support already existing federal legislation encompassed in the Uniform Anatomical Gift Act. This makes it mandatory for a donor to sign a consent form for an organ to be used after his or her death.

But such legal requirements did not take away from the reality of demand exceeding supply. Theoretically, there is no actual shortage of organs. Each year about twenty-five thousand healthy people die unexpectedly in America, usually in accidents. The problem is that fewer than 20 per cent have previously agreed to donate organs.

Susan could understand how the organ traffickers saw a market opportunity – and filled it from the kind of source Bermundez had exposed.

She believed bringing the organs into the United States to be a simple matter. Packed in saline and ice, they could be flown across the border in the planes which regularly airlifted drugs into the US from Central America. Men who could traffick in drugs would have no compunction about dealing in human organs.

The accusations of underground trafficking in human organs had continued to increase. Throughout 1989, a number of Latin American countries were reportedly implicated in the traffic. Among them were Panama, Guatamala, El Salvador, Nicaragua and Brazil. But it was from Costa Rica, in late December 1988, that the most sensational allegation came.

Bruja Goldman, a research worker at the Friends World College in San José, claimed that, 'children as young as four months were either being kidnapped, deceptively adopted or brought into the United States, Israel and European countries as live donors to be dismembered for their organs. Children have been bought for twenty dollars and their organs sold for seventy-five thousand dollars.'

The governments of the countries named insisted the allegations were propaganda by their political opponents.

In January 1989, widely separated incidents brought the traffic into sharper focus.

From Hong Kong came the revelation that wealthy Chinese were paying around the equal of £7,000 a time to two Canton hospitals in mainland China to receive the kidneys of executed criminals. The Peking government confirmed the organs were removed from the condemned men immediately after death without their prior approval or the knowledge of their relatives.

In London, the Humana Wellington Hospital was implicated in the trafficking of kidney donors from Turkey, where selling organs carries a heavy fine and often imprisonment. The Turks brought to London each received an average of £2,000 to donate a kidney. The organs were then taken and used for patients at Britain's privately-run National Kidney Centre. The British government took swift action to stop the trade.

In Paraguay, the police raided a house in Asuncion and discovered seven Brazilian baby boys, aged between three and six months. A respected juvenile court judge, Angel Campus, said he had 'good evidence that the babies were going to be sold in the United States to private clinics for fifteen thousand dollars each.' He refused to name the clinics, but he knew the type of patient they catered for. 'The son of an American multi-millionaire gets kidney problems. The father is not going to spare any effort to pay a millionaire sum for a healthy new kidney. Our investigations have led us to conclude these babies were going to be butchered in the United States for their organs.'

When Susan heard such claims, she was not surprised.

For years baby farms have successfully operated in South America, where girls are deliberately impregnated and kept, pending the birth of their babies. These are then sold-off to childless foreign couples, mostly from the United States, West Germany and Britain. Economically, it makes more sense to use babies for their organs. A baby for adoption has nothing like the value of the child's organs. A perfectly healthy child, cut up into pieces, can have a market value of $200,000.

The doctors involved were, she still believed, highly adept at covering their tracks from even the experienced investigators of Amnesty International. Susan remained satisfied that a physician who had

75

sufficiently departed from his ethics to electro-shock a prisoner or inject mind-bending drugs, will have little hesitation over removing an organ from a child.

The list of countries where such doctors are now said to work includes Bolivia, Burma, Chile, India, Iran and Pakistan. Organs removed from Asian victims are reported to be used as transplants for wealthy Arabs, the operations performed in private clinics in Damascus, Baghdad and Riydah. Organs from Latin America are said to be for wealthy North American patients. Some reports claim these patients are flown to private clinics in Central and South America for surgery. But Susan knew only too well that without proof they remained – only reports. In the hope of acquiring hard evidence she had been amassing information. Now, along with all her's and Pamela's data on the Ranch, it had gone.

Susan led Pamela to the door of the conference room.

'Uh-uh,' said Pamela, counting. 'Quite a little party.' The light-tanned skin stretched more tightly over her high cheekbones.

Pamela walked into the room and quickly gathered up the cups, dumping them in a trash can. The women crossed the corridor. Pamela surveyed the scattered papers on Susan's desk. 'Not very professional.'

Susan's mirthless grin returned.

They walked back to Pamela's office and stood before the screen. Susan broke the silence. 'We're getting closer than they want us to be. They want to scare us off. But they know that if they go too far, like wrecking the whole place, we'd have to call in the police. They may have a lot of cops buttoned up, but they still wouldn't want to risk that. This was a back-off warning.'

Pamela looked at Susan. 'And we do?'

'What?'

'Back-off?'

Susan's response was to widen the mirthless grin.

Pamela leaned against the desk. 'I don't think we should tell anybody.'

Susan looked at the screen. 'What about the staff? Karen's sensible.'

Pamela moved to the computer keyboard. 'Sure she is.' She pressed a key. The words finally disappeared. 'So is Marsha.'

Karen Kalley was the Center's Resource and Reference Director, responsible for liaising with some fifty child-care agencies throughout California. Marsha Davis was the office manager.

Pamela returned to lean against the desk. 'If we tell one, we have to tell them all. I say we don't tell any of them. There's nothing they

76

can do. It would be only one more thing for them to worry about. And this sort of thing could spook Allen.'

Susan nodded. Allen Simmons was a great deal more complex than he appeared. The former priest sometimes hinted he had been sent to Rome on the Pope's business and finally asked by John Paul to choose between his vocation and a nurse Allen loved back in Orange County. He implied he had chosen love. He had resigned his holy orders, but somewhere between returning to California and taking up his job at the Center, the nurse had married a doctor. Susan had not probed, because she had a rule of distancing herself from the private lives of her staff.

She stared briefly at the blank screen. 'I want to tell Lee. But first I want to hear about what's going to happen to Charlie.'

Pamela started describing her visit to the Reverend Sempstrott.

A couple of hours after Sanders telephoned, Gallant came out of the elevator on the fourth floor of Headquarters and made a left turn into a corridor. She wore cream slacks, a white blouse and red cardigan, her hair was combed up off her face but apart from a touch of lipstick, she wore no other make-up. There was no badge or shield pinned to her chest or gun at her hip. Some of the women officers roamed the corridors of the Hall of Justice as if they were going to war. That was fine by her, as long as they didn't ask her to join their game.

Driving to work she had considered what Sanders had told her. It wasn't much to go on.

The pentagram is a favourite symbol for all cultists. They use it to either protect themselves against evil, or to control others in their spell. It depends how it is drawn. If one point was directed upwards, that was Mind ruling over the World of Matter, what the early Christians regarded as representing the Five Words of Christ. The symbol is still found in church architecture. She'd seen a particularly striking photograph of a pentagram in one of the windows of Exeter Cathedral in England. Freemasons and Rosicrucians regularly use the sign among their symbols. That sort of pentagram had been around well before them. Pythagoras used one to form his distinctive letter 'A'. Medieval English knights engraved pentagrams on their shields. There was even a folk-song devoted to it, 'Green Grow the Rushes-O'.

Upward pointed pentagrams appeared all over the place. England's Queen Anne used one when she had carried out public healing ceremonies. King James the First had slept with such a pentagram over his bed. One of the ancestors of the present Queen of England, Lady Janet Glamis, had been burned at the stake as a witch clutching her upward-pointed pentagram, convinced it would ensure her life in the hereafter.

Gallant always liked to sprinkle her lectures with a little history, just as she could be deliberately low-key when she described how a pentagram with the point facing downward, or in the form of goat's horns, is a symbol of total evil. It is the sign of Kali Unga, of the Goat of Mendes, ruler of all Satanic forces. Sometimes, she sensed even seasoned investigators breathe a little faster when she said that.

Sanders had not described the pentagram on the body, and she had not thought to ask. She'd know soon enough.

Room 450 had a frosted door with a sign above: Homicide Detail. The door opened on to a waiting area. It has a short row of moulded black plastic chairs against one wall, a low table with some old magazines. It is the Detail's version of a doctor's waiting room. People could sit there while their friends waited to be questioned in the interview room nearby, or in the squad room beyond the partition wall.

She stood for a moment longer, arranging in her mind answers to questions Sanders could ask.

Sometimes a Voodo *hougan*, a high priest, marked a body about to be sacrificed. But those ritual killings were usually of babies. Only if an adult had violated a *duok*, a Voodoo priestess, would he be ceremonially killed, his throat cut and his body eviscerated on the cult's altar.

There are Voodoo cultists in the Bay area capable of such an act. But there are other groups who could just as easily have carried out a ritual murder. Among them are those who follow the beliefs of ancient Egypt, where human sacrifice was an integral part of worship; those who continue to worship Kali, who could only be appeased by ritual murder. There are a number of other mystical Oriental religions practised around the city in which ritual killing plays a part. The great majority of the sacrifices are of animals. But once in a while a group had been said to use humans.

It was possible, she would tell Sanders, that these are the cultists he should be looking for. But, she would add, ritual crimes broke all the rules.

She walked into the squad room. Desks stood back-to-back surrounded by metal filing cabinets, their tops piled with boxes of papers from old cases. The walls were covered with duty rosters, copies of memoranda from the Chief's office, bulletins from the District Attorney's office, clippings from law journals, faded cartoons from the *Chronicle* and *Examiner*, a few postcards. The room was empty except for a uniformed policewoman typing at a desk in a corner of the room.

'They're waiting in the back room,' she said, not bothering to look up.

Gallant left the squad room and took the lift down to the Necropsy Department in the rear of the building, thinking why was it that she could cope with the supernatural, but dreaded looking upon the newly dead? She made a conscious effort to control her anxiety as she approached the morgue.

SEVEN

Breakdowns and Procedures

Sanders and Hendrix were two of four men grouped around the body of John Doe Sixty, lying on a stainless-steel table in the necropsy suite at the rear of police headquarters at 650 Bryant Street. The others were the pathologist, Dr Ferrar, and his assistant, Pringle. They were about to perform an autopsy. First each man conducted a long and careful study of the corpse.

It was an integral part of the investigation – among the essential procedures which could lead to the arrest of John Doe Sixty's killer or killers. The scrutiny was to try and discover clues which would help to determine the number of persons involved in the murder.

John Doe Sixty's arms had been untied and placed at his side. The body lay on a table in the centre of a brightly lit room with floor-to-ceiling tiling and a hard composition floor. The table had a lip to catch liquids. Weighing scales were suspended above. A large stainless-steel basin hung from each scale. Powerful fluorescent lights on adjustable arms provided further light. A perforated stainless-steel sheet ran the length of the table and drained into a shallow well beneath. Double stainless-steel sinks with taps were close-by. Over the table was an adjustable microphone.

Positioned to one side was a standard surgical trolley. It contained an assortment of scalpels, bone cutters, bowls and pots. The single largest instrument was a small electric saw, connected by a flex to one of the many power outlets in the tiled walls.

'Height okay, Dr Ferrar?' Pringle asked, one hand raised towards the microphone. In his other he held a camera.

'Fine. Just fine.' The pathologist continued staring at the body. Dr Ferrar wore a green surgical smock but no cap or mask.

'You're most welcome, Dr Ferrar,' Pringle said.

Sanders wondered why people who worked with the dead were so overly-polite. A reminder of their own mortality – the hope that when their time came they would be shown the same deference?

The pathologist told Pringle to photograph the body. He began to take a series of close-up shots. They would be included with the CSU photos as part of the evidential chain. When Pringle finished, the pathologist looked towards the door.

'Gallant going to be long, Earl?' Dr Ferrar stood at Sanders' elbow, still running his eyes over the body.

'Should be here soon,' said Sanders. He clutched a slim file; it contained all the paperwork on the case so far.

Hendrix turned to Pringle. 'Take a look outside.'

'My pleasure, Mr Hendrix.' Pringle walked to the door. He could have been a butler in one of the mansions on Nob Hill, thought Hendrix. He turned to Dr Ferrar.

'Business slack, Doc?'

The pathologist continued studying John Doe Sixty. 'Slowish on the homicide front, Nap. Usual number of ODs. A hanging. And a guy who fried himself with his toaster. Stripped off the covering, taped the elements to his chest and took a shower. He was still dancing when they found him.'

Hendrix enjoyed the gallows humour of the Medical Examiner. He supposed it was a prerequisite for doing an average of a dozen autopsies a day.

Behind them the door opened to admit Pringle and Gallant. He went to a glass-fronted wall cupboard and removed wooden probes, swabs, vials and slides, bringing them to the table. Gallant hesitated at the door.

'Come on over, Officer Gallant. He isn't going to bite you,' said Dr Ferrar.

Gallant walked slowly towards the table and stood at Sanders' shoulder, peering at the body.

'OK! All present,' cried Dr Ferrar, brisk and bustling. 'Assume paperwork's OK, Earl?'

Sanders nodded, tapping the file. He had checked the PI, the Police Identification form, a legal-sized document which Criminal Procedure insisted must be completed by the Investigations Officer before an autopsy could begin. The PI confirmed that the body of John Doe Sixty lying on the table was the same one Sanders had seen by the semi-trailer.

Dr Ferrar was always most careful about documentation. His acceptance of Sanders' word was a sign of the high regard he had for the detective. Sanders, for his part, enjoyed working with the veteran pathologist. Dr Ferrar not only thought like a detective, but often asked the sort of questions defence counsel would put. Over the years they had come to know better than to challenge Dr Ferrar's forensic evidence.

'Any ideas, Sandi?' asked Sanders.

Both detectives had their notepads open, eyes on Gallant.

She forced herself to concentrate a little longer on the body. When she spoke, she lapsed into her lecturer's voice – a calm, authoritative tone, which has become natural over the years.

'The wax in the eye and the cut on the lip are classic in Satanic ritual. It's the "see no evil, speak no evil" thing. Satanists use it to symbolically silence a person.'

After writing in his pad, Sanders spoke. 'Is this symbolic silencing always the prelude to killing?'

Gallant considered. 'Not always. The wax and cut are often used to show a person just belongs totally to the group.'

Hendrix interposed. 'Could he have gotten into this voluntarily, and then become a sacrifice?'

Gallant shook her head. 'Satanists don't usually turn on their own. My bet is, they took him as a sacrifice from the beginning.'

There was silence around the table, broken by Sanders. 'What about the pentagram, Sandi?'

'The pentagram's a reversal. So that further suggests Satanism. But it's badly drawn. The points are not in the correct place. Either whoever did it didn't know what he should be doing, or didn't care about the niceties.'

Sanders and Hendrix noted the observations.

'Why take out a testicle, Sandi?' asked Sanders. 'And why the right one?'

Gallant stepped back from the table, and looked directly at Sanders. 'Whoever did it knew enough about black magic to know that the testes are regarded as luck-bringers. Something to ward off the Evil Eye. The right testis is held to be specially lucky by some cultists. The other possibility is that it was removed as part of moon worship. The moon has always been regarded as feminine, although there are many moon gods as well as moon goddesses. A lot of cultists swear there is a link between the moon and human fertility. The twenty-eight day menstrual cycle is a good example. Again, cultists believe the moon influences the other fluid secretions in the body. This includes seminal fluid. So semen and menstrual blood are highly prized essentials of moon worship.'

Gallant paused for the detectives to catch up with their writing. Dr Ferrar continued listening carefully before putting a question.

'So they could have taken out one of his testes as some sort of sacrifice to the moon?'

Gallant nodded. 'And ate it to give that person, or persons, a greater fertility. They often slice up a testicle so that everyone gets a piece.'

Hendrix shook his head. 'Sounds like something they do in Chinatown.'

Gallant smiled quickly. 'The Chinese only eat animal testes. You could be dealing here with one of the Caribbean cults. Or out of Africa. Or just crazies.'

Sanders exhaled a long, slow breath. 'Then we're looking for just about every other guy on the street.'

Gallant nodded. 'Right. But like I said, it could be Caribbean or African based. They all use blood to purify altars, sprinkle over their gods, and to drink. They use pints in one ceremony. They often bleed a victim. Sometimes to death.'

Sanders and Hendrix wrote in their pads.

Dr Ferrar intertwined one rubber-gloved hand with another. 'From what I've read, that points to Voodoo. Would that explain the patterns on his buttocks and lower back area? The transverse cut on the right ankle and the contusions on his wrists?'

Gallant shrugged. 'There's nothing specific to Voodoo, witch-craft or Satanism about that. But people adapt. Borrow a piece of ritual from here, a bit from there, to make up their own brand-new cult.'

Hendrix interrupted. 'This blood thing. Could it be something like werewolves or vampires we are looking for?' His face was sombre.

Gallant was equally serious-faced as she pondered. 'If you put aside that garbage about stripping naked and being anointed with a magical unguent, and putting on a wolf's skin, then, yes, some cultists really believe that, in a certain sense, werewolving is possible. They say that what is transposed, in their case, is not the physical body, but their spirit. And they do this by drinking blood.'

Hendrix groaned aloud.

'And vampires,' pressed Sanders. 'How about them?'

Gallant risked another smile. 'Again, it isn't like the movies. But there are a number of cultists who practise a kind of vampirism. Drinking a person's blood to drain the vitality of that person.'

Sanders made a further note. Once more there was silence around the table. The men stared at John Doe Sixty. Gallant looked at Sanders and Hendrix.

Dr Ferrar finally asked her if she had any more observations. She shook her head and glanced towards the door.

Sanders gave a sympathetic smile. 'Sandi, I hate to ask you this, but I'll need you to stick around. When Dr Ferrar gets inside, he may have further questions which only you can help on. The more Nap and I know now, the easier it will be later.'

Gallant took a deep breath. 'O . . kay.'

'Don't think of him as being alive,' said Dr Ferrar, as he switched on the microphone. A certain heaviness came over the pathologist. He bowed his shoulders slightly and his voice and movements became more deliberate. Standing over the body, he began to intone.

'This is Dr Ferrar, Assistant Medical Examiner for the city and county of San Francisco. I will now conduct a post-mortem examination on the body of a male Caucasian, unidentified, but known for the purpose of this examination as John Doe Sixty. Subject is approximately twenty-five years of age, height five-five, weight one-thirty pounds. Subject bears case tag number o-eight-two-four. The investigating officer is Inspector Prentice Earl Sanders of the Homicide Detail, San Francisco Police Department. His star number is nine-o-one. I will begin by external examination.'

He reached up and switched off the microphone. It was linked to a tape-recorder in his office. When the autopsy was complete Dr Ferrar's secretary would type up the tape and distribute copies to those who would want to know what Dr Ferrar had discovered.

The pathologist began to run his gloved hands over John Doe Sixty's torso, arms and legs, systematically squeezing muscle and fat. He peered between toes, under the arms and in the groin. He asked Pringle to help, and together they manoeuvred the body on to its stomach. Dr Ferrar ran his hands over the head, the base of the neck, the spine, the rib cage, the buttocks, the thighs, legs and feet. He and Pringle then returned the body to its former position. The pathologist took swabs from John Doe Sixty's nose, eyes, ears, mouth and rectum. He switched on the microphone and once more assumed a sombre voice.

The body is poorly developed. The head contour is symmetrical. There is no evidence of trauma. The hair is long, brown and of male distribution. There is a brown moustache. The right eye shows wax drippings. The conjunctival sac and scleral membranes reveal minimal congestion and the pupils are equal at three millimetres. There is minimal vitreous humor in each eye. Swab taken. The nose is symmetrical and shows no evidence of fracture or haemorrhage. But there is a minimal amount of mucus secretions exuding from the nasal cavities. Swab taken. The glabella shows no evidence of fracture or trauma. The mouth has lost its rigidity . . .

Dr Ferrar continued his careful commentary. He described John Doe's lips, teeth and ears. He mentioned the neck wound, and said he would deal with it separately. He drew attention to what appeared to be burn marks on the skin around the wound. He reached for a rule from the trolley and measured the area: 2.5 centimetres by 3.2 centimetres. He noted the pentagram adding he would deal with it later. He measured a surgical scar on the right lower abdomen: eight centimetres. He paused to clear his throat and continued.

'There are no needle tracks or marks in the antecubital fossae.'

84

'No drugs, then,' murmured Hendrix.

Dr Ferrar looked up sharply. 'I get paid to do this voice-over without interruption.' He smiled, the irritation gone. 'No, No drugs.'

The pathologist continued. He described the scarring on John Doe Sixty's wrist and elbows. He took and identified scrapings from under the fingernails and toenails, putting them into vials.

Pringle labelled and placed them with the other samples on the undershelf of the trolley.

Dr Ferrar and the attendant once more turned over the body. The pathologist took a snippet of hair from the back of John Doe Sixty's scalp. Pringle fixed it on a staining glass. The hairs would later be compared with those Hendrix had removed at the scene of the crime.

Working slowly and meticulously, the pathologist described the cluster of criss-cross cuts on John Doe Sixty's lower back and buttocks. When he finished he switched off the microphone and looked at Gallant. 'Any further thoughts about the markings, Officer?'

Gallant forced herself to once more peer at the deeply scarred skin. The others watched her expectantly. She addressed Sanders. 'I've heard the Piquets sometimes do this to someone before they kill him.'

'Piquets, Sandi?' Sanders asked, pen poised.

'Nobody knows much about them. They're usually based in Haiti and operate like the Klan does in the South. Except the Piquets promote black supremacy and kill whites. I've not heard they'd come this way.'

The two detectives made further notes. Dr Ferrar pointed to the markings on the buttocks. 'Some sort of branding iron could have done that.'

Gallant ventured. 'Could be a pince. That's a wrought iron bar Voodooists heat in a fire. The Petro Society often use it to mark their sacrifices.'

Hendrix asked what the Petro Society was, and Gallant explained it is the most violent and bloodthirsty of all Voodoo groups, a cult of devil worshippers among whom human sacrifices are common. The cult exists widely in Africa and Haiti.

'Think they've opened a California branch, Sandi?' asked Sanders.

'I'll check.'

Dr Ferrar glanced around the table, smiling at Gallant. 'I learn a little every day. Today, I learn a lot.'

He nodded to Pringle. They returned John Doe Sixty on to his back. Dr Ferrar switched on the microphone and described in detail how the testicle had been removed. He shook his head at Sanders.

'Before you ask, the answer's – no. No doctor I know would be responsible for such butchery. Not even a pre-med student. Not even a paramedic. The guy who did this knew as much about the art of evisceration as I know about rocket building.'

Sanders scribbled. 'Testis removed non-surgically.'

Dr Ferrar stared questioningly at Gallant. She looked at Sanders.

'Earl, I don't think a goofer could have done this. Unless he was in a great hurry. A goofer's usually very careful how he takes an organ.'

Hendrix' baffled look drew another quick smile from her. 'A goofer's a Voodoo doctor.' She looked at Sanders. 'Down in Texas they call them root doctors.'

Sanders smiled back. 'They used to call them nigger doctors. Then we got Civil Rights.'

Dr Ferrar nodded equably. 'I hate to break this up. But I've got other customers waiting.'

He switched on the microphone and began to describe each wound on John Doe Sixty's body.

'Stab wound number one. The entry is located on the right lateral neck . . .'

For the next fifteen minutes the pathologist probed and measured and described the wounds. Swabs and scrapings were taken from each entry point and labelled by Pringle and joined the growing number on the trolley. Dr Ferrar straightened and switched off the microphone. He did so each time to avoid extraneous conversations appearing on the tape.

Sanders pointed to the neck wound. 'This the one which killed him, Doc?'

Dr Ferrar nodded. 'Probably. But he was already well gone by the time it was done.'

Sanders pressed. 'You think the other wounds came first? Then the final one in the neck?'

Dr Ferrar looked at Gallant. 'Any views on that?'

She spoke across the table.

'It could have gone like this. The eye wax and lip cut were temporary. But the pentagram marked him forever as theirs. It's important with cultists to stake-out their human property. They could have made one of the smaller body wounds to get the blood running. When they realized he was dying on them, they could have made the neck hole to get the rest of his blood out fast. That's the logical route for most Satanists. But you can never be certain.'

Dr Ferrar nodded. 'That would explain the position of the post-mortem lividity. There was no blood to sink to its natural position after death.'

Sanders noted the explanation.

'You say "they", Sandi. How do you know more than one is involved?' asked Hendrix.

Gallant sighed. 'I don't, for sure. It could be a one-to-one. But if this is cult-related, then a whole group will be involved. And I think this *is* cult. Satanic cult or Voodoo.'

Hendrix noted her reply.

Sanders turned to Dr Ferrar. 'Any idea on ETD?'

The pathologist nodded cautiously. 'Probably a few hours before he was found. Maybe longer. The lab should tell us.'

Sanders noted that the exact time of death was still unknown. Dr Ferrar switched on the microphone, and continued to dictate. 'There is a six-point small monochromatic tattoo of a star between the web of the left thumb and second finger . . .'

For a few minutes longer he continued with his steady rhythmic description. Gallant began to feel more relaxed. She started to think about how John Doe Sixty could have ended up in the hands of his killers. Most probably, he would turn out to be a drifter, another of those young people who hitch-hike to California, seeking work, or more likely, excitement. He could have been picked up well outside the city and brought in, already a prisoner and doomed. Equally, he could have been snatched within the city. No one would have noticed a drifter who suddenly disappeared.

'Let's open him up.'

Dr Ferrar's words drove all else from her mind. Sanders looked at her reassuringly. She wished she could be like Hendrix, standing perfectly still, arms folded, face settled. She watched Pringle take a scalpel from the trolley and hand it to Dr Ferrar. She willed herself not to look away.

The pathologist made the first cut. For the next ten minutes he used the scalpel and the electric saw.

Gallant closed her eyes. There was no escaping the smell of singed bone, or the sound of the saw.

Sanders watched the work progress. There was little blood. The first time he had stood at an autopsy there was blood everywhere. A child had been raped and then shot by some stranger who had picked her up off the street. He couldn't remember the little girl's name now, or that of the man. All he could recall was what the ME had said. 'This is the time when we get to see how God made us. As long as we remember this is all part of God's plan, then we won't have a problem with doing what we have to do here.' It hadn't made it any easier to watch the ME cut into her.

The sawing over, Dr Ferrar took a pair of bone cutters and began to open up the chest.

Hendrix wrinkled his nose, thinking he had smelled worse down at the market than this stench which so clearly reeked of mortality.

The pathologist exposed the organs, and turned to John Doe Sixty's head. Dr Ferrar took a clean scalpel and set to work once more, alternately using knife and saw.

When he decided there were enough openings in the skull, he took a steel lever, shaped rather like a shoe-horn, and worked it between the first pair of holes. With some difficulty, and accompanied by a sucking noise, a sound which made Gallant tremble, Dr Ferrar prised off the crest of the skull. He used a knife to expose the brain covering. Then he took a larger scalpel to cut through the tissue and arteries which held the brain in place. In less than five minutes he removed the brain.

Sanders looked at Gallant, silently mouthing it would soon end. She continued to stare frozen-faced at what Dr Ferrar was doing.

After minutely inspecting it, turning it in his hands, Dr Ferrar placed the brain in the bowl. He switched on the microphone once more, and began to describe his findings.

> Internal examination. Central Nervous System. The brain weighs thirteen hundred grams. No evidence of epidural, subdural or subarachnoia haemorrhage. The subgaleal and galeal tissues show no evidence of trauma. The leptomeninges are thin and delicate. The blood vessels have collapsed. The tentorium, cerebellum and falx cerebri are intact. The circle of Willis shows no aneurysm. There is no subfalcial herniation or uncinate grooving. The basal ganglia, lateral ventricles, mamillary bodies and hippocampi show no abnormalities . . .

While Dr Ferrar continued with his litany, Pringle took the brain out of the bowl and placed it in a large jar. It would be sent to Pathology for further examination, along with any other organs the pathologist would specify. The stomach contents, cerebrospinal fluid, bile and urine specimens would be sent to Toxicology.

Dr Ferrar removed the lungs. He inspected them and dropped one into the bowl, noted the weight, waited for Pringle to remove it, and then weighed the other.

> Respiratory System. The right lung weighs three hundred grams. The left lung weighs two hundred and fifty grams. There is an incisional wound on the medial surface of the left lobe, measuring 2.5 centimetres in length . . .

How had John Doe Sixty survived that, Sanders wondered? That was a killing wound.

Dr Ferrar removed the heart from the body cavity and examined it. He waited for Pringle to remove the lung from the bowl and then placed the heart in the receptacle.

Cardiovascular System. The heart weighs two hundred and eighty grams, is soft, flabby and demonstrates no evidence of penetrating stab wound. The epicardium is smooth, glistening and contains adipose tissue only along the course of the coronary arteries . . .

In succession Dr Ferrar removed, inspected, weighed and described the liver, gall bladder, pancreas and the kidneys. Next he dealt with the neck area.

The tongue and neck organs were removed 'en bloc'. The pharyngeal and laryngeal mucosa show no focal lesions. The vocal cords, larynx and trachea are not edematous, and no petechial haemorrhage is noted in the upper respiratory tract . . .

Gallant wondered how much of this would help the two men opposite her find the killers.

Musculoskeletal System. The body framework is well developed and well retained. No evidence of fracture, focal trauma, or diffuse osseous lesion. The vertebral bone marrow is a uniform brown-red and shows no focal change or excess fat . . .

Sanders continued to listen carefully as Dr Ferrar came to the end.

Diagnosis. Multiple penetrating stab wounds to neck and left chest. Transection of right external jugular vein. Incisional wound of right stenocleidomastoid muscle. Incisional wound of aortic arch. Penetrating stab wound to left lower lobe of lung and left leaf of diaphragm. Massive left hemothorax. Minimal hemopericardium . . .

Pringle walked to a cupboard and returned with a newly pressed white folded sheet. He placed it on the trolley.

. . . Remote hesitation scars on left wrist. Moderate pallor of abdominal viscera. Cerebral edema and congestion . . .

Dr Ferrar paused and glanced at Gallant. Then in the same measured tone, he concluded, 'Patterned incisional wounds on chest. Five-pointed star shaped.'

Dr Ferrar dictated the list of specimens he was sending for laboratory analysis. He switched off the microphone and stepped back from the table.

Pringle picked up the sheet and opened it with a starched snap and flutter. He threw the shroud over the ruins of John Doe Sixty.

Gallant gave an involuntary sigh of relief as the sheet settled slowly over the form.

Sanders looked quickly at Hendrix. In unison their lips mouthed the question. 'Forever, forever, forever?'

O'Malley sat in his office in Chicago. Until now it had been a relatively uneventful week during which he had finally come to a decision over Susan Davidson's request. He was going to pass. He had called her and said he would always be ready to review her request based on further evidence. He tried to sound positive. That way he left his options open, the way he liked them always to be. He'd sensed her disappointment. After the call he continued doing what he always did on a slack day, studying the files on current operations.

Thirty-one days had now passed since he had last heard from Sturmer, and he had all but given up hope of doing so. Now, on this early day in September, the air fresh after heavy overnight rain, the video had arrived to rekindle O'Malley's hopes.

It came on the overnight flight from Frankfurt, travelling in the forward hold in a pouch, separated from the other couriered mail. The pouch had been given priority clearance at O'Hare by Customs. Ninety minutes after the plane reached its gate, the packet was delivered to the eighth floor.

As well as the video came a photograph and a Bundesrepublik certification that it was a copy of the one in Sturmer's current passport. German Customs had also provided a report that the master tape of the video was made in Asia, and seized as it was being smuggled through Frankfurt Airport by a Filipina.

Copies would have been made in West Germany and shipped across the Atlantic by the couriers who carried vast quantities of pornography around the world. One hub of their operation is Paris. Another, London. In both cities US Customs agents work closely with local forces to try and stop the traffic. But, realistically, the chances are low of spotting tapes being carried through busy airports like Orly and Heathrow. They are often smuggled singly, and labelled as a wedding or family christening cassette. Sometimes they are disguised as a child's cartoon tape. The couriers are expert at manufacturing suitable packaging to hide obscene material. Faking Disney logos is a favourite method.

O'Malley knew not only were there continuous technical advances – 8mm silent loops had long given way to full-length colour extravaganzas with music and special effects, such as running a copulation scene at slow speed – but the content had become even more depraved. With Hollywood itself increasingly catering for the soft porn market of the so-called *Pussycat Theatre* network, hard-core pornographers are pushing ever wider what O'Malley called 'the frontiers of filth'. There were now over a hundred companies around the world producing several hundred new hard porn films a year. Their average budget ran between $100,000 and $200,000.

Whoever financed them, they were no more than a succession of sex acts, clearly shot, involving every possible kind of deviation. A key member of the film crew was the 'coozie spot' operator – the man who focussed a pencil spotlight for genital closeups.

The last time he had passed through London, his old friend, Superintendent Iain Donaldson, then head of Scotland Yard's Obscene Publications Squad, had said he had reports that film editors working for the BBC and ITV networks were moonlighting – putting together what Donaldson called 'really serious hard stuff' in the city's film quarter. Donaldson added he did not have the manpower to mount a concerted surveillance on all the editing rooms around Soho Square. He suspected if he went to the Commissioner and asked for more men, he would be told they could not be taken off other investigations. With London increasingly one of the capitals for all types of terrorist activity, its police force was stretched to the limit protecting the public.

On the flight home, O'Malley had wondered whether terrorist organizations were actually financing the manufacture and distribution of hard porn into Britain, Europe and the United States, as part of their avowed policy to destabilize democracy. As far as he knew, no one was looking for such links. He added this possibility to his constantly lengthening list of points to be alert for in any of his own operations.

He still read everything he could about pornography. Earlier that week another report from the Anti-Slavery Society in London had made its way across the Atlantic on to O'Malley's desk. It warned there was a significant increase in the number of children being kidnapped in the Third World to be specifically used in hard-porn films. He admired the way the Society persevered in trying to alert the public. But, by and large, people did not listen.

In the end, O'Malley knew, it all came down to money. No money to set-up an international task force to tackle pornography. No money to publicize the problem. No money to bring people together to discuss the crisis. American investigators sometimes went to conferences in Europe and Asia, but there were seldom reciprocal visits – unless Washington picked up the tab. No money to conduct research into the long-term effects of pornography on society. No money to pay for more investigators. No money to go on the offensive. Simply no money.

On the other hand, pornographers channelled part of their profits into organizations like NAMBLA, or supported conferences where another damned psychologist came grunting out of the woodwork arguing pornography was a good thing. O'Malley studied their arguments to justify using children for pornography: that in doing so, it allowed adults to indulge their fantasies without encouraging them to act out their yearnings. But children were used to produce this pornography in the first place.

By 1989 most of the material came from a dozen suppliers in Europe. They now controlled about two-thirds of the world's multi-billion dollar child pornographic industry. The Germans were its leaders.

O'Malley wondered who among them was acting as distributor for the video German Customs had sent.

O'Malley viewed the tape on one of the machines in his office. Then he fetched an agent to watch it with him. The man was a newcomer to the team, transferring from the Secret Service in Washington. During the formal interview O'Malley had been impressed by his enthusiasm for long days, and irregular meals.

But there were other tests an agent had to pass, none in the rule book, before being accepted on the eighth floor. Could an agent maintain control in any given situation? Had an agent already made a mark on the street? The guts to go in first? But was an agent stupid enough to go in first *every* time? He did not want Rambos. The final test was one of loyalty. Was an agent loyal? And if so, to whom was that loyalty pledged? If it was just to the Commissioner and the service, that was not enough. But if an agent found his or her loyalty placed on the line, between doing it by the book or the street, and chose the street because there was no other way to do the job: if an agent understood that to be the meaning of loyalty, then he or she was warmly welcomed in the Parish House. O'Malley made those decisions about every man or woman who came to work for him. Those who passed his tests remained, in his eyes, men among men, women above women.

Walking down the corridor back to his office O'Malley asked how the man had settled in.

'Glad to be here, Jack.'

The agent was built like a football player, with an abrasive voice and a chest which stretched the waistcoat of his three-piece suit. At the formal interview he had been taciturn. But he now sensed the man had a driving purpose in him. That was reassuring.

O'Malley gave his pirate's smile. Then, ever so gently, he delivered his punch. 'That's good to know. Because there is something I want you to try and work up. Do you think there is any way we could use your Washington experience to get us a little closer to the action?'

The agent smiled. 'Absolutely. There's a lot my old people should be able to do for us.'

O'Malley liked the way he spoke about 'us'.

The agent had not spoken since the video began.

O'Malley watched the man on the screen, thinking how he had aged. The thick-necked figure had first come to his attention in photographs showing him raping under-age Asian girls. Thousands of prints had been shipped to paedophiles in America. At the conclusion of a sting operation every bit as elaborate as the one he was running against Sturmer, O'Malley and another agent had flown to Bangkok. Working alongside Thai detectives he had led the raid on the studio producing the photographs. But their 'star' had escaped the dragnet.

Now, four years later, his lifeguard muscles had turned to flab and his beard a yellowish-grey. He looked like a man who was well into the fish-hook pain of venereal disease.

O'Malley regarded him as just another of the foot soldiers of porn; the generals sheltered behind off-shore companies and high-priced lawyers.

On the video another man appeared with a large gift-wrapped box. He explained it contained 'the ultimate in sex technology – the world's first humanoid nymphomaniac'. The man went into a sales pitch, talking about the 'genetic research which had created an orgasmic partner'.

The agent at O'Malley's elbow scribbled steadily, noting everything that was said and done on screen.

The process is called 'the breakdown'. The transcription is a legal requirement in any court case involving pornographic films or videos.

The salesman said 'the humanoid enjoys being abused, tortured and violated in every way possible'. His aged companion ripped away the wrapping to reveal a vulnerable looking and completely naked Asian girl.

'Hold it right there!'

O'Malley rose in a smooth movement, not once using the arm rests on his chair, and strode to the video player. He pressed a button, freezing the frame. The girl remained caught with her mouth open, one hand extended as if in supplication, the look in her eyes glazed.

Pointing at the screen O'Malley yelled. 'She's gotta be no more than twelve. Maybe less.' He pressed a button and the video resumed. Both men had sex with the child.

On the screen a third figure joined the party. The tall sombrely-dressed man had his back to the camera. But O'Malley had glimpsed a narrow face dominated by thick heavy glasses. The man looked like a book-keeper. O'Malley put his age at around thirty. He made a note on his pad. The girl performed various obscene acts with the man.

He continued staring at the badly-lit figure, glancing from the screen to the passport photograph on his clipboard.

When the video ended, O'Malley rewound it. Once more they watched and listened intently to every exchange and action. Those scenes where the man's face was clear, O'Malley stopped the tape and each time compared it carefully with the photo. He noted the footage-counter number on the player so that later a frame could be taken from the tape as evidence.

'It's Sturmer. It has to be!' O'Malley finally said. 'But for all the good knowing that is, he could be on the moon.'

He rewound the video and continued to vent his frustration.

The Dutch don't have a law which stops this sort of thing being sold openly. So they say *they* don't have a problem. The Germans say how do you tell from a film if a kid's underage? Especially a Thai? So when in doubt, let it go. So *they* also say they don't have a problem. The Danes and Swedes say – don't blame us. We didn't start this. So *they*, too, say they don't have a problem.

O'Malley removed the cassette from the machine. He began to pace around his office. Its stained-wood panelled walls were covered with plaques from various civic organizations commending his work. A German Customs Service sign hung beside a Scotland Yard pennant. They were mementoes of joint operations.

O'Malley continued to address the agent.

It's not the fault of the cops in Europe. They'll bust a gut to help us. But too often they work in a pig-in-a-poke situation. Their politicians make a lot of noise. But in the end it doesn't amount to a can of beans. They say it's an American problem. That most of the filth is directed at us. So we should deal with it here. We got a hundred knuckleheads in Europe who just don't want to know. Nobody's dumping on their doorsteps. Only on ours.

94

O'Malley tossed the clipboard on to his desk and suddenly sat down in his high-backed chair, breathing deeply.

'You see the look on Sturmer's face? He really enjoyed brutalizing the kid. Him, I have to get!'

After the agent left, O'Malley sat staring at Sturmer's photo. It was unusual for a pornographer to appear in photographs or film which could incriminate him. Whatever made Sturmer do so, clearly indicated he had become careless or over-confident his pornography was secure. A number of people were now in jail who had forgotten that certainty often bred mistakes. O'Malley began to think how to persuade Sturmer into making one.

EIGHT

Suffer the Children

Susan sat on the couch in the Center's interview room and thought how best to frame the right question which would draw out Danny – the clincher question which would get him to reveal still more about the Ranch.

He hadn't touched the books and games she had placed beside him, including his favourite, checkers. They would usually sit on the floor, he determined to win, she gradually asking questions. When the game ended, she would move on the couch and continue putting them, as if it was part of the game. She tried again.

'Bet I beat you this one time.' He was precociously quick at checkers, able to think out several moves ahead. Whatever they had done to him, those who had abused Danny had not been able to destroy his intelligence.

'Don' wanna play.' Danny lowered his eyes.

If she had not known Danny was nine, she would have put his age at five-and-a-half, no more than six. Was that why his abusers had not worried, because he looked so young no one would have believed him?

There came a time when there was never an easy way to ask questions. The skill was to continue putting them in a non-threatening way.

'Do you win with your mom?'

From beyond the walls came familiar sounds: phones ringing, the cheerful voices of volunteers escorting parents and children to and from offices for their consultations, doors opening and closing. But in the interview room the silence stretched.

'She don' have time to play.' Danny's voice was the merest whisper.

'Ever play checkers with your dad?'

Danny shook his head and wiped his eyes with the back of his hand.

She bent forward. 'You want to cry, hon, that's okay.'

Danny's head dropped lower. 'Don' wanna cry.' He sounded close to tears.

She moved off the couch on to the floor and held him, running her hand gently over his face. She knew who had been evil enough to have done those things to Danny.

'Is it real hard to talk about your dad?'

She felt him flinch. 'It's okay, hon. No one's going to hurt you any more. Promise.'

He clung to her wordlessly.

'Danny, you know why I ask you questions?'

He gave a perplexed frown. ''Cos you wanna know things I'm not supposed to tell.'

She smiled. 'Well, yes. That too. But I want to help you.'

Last weekend she and Lee had gone to an exhibition of paintings by survivors of the Holocaust. She had remarked at the way after all those years they had still been able to reproduce the details of camp life. Lee said that kind of experience never faded from memory.

Looking into Danny's eyes she wondered if he would ever be able to forget.

'Danny, was it your dad who mostly drove you out to that place?'

The boy shook his head. 'Mustn' tell.' Danny's voice was small and distant. The volunteer who transcribed the tape would have difficulty getting the words.

Susan tried again. 'Did he say why you weren't to tell?'

He stared at her.

'Danny, if I said it was okay to tell, would you?'

He lowered his head. 'Dunno.'

She spoke with quiet authority. 'Well, I do know. If you talk about it, things won't seem so bad. Talking's good for everyone. People can help when they know things. And I just want to help you. That's all, hon.'

Danny kept his head lowered.

She continued sounding positive. 'Lots of little boys and girls have come here and they've been helped. I can help you, if you let me.'

Susan continued asking questions.

'When he took you out, did your dad buy you soda-pop? Or coke?'

Danny looked uneasy. 'He always brought alon' a drink.'

The large blue eyes drifted around the room, moving from the checker board to the walls painted in strong primary colours, back to her face.

She smiled at him. 'Did you like the drink?'

'Didn't taste much like soda.'

97

She knew it was too soon to probe further about the drink that had probably been a sedative.

The silence stretched.

Susan was facing a familiar problem: how to coax from Danny further vital information – but which would not distress the boy. One result of that could be for him to embellish what had actually been done to him, or what he had really seen. Susan called it the I-Want-To-Please syndrome.

It seems from the grey and often uncharted area of knowing that, while children seldom lie about what they have endured, they are not always able to tell the truth. Usually it is because what they have suffered is so awful they cannot speak about it. Instead, they often describe something they have seen or have heard happen to another child.

The condition is clinically know as *projection*, a complex defence mechanism which diverts unpleasant experiences away from what Freud has called the *me* to the *not me*. He identified it as a common way for children, in particular, to cope with emotionally charged encounters. Susan had become adept at spotting projection, enabling her to deal better with the anxiety many children display, and to understand that in cases like Danny's, one of their strongest defences is that of denial, what she calls *psychic reality*. It was another Freudian term to describe the kind of refusal to admit the true situation. It makes children like Danny all that much harder to help.

In cases like his there was the further problem that Danny could be confused easily, especially if the questions were deliberately designed to unsettle him, as she had seen policemen and defence lawyers often try and do to young victims.

Even FBI agents specially trained to interview children, still did that with their questions. It is part of any policeman's training to cast doubt.

It still made Susan angry to know what had happened at Jordan in Minnesota in 1983. Children told the local police they had been forced to witness ritual murder. They were exposed to the full rigour of investigation. Under its unremitting pressure she thought it inevitable that they had begun to produce different stories about how the sacrifice was performed, and where the body had been buried. The investigation finally ended up the way so many others had – a closed file marked: 'Insufficient evidence to proceed.'

She knew how close that had come to happening in the now celebrated Fuster case. Ileana and Frank Fuster had run a baby-sitting service in the fashionable Miami suburb of Country Walk. In their home they looked after a couple of dozen children whose parents

98

included local police officers. A simple check by one of them would have revealed Frank Fuster was a convicted child molester who raped his own wife before they married.

The allegations against the couple surfaced when a four-year-old boy suddenly asked his mother to kiss his penis. When the horrified parent asked where he had been told to do such a thing, the child had said 'Aunty Ileana does it to me.'

The police finally put together a case. But it all sounded, to them, so incredibly bizarre, that some officers still half-expected it to be thrown out of court. After all, who could possibly believe children who said they had been asked to drink something called 'demon slime', which had made them sufficiently sleepy to enjoy playing with 'Uncle Frank's' excrement and urine? Or watch the couple have sex? Or 'Uncle Frank' stamp to death birds on the floor of the play school? And, most incredible of all, were the children's stories about 'Uncle Frank' holding a knife to their throats and saying he would kill them if they ever 'told'. Who was going to believe any of *that*?

In court the lawyers who defended the Fusters attacked the therapist who was trying to help the children rebuild their lives, suggesting his real motive was extracting information which could help the prosecution.

The defence team insisted their clients were being pilloried, claiming 'someone had somehow brainwashed' the children to make 'such monstrous and patently unbelievable allegations,' or the children had 'somehow' been subjected to 'a more subtle form of coercion than the North Vietnamese did to our prisoners of war.'

The case looked doomed. Suddenly, and inexplicably, Ileana Fuster confessed that everything the children said was true. Standing on the witness stand, her deep-set eyes and long, braided hair giving her a curiously waif-like appearance, the young woman described how she had indeed been forced to undress in front of the children and made to perform oral sex on them. The 'demon slime' was a concoction of crushed Valium tablets, urine and lemonade which the children were forced to drink before being made to watch Fuster rape his wife with a crucifix and an electric drill. Afterwards he had killed another of the parakeets the couple kept as pets. Fuster was convicted on multiple counts of child abuse and was now serving the first of six consecutive terms of life imprisonment.

Though the children in that case had been vindicated, Susan knew all over North America and, she knew from reports, in Britain, Europe and Australia, other children were still having their stories regularly challenged or openly disbelieved.

Susan looked at Danny, thinking again who would believe him if it ever came to the day when he would stand in court and testify?

And would the defence attorneys try and suggest that the boy had been manipulated by her?

Danny broke the silence. 'You mad at me?'

'No, of course not. Why should I be?'

'Cos I don' wanna talk.'

'Did your dad get mad at you for things like that?'

'Uh-huh.'

'What sort of things, hon?'

Danny bit his lip. 'Like when I told him about not wantin' to go there.'

'The place out in the desert?'

'Uh-huh.'

'Where they took the photos? And made you watch what happened to the baby?'

After a long pause: 'Uh-huh.'

'Was your dad there?'

Danny looked away.

Susan tried to decide whether Danny's silence meant he was either embarrassed, or did not fully understand the importance of the question. The session with Danny, as with any other child, involved a complex interplay of questioning, counselling and comforting. Danny was a confused and traumatized person whose level of communication and comprehension were years behind that of an adult. The important thing was constantly to show him she understood his feelings.

'It must have been very upsetting,' she said.

After a while Danny looked at her. 'My dad said I wasn' be upset.'

This time Susan remained deliberately silent. She calls it 'reflective listening', a technique which allows her to absorb what has been said and to try and decipher the emotional content of the words. From experience she knew any interview with a child victim of sexual abuse is likely to be laden with emotion. The important thing is not to deflect it. Unaddressed emotional issues could block the collection of information essential for therapy – and hopefully, a successful prosecution of those responsible.

She is always careful to make sure her questions are non-judgmental. One of the many characteristics of sexual exploitation which hampers therapy is that the abuser has usually established a bond or 'secret pact' with the child, either through affection, coercion or guilt. Such a bond is often so severe a source of trauma for a child – to tell or not to tell – that it inhibits disclosure of what happened.

Despite all he had suffered, Susan suspected that bond was stopping Danny from talking about what his father had done to him, and had allowed others to do.

'Did your dad make you watch what happened to the baby?'

Danny once more looked away.

Not only did she try to keep her questions direct and simple, but she was careful to make sure they did not suggest any active participation on Danny's part. That would reinforce feelings of guilt in the child.

But she had devised a list of questions to obtain specific and complete details which are essential for any prosecution to succeed. They include a description of the abuser, his clothing, vehicle or house; the number and specific nature of acts of abuse; whether pornography or erotica, such as pictures or films, were used during the offences; if drugs were administered; if the child was photographed; if other children were involved.

She tailored the guidelines to individual cases. What she called 'when' questions – those designed to obtain dates and times – were put sparingly. Most children, she had discovered, have difficulty remembering such details. She found that a good way to obtain reliable 'when' information is to associate questions with familiar events: holidays, a child's birthday, those of family members, the school year and grade levels, the seasons, even mealtimes and bedtime.

In the early interviews with Danny, Susan had put a number of 'when' questions to try and pinpoint dates and times, and to try and find out who else had been present when Danny said he had been made to witness the baby being killed and eaten. Once more she returned to the matter.

'When your dad first took you out to the desert was that the day after you got your cold shot?'

Danny shook his head. 'Two days. I was sick the day after my shot.'

Susan smiled. 'I feel the same when I get my shots.'

Danny looked around the room. 'I'sn' cold in here.'

She smiled and nodded. 'Was it cold out in the desert?'

'Uh-huh.'

'Was that in the summer? Did you go often? During school holidays?'

'Uh-huh.'

'On your birthday?'

'Uh-huh.'

'On Thanksgiving?'

'Uh-huh. We went lotsa times. Lotsa, lotsa times.'

'More times than you can count on all your fingers?'

Danny nodded.

'And your toes as well?'

'Uh-huh.'

Susan knew children are prone to embellish, because they believe that the easiest way to get along in the world is to try and please adults. One way to do this is to tell grown-ups what they imagine adults want to hear. The important thing is to recognize when a child is doing that.

Danny looked up at Susan. He whispered. 'After the baby, we didn't go any more.'

Susan considered how next to proceed. Though she had more practical experience than many investigators, she accepted that dealing with Satanic abuse is still largely unknown territory. The rules are not only still to be written, but even seasoned investigators became often bogged down in assessing the symbols and paraphernalia of Satanic ritual. She always tried to use old-fashioned fact finding. The most important point, she told her staff, is to always remember that a specific incident may *not* have happened, but that did not mean a very similar incident has *not* occurred. Their attention must constantly be focussed on trying to establish the consistency and credibility of a child before, during and after the actual crime. When a child like Danny could not easily verbalize what had happened, other means had to be found.

'How about if I fetched a pad and pencil, and you could draw anything you want?'

He averted his eyes. 'Don' wanna.'

She smiled reassuringly. 'I know it's not because you are bad at drawing. Your mom said you are best in the class.'

He lowered his head. 'Don' wanna draw.'

The silence returned.

Susan tried again. 'If you tell me, maybe I could draw it. And you could see if I get it right.'

Danny gave no response.

She thought he had the bluest eyes she had seen. His small, pinched face was topped with a cascade of waves which flowed over his ears and were cut in a curiously old-fashioned bob. He looked like a page in some painting of a medieval court scene. Susan had no difficulty in imagining others would have seen in the little boy a reflection of the Child Jesus. That was probably another reason why they had taken him, and done to him what they had.

The concealed reel-to-reel tape continued to record the silence.

Two months had passed since Danny had sat here and described how he had been made to watch a baby ritually killed and devoured by his father and other adults, and then how he and other children were forced to eat the remains of the infant.

That had been the evening of the break-in.

In its aftermath Susan had made a number of decisions. She had decided not to change the lock on the Center's front door, because she did not want to alert, or alarm, the other staff about the incident. She also concluded that even if she replaced the lock, it would make no difference. Whoever had broken in, could do so again. She had decided not to tell the police, because that would require from her a greater faith in the open-mindedness of law enforcement than she possessed.

She had tried to reconstruct from memory what was in the stolen files. She thought she had remembered most of it.

There had been an agonizingly painful session with Bonnie. Bonnie had suddenly burst out that the death of her daughter was all her fault because, she, too, had a dark and terrible secret: she had been abused by her own father, and had never gotten over being molested. When she realized what was happening to her little girl, Bonnie thought it was somehow 'God's punishment' for what she had allowed her father to do.

Susan had seen Bonnie three times since then, encouraging her to talk, gradually beginning to remove the woman's guilt, telling Bonnie her feelings were understandable, and that adult survivors commonly experience them. She had told Bonnie about those nights she had herself sat with Lee, describing her own experiences. Bonnie had looked at her wonderingly, and then smiled through her tears, saying thank God she was not alone. Susan often shared her memories for that very purpose.

Though Bonnie would need many weeks more of intensive counselling, Susan was optimistic that, now she had begun to talk her case would be relatively straightforward. Having finally confronted her biggest, darkest secret, Bonnie should be able to face up to the loss of her daughter.

Danny's response to therapy, on the other hand, had been disappointingly different. Just when she thought she was making real progress, the boy had lapsed back into his shell.

Looking at him now, Susan felt again that he would be putty in the hands of some already unconvinced police officer or smart defence lawyer. An experienced trial attorney would tie-up the boy in knots – presenting Danny's silences and hesitations as further proof he was lying.

She could imagine what a lawyer would say to the boy. 'Danny,' a lawyer might ask, 'do you know what a lie is?'

And the boy would nod, the way he had sometimes nodded in this room over the past weeks. The lawyer would press. Did Danny know the difference between a small lie and a big lie? What was the biggest lie he had ever told? Had he ever told a lie to his mother? One about his dad? The politely framed questions would be designed to trap Danny. No matter how he would respond, doubts could be sown in the jury's mind. Later, the lawyer would tell the jurors, his voice still gentle and kindly, that all children lied. So why not Danny?

Susan knew defence lawyers are no longer brutal or hectoring in their questioning. They use instead a professional veneer of courtesy and patience. In many ways that is far more effective. A child often trusts the attorney who talks nicely to him in the dauntingly unfamiliar surrounds of a court.

To improve their techniques, lawyers who specialized in defending child abusers, attended seminars in the art of destroying the credibility of young witnesses. She had listened to a lecture where the speaker had not minced words.

> Children are insidious liars, and they're practised liars. They are the best. They can lie at the drop of a hat. In order to effectively discredit such a child you want to know the child's history. You want to know about the people who don't like the child. You want to know what those people have to say about the child. Subpoena the school records. Then insist upon your right of confrontation. Insist that you must be able to cross-examine this child in an adversarial position. That's what a trial is all about. I find that children do not have good memories, and to show that these children do not have real good memories, I ask them about specific occurrences in their life, such as their birthday, Christmas Day and so forth. I ask them where they were, and what they did on those days, and I try to show that they really can't remember. So they make it up. Show through your cross-examination that a child has a vivid imagination. Be prepared to lead the child into a situation that could not possibly occur. What you want to project is the feeling that this particular child cannot be trusted to tell the truth.

She had come away disgusted that so much energy and effort was being put into defending the abusers while so little was still being done to establish the truth of the kind of story that Danny had told her.

Danny's parents were divorced. His father lived with a woman out on Buena Park. He was in the aerospace industry: she worked with a nationwide property company. They led the lifestyle of the comfortably off. Danny, on the other hand, had a cramped and restricted existence. His mother was the manager of an apartment block, a singles-only complex for the successful and upwardly mobile. Her hours were long and she had little time to take the boy out. Danny spent most of his time at home watching TV.

104

Mother and son lived at the rear of the building, in what she called the Manager's Apartment. After visiting, Susan thought the description a huge overstatement. Danny's home was three small boxes, one where his mother cooked and they ate, another where they showered and used the toilet, the third where they slept, Danny on a fold-down bed, his mother on a divan. The place was neat and spotless on the day she called. Even so, Danny's mother, when showing her around, constantly straightened items in a nervous distracted manner. Susan wondered how much a part that had played in the break-up of the marriage.

Danny's mother clearly loved him, and kept on saying that she only wanted the best for the boy. She explained that was why she had swallowed her own bitterness over the divorce, and allowed Danny's father back into their lives.

Susan had sensed something and she asked what access arrangements the court had granted the boy's father. Danny's mother replied that she asked the judge to allow the father to see her son as often as he liked. Not bothering to hide her own anger, the woman added that, for a whole year, his father had nevertheless neither called nor sent a present at Christmas or on Danny's birthday.

Then, one day he had shown up, in a shiny new car and said he would like to start taking Danny away for weekends. She remembered how he stood in her doorway, in expensive sports clothes, tanned and looking fit, and over his shoulder she glimpsed a blonde woman in the passenger seat, dressed completely in black with matching sunglasses. Danny's mother thought it strange for a woman to dress like that in daytime. Danny's father made no move to introduce them.

The weekend outings became a regular occasion. Danny's father picked him up after school on a Friday and brought him back on Sunday evenings. His mother forced herself not to question Danny over what he had done, or where his father had taken him, because she couldn't bear to think of that woman being with her son.

At this point, she had smiled wanly at Susan who, as she often did, reached for the hand of Danny's mother, squeezing it and silently encouraging her to continue.

She described how she had begun to notice Danny was quiet when he came home. It would be a day or so before he returned to normal. She had supposed it was the boy's conflict over being torn between his parents. She had read an article in one of the magazine digests that the best way to handle the situation was to say nothing. Another hand squeeze. The world was filled with writers offering pop-psychology solutions. If only life was as simple as they portrayed it, Susan had thought.

After a few weeks, his mother continued, Danny had his first nightmare. He sat up in bed, shouting and crying, 'No, no, no. Don't do that! It's alive!'

She had spent the rest of that night trying to calm the trembling child. The nightmares persisted and became worse, with Danny screaming out frightening words about not wanting something killed, and that he did not want to eat what he had seen killed. When she tried to question him, he became withdrawn and anxious.

Finally, she had taken him to the local hospital, which ran a community mental health programme offering free consultation. The doctor who saw Danny recommended he should be brought to the Center. Susan had taken on the case and had told his mother she was certain that Danny's trauma resulted from what had taken place during those weekends with his father.

His mother had wanted to call in the police. Susan persuaded her not to, explaining they would interrogate Danny, which might further traumatize him. She suggested instead that she should continue to explore quietly with Danny what had happened. Then, after she judged he was sufficiently able to cope with his experiences, they could consider going to the police.

In the meantime, Susan advised, Danny's mother should refuse the boy's father further access. If he resisted, the Center would provide her with free legal help.

When Danny's father next called, she told him she would no longer allow the boy to go away at weekends. He had turned on his heels and walked back to the car. As they drove off the woman in black had turned and looked at her. Then she had slowly removed her sunglasses. Danny's mother told Susan she felt more frightened then than she had ever been in her life.

During her years in law enforcement, Susan had learned how to obtain information quickly and discreetly. She soon collected a considerable amount of data on the woman in black. Susan now knew her credit rating, her bank account number, social security status, her present position and salary and her previous posts. In all the places she had worked, she had been employed in the shipping department of a property company. Susan had discovered she was responsible for moving its fleet of trucks across North America. Sometimes they crossed into Mexico and Canada. Susan made further discreet enquiries. One of the routes the trucks regularly used was the highway which ran through the desert. It passed the turning off into the mesa which Pamela told her led to the Ranch.

In Pamela's office, Charlie's mother, Lili, sat straightbacked on her chair, facing Pamela across the desk, listening intently, occasionally wringing her hands together.

'What's this gonna do to him?' Lili moved her lips, trying out

106

several unspoken words, finding none of them suitable. Finally she settled for: 'I saw *The Exorcist*. I don't want that to happen to Charlie.'

Lili worked one hand into another.

Pamela continued to frame her words carefully, 'It isn't anything like that. Spiritual reversal is very rewarding and reassuring. The children always feel better afterwards. And sometimes we learn a lot. The Reverend Sempstrott is a recognized expert in the area and he is especially good with children. Spiritual reversal is just what it says it is. It'll bring to the fore once more all that is good in Charlie.'

'I see,' Lili took off her glasses and polished them on the sleeve of her dress. She stared myopically. 'No hypnosis, nothing like that?'

'Absolutely not. It's all to do with the power of prayer.'

'I see,' Lili chewed her lip, 'I really don't know.'

Pamela waited. She had seen the hesitation in others.

'You understand, I'm worried for Charlie? What this could do . . . what people will say.'

Pamela interrupted, 'No one will know, Lili. It's totally confidential.'

Lili put her glasses back on, and her eyes became larger and curiously softer.

'You're absolutely certain?'

Pamela nodded, 'Absolutely.'

The conflict faded from the magnified eyes. The tug-of-war passed to Lili's lips.

'People don't understand these things. His dad doesn't. Thinks Charlie will be ostracized if people get to know. You can understand that, can't you . . . ?'

Pamela heard herself reply, so certain, so very sure, 'I can understand that. But I know it's going to be fine.'

Lili began to nod.

NINE

The Counter Network

Along a narrow corridor from Pamela's office, Allen Simmons sat behind a metal desk in an alcove. On the Center's list of employees he was described as Community Resource Director. The title gave no indication of the thirty-eight-year-old former Catholic priest's responsibilities on this September morning.

He also was the subject of continuous speculation among some of the younger women staff over why he resigned from his Order. He liked to kid them it was over a woman – the truth was more prosaic. He had found the discipline of religious life too harsh.

At the Center, whatever he was engaged upon, he did with unfailing cheerfulness. His main job was fund-raising, keeping in regular contact with corporations and organizations throughout California. He had a natural skill for sensing where funds are available, and how best to persuade executives to divert them to support the Center. Some weeks he pulled in several thousand dollars; the money was carefully entered in his record book.

He was also the Center's archivist and like his desk, the alcove overflowed with reports and documents. They were piled on every available inch of floor not already occupied by the wall of filing cabinets, themselves stuffed to capacity with more papers. Most were from child-care agencies around the world and the information was often stomach-churning. But he could remember reading nothing as horrific as this description of the cold-blooded murder of helpless slaves. He slumped lower in his chair, holding the report in both hands, the way he had once held a missal.

His bulk gave him an almost squat appearance. His face, however, would not have disgraced the back of a coin. Its dominant features were a powerful out-thrust chin and the nose of an imperious cardinal, with high-coloured cheekbones to match. His dark hair drew back from a wide brow which, in turn, rose from eyebrows that were twin thunderclouds. Only his eyes seemed out of place in such an autocratic face, they were soft and moist, as if they alone knew of an inner, and altogether gentler man than his other features suggested.

He was close to tears as he continued reading the report from the Sudanese relief agency about how a thousand Dinka tribesmen, women and children, had been herded and locked into wooden rail trucks, which were doused with petrol and set alight. The wagons had burnt for a day. The incident was now over a year old, but it had taken that long for the agency to piece together what happened on the night of 27/28 March 1987, at a place called Diein in Western Sudan. Attached to the report was a map of the massacre site. Allen took an atlas off a shelf and opened it at a map of Sudan and began to run a finger over the desert region, trying to pinpoint Diein.

One of the women volunteers stood over his desk.

'Susan wants these stored.'

She dropped a pile of folders on the desk, then bent over and squinted at the map. 'Looking for a good vacation spot?'

She was pretty, fresh-faced, with frizzy hair and dark eyes. He always thought she smelled of newly-mown hay. He told her about the report.

'My God,' she said, 'what kind of people could do that?'

'The people who did that are no different to those we have to deal with.'

His voice was soft; smooth and reassuring, it had been honed in the priest's cubbyhole of a confessional.

He rummaged around the desk top. 'I picked up another story this morning for Susan that may help her with the Ranch.' He found the newsclip and placed it in a folder, handing it to her.

He watched her sashay down the corridor, wondering why some women chose to play Delilah to former priests. Sighing, he put aside the Sudanese report, and placed the files on the floor before concentrating on another of his morning tasks – sorting through newspapers for further clues about the Ranch.

There was a mention of the San Francisco mass murderer Leonard Lake.

He had been caught shoplifting in 1985 in a city store and had promptly swallowed a cyanide capsule. Their suspicions aroused at such a response to a minor offence, detectives went to his cabin in the Sierra Nevada mountains. They discovered racks of videotapes showing Lake sexually abusing people. Each victim was then ritually killed. He had rigged his camera to capture it all. Police had found mass graves of two dozen men, women and children.

The latest report said Lake may have worked at a ranch in Southern California which was suspected of being used by paedophiles. The ranch was not named. A New Orleans group of paedophiles had formed their own Boy Scout Troop and turned it into a sex-for-sale ring which had travelled across the country. Finally arrested, some of its members told police they had visited a ranch somewhere in the deserts of California, and now the police had told reporters they were not taking the claim seriously.

Another clue surfaced in a story about a conviction of a clergyman who ran a home for fatherless youths in Winchester, Tennessee. He had kept the place going by sending pornographic photographs he took of the boys, in return for tax-free contributions to the home's upkeep. For larger donations, he arranged for boys to be 'loaned' to sponsors – paedophiles throughout America. When the police arrested the minister, several of the boys spoke of a ranch where, they claimed, they had been sexually assaulted. Once more the reports did not pinpoint the whereabouts of the place; once more police expressed doubts about its existence.

Allen remembered reading of Lauren Stratford's experiences at the Ranch. She insisted she saw babies being skinned alive and children raped on altars and other kinds of sexual perversions, so horrific no one, he was certain, could have invented them. Yet Lauren said no one would believe her, and therefore nobody would bother to investigate the Ranch.

Yet Susan doggedly went on collecting these snippets of evidence, convinced one day they would form the basis for a criminal case. He could only admire her tenacity.

Yet after six months at the Center, Allen remained uncertain of their relationship. She was polite and friendly and never seemed to mind when he called her at home, sometimes late in the evening, with news of another donation. Yet, he sensed a distance between them, as if she was still assessing him. It made him wonder if he really had a future at the Center.

Every day brought police and FBI leaflets on missing American children. Other reports showed the problem was worldwide, and on the increase. There were envelopes bearing the bold red and black logo of the National Center for Missing and Exploited Children, and those with the cheerful one of Italy's national child-care organization. There were letters franked in Mexico, Brazil, Germany, France and Australia – on a good day the mail brought stamps from fifty, and more, countries.

The reports often provided tantalizing glimpses, making him want to know more. From London came news that the Commission for Filipino Migrant Workers had discovered a two-year-old Asian boy had been smuggled into England to be used as a ritual sacrifice. He had asked himself what happened to the child? Susan said there was no point in writing to the Commission asking for more information; there was nothing the Center could do with it. To follow-up every lead would require a staff many times greater than was available. It reminded Allen of how restricted the Center was by its budget.

Nevertheless, from a village in Cumbria, one so tiny his atlas did not list it, Chris Strickland continued to send detailed reports on Britain's Satanic underworld. She had originally written seeking support for a child-care agency she had started, to help cases of ritual abuse in her own community, and the Center provided her with guidance on how to counsel victims and their families.

Recent letters from her contained the names and addresses of English clergymen, Freemasons and even members of the Salvation Army, all of whom Chris feared, were involved in Satanic practices with children. Her descriptions showed the pattern of abuse was almost identical on both sides of the Atlantic. In her latest report she wrote that, when she had tried to bring the matter to police attention, she was politely brushed aside. Cumbria was really no different from California, he sighed.

Allen had ample evidence to show Britain had established itself as the European centre for Satanic activities. In 1989 there were an estimated one hundred thousand cult members, with London as their main centre. Sizeable groups were centred on the city's Notting Hill and Camden areas; smaller ones existed in Bloomsbury, Wimbledon and Ealing. Other covens met in Birmingham, Manchester, Glasgow, Leeds and Brighton. So serious was the problem in the seaside resort, that Canon Dominic Walker, Vicar of Brighton, had set up a team to fight Satanic activities. They had so far dealt with fifteen hundred cases 'of occult oppression'. Walker feared that, as the year 2000 approached – heightening interest in not only Christian belief at the dawn of a new millennium, but among Satanists too – Britain would see an increase in paganism and a return to that time 'of fear in a world where God was far away and the earth was abandoned to demons.'

In one of the few investigations into Satanic activities in Britain, another clergyman, the Reverend Kevin Logan, discovered that in a survey of several hundred school children, 89 per cent admitted to having 'dabbled' in the occult, and six per cent habitually used it to try and influence events. Children in Britain were praying to the Devil to help them pass examinations and obtain jobs. Logan also discovered that a number of British Satanists are lapsed Catholics – who have reversed the liturgy and celebrate black mass with an inverted cross and consecrated hosts stolen from churches.

Childwatch, the charity which monitors child abuse in Britain, reported there existed 'a horrific occult problem in these islands. Satanists believe that children, by virtue of their innocence, increase their power. Paedophiles, posing as Satanists, are using children

111

through an underground network that extends to all corners of the country – and beyond.'

Evidence to support Childwatch's claim was reinforced by an account, in 1988, by Audrey Harper, a woman who described herself as 'a former black witch'. She claimed that at her initiation ceremony in London's now-fashionable Dockland, a nine-day-old baby was slaughtered. Harper also alleged a thirteen-year-old girl was raped on a Satanic altar. She insisted that throughout Britain, 'teenagers just disappear. People think they have run away from home. In fact they have been snatched for sacrifice. Afterwards their bodies are consumed. What bones remain are totally destroyed.'

Harper also claimed her coven had included a doctor and a lawyer with 'close connections' to various police forces. That, she insisted, 'will explain why it is pointless for me to go to the police'.

From West Germany Allen received reports from Catholic organizations stating there were 'at least' 10,000 practising Satanists in the country, and the figure was on the increase. Many were young and raised in the Church, but had ceased to practise their faith. Black masses were being regularly held on the campuses of the country's leading universities, including those in Munich and Saarbrucken, both traditional Catholic seats of learning.

In Westphalia, a fifteen-year-old girl had cut her wrists on a Satanic altar and died of loss of blood. She belonged to a coven called 'Luzifaciner'. Again, its members were mostly lapsed Catholics. After the girl's death, the cult membership increased.

The Catholic diocesan office of Augsburg reported, in 1988, 'an unprecedented increase' in the number of calls from parents frightened their children were involved with occult practices in the city.

From French agencies Allen received reports there are now a record number of separate Satanic cults – as many as 400 – in the Republic. The majority were also made up of disaffected Catholics.

But it was from the supposed heartland of Catholicism, Italy, that he had received the most disturbing news. There were now said to be 40,000 Satanists in Turin alone – forcing the diocese's chief exorcist to increase his number of exorcists five-fold. The city's cardinal-archbishop Anastasio Ballestero, had publicly stated Turin was in a 'fever of occultism and black masses'. He said there was at least one authenticated murder of a victim of satanic rites in Turin.

Whatever paper writ ran, it seemed to Allen, Satanic practices are on the increase. Many involved the young, often children. He had formed the opinion that there was a definite link between the failure of organized religion, particularly the Catholic faith, and those practices.

Other reports reaching his desk showed children continued to be abused in other ways.

An American oil worker in the Gulf described camel races in Dubai in which terrified boys were lashed to the back of animals, like Shambu had been. On the day the rigger had watched, several fell and were seriously injured.

The Under-Secretary for Child Welfare in Ecuador, Elsa Maria Castro, had sent an urgent warning announcing the suspension of all adoptions to foreigners following the discovery within the country of a well-organized gang which kidnapped babies and sold them to childless couples in Britain and Norway. At least thirty children had been disposed of before the scandal had come to light.

The same post brought a warning, from Piet Stofflen, a Dutch member of parliament, claiming similar gangs operated in Guatemala – and that this time the stolen children were being sold-off to pro-curers in the United States. Each child reportedly fetched an average of $15,000.

The Center's counterpart in Bangkok, the Center for the Protection of Children's Rights, reported some six thousand Thai children were kidnapped off the capital's streets over a period of a few months in 1988. The agency traced them as far as the Middle East. Allen suspected some of the children were also destined for Europe's and North America's sex rings.

There were hundreds of names of traffickers on file at the Center – evidence of the sheer global extent of slavery. There was evil in the world Allen Simmons had not realized until he came to work in the Center.

Allen looked at the list of names he had targeted for his next round of fund-raising calls.

The phone buzzed.

'Allen? Marcia Lombard's father's on the line.' The receptionist sounded anxious. 'Will you talk to him? He's about to do something crazy.'

Even before he lifted the phone, Allen guessed what Sam Lombard was about to do.

In the interview room Susan continued trying to question Danny.

The fifty-minute session was coming to a close. Susan sensed it was time to press.

'Was Tom with your dad all the time when they did that to the baby?'

Danny nodded.

Susan leant forward and spoke very slowly and deliberately, 'Just tell me what happened.'

'Tom said wasn't to tell,' Danny returned to staring at the floor.

Susan glanced at the case file on the couch beside her. It was open at a page:

> Transcript/summary of tape, 5/3/88. Danny spoke about Tom. Said he had taken him to room out at 'the place' and showed him 'baby on table'. Tom said baby was dead, to 'make us strong'. Danny then mentioned a 'church'. I asked where the church was, and he said 'my dad's church is where the bodies are'. I showed him the album we had assembled, and while he was going through it, he stopped at Charlie's drawings of the Ranch. He pointed at them and became frightened. Then I showed him a photograph of a church and one of a cemetery with headstones. He pointed at the pictures and said, 'Tom lives here . . . '.

Tom was a local businessman whose name already appeared in several of the Center's files as being a suspected Satanist.

There was a knock on the door. Susan looked up, surprised. There was a strict rule that no one interrupted a counselling session. Concealing her irritation she walked to the door.

Allen stood white-faced and tense in the corridor. 'Sam Lombard has gone off to look for the Ranch, to try and find his little girl.'

O'Malley slumped back in his office chair, listening, the phone pressed hard against his ears, thinking people remembered only the high points of any operation; how successful it had been, never when it had run its course. Whenever he had to, he always told his agents what he was telling Richard Rivera in Mexico City.

'Come up with something new, Dick, and we'll give it another shot.'

He sensed Rivera's juices flowing, already thinking of some way to maintain International Enterprises, the name of the dummy company which had been at the heart of Operation Cameo. As stings went, it hadn't been a big one. The entire corporate assets of International Enterprises were virtually contained in the rental cost for a mail box in Mexico City's central post office. O'Malley had named the fake company and placed advertisements for its wares in porn magazines in North America, using another of his aliases to do so. Every day Rivera had checked the box for orders for sexually explicit magazines.

He was 'Erik' to the paedophiles who wrote for material. Those who appeared cautious were reassured by Erik's story of having moved from Copenhagen to Mexico City so that he could operate without 'government pressure'. Over several months, Operation Cameo had led to the arrest of a score of American paedophiles who had ordered pornography through the mail. Suddenly, the orders stopped.

Rivera, an assistant Customs attaché in Mexico City, wanted to keep the sting running just a little longer.

O'Malley could imagine Rivera, sitting in his office, feet up on his desk, staring out of the window at the smog which always gave Mexico at this time of year the appearance of an old tinted photograph. Up there, on the top floor of the embassy, the chorus of horns would be muted, and the vastness of the city less daunting. Later, when he went to close down the post office box, Rivera would be back among the burning smog and diesel fumes, and that indefinable tension which only comes when twenty million people are forced to live in close proximity.

O'Malley respected Rivera. Like himself, the agent had worked in places where the streets did not have pavements. Rivera had chased contraband, gun and drug runners up and down Central America and there was now a price on his head – a half-million dollar contract – after he bust an arms smuggling gang. When he heard, Rivera laughed and said that was par for the job. O'Malley liked a man with that attitude.

'Think of something good, Dick, and we'll work it together again.'

'We okay for stock?'

'Sure. Got a room full of stuff. Magazines. Videos. Filth for all tastes. You just think of a good sting and I'll supply the goods.'

There was another echoey laugh from Mexico. Rivera's voice was suddenly serious.

'Got another goddam call from Washington the other day about this kids' organs scam. Damn thing just won't die.'

O'Malley's voice was crisp. 'Not our brief, Dick. We've got to stick with the porn stuff.'

More reports had surfaced that children were being stolen in South and Central America, flown across the border in light aircraft and sold to child sex rings or for their organs to be used for transplants.

There was no shortage of rumours about who was involved. One named was Air Force Colonel Phil Willer, a World War Two veteran turned contraband-runner whose twin-engined Beechcraft had finally been shot down by a Mexican anti-aircraft unit – Willer died strapped in the cockpit. Ironically, there was no one else on board. But the story persisted that other fliers had inherited his role, and substantial income. One was known as the Desert Jackal, a sixty-year-old American who learned his flying against the Japanese in the Pacific in World War Two. Another had flown a helicopter gunship in Vietnam.

115

A pilot could make two thousand dollars on a ninety-minute round trip from some Mexican mountaintop or jungle clearing, and skim over the border to land at a remote landing strip in New Mexico or Texas. Some made two or three flights a day. The more experienced used Beech-18s, because of the aircraft's capacity and manoeuvrability. The majority of the fliers were mercenaries who had flown for the CIA.

Catching them was almost impossible. They flew their sorties like fighter aces, hugging the terrain to avoid radar, choosing a landing site at the last moment, keeping their engines running while their human cargoes were unloaded and driven off. By the time a Border patrol reached a landing strip, there was usually nothing to be seen but tyremarks. The fliers were like will-o'-the-wisps, protected by the community who lived in that twenty-mile strip which ran for more than two thousand miles, a nation unto itself, long and narrow, only nominally ruled from Mexico City or Washington. No one in that closed community doubted they were certainly ruthless enough to either carry organs for transplants or even living human donors. But in places like El Paso, Ciudad Juarez, Mexicali and Calexico, those who flew the planes knew their secrets were safe. People had been killed for talking about less.

Elsewhere the allegations about organ transplants continued more publicly. The matter had been raised at the European Community's headquarters in Brussels and debated in the Italian Parliament. The controversy was further fuelled when the Soviet newspaper, *Izvestia*, published a lengthy article based, it claimed, on information supplied by Defence for Children International. The story alleged the United States was the world's biggest market for organs illegally removed from children.

The State Department furiously insisted that DCI should publicly renounce the report. The agency refused to be intimidated by the ferocity of the attack and informed Washington that DCI would not issue a public disclaimer, but would 'mention the affair' in the next edition of its newsletter, *Monitor*. In the newsletter DCI argued, that a public rebuke to *Izvestia* would only further the controversy and that, in any event, any retraction DCI demanded would almost certainly not be published in the Soviet newspaper.

The Reagan Administration was outraged.

Within hours DCI found itself beleaguered by the world's press; reporters claimed they had 'damning information' that DCI was 'a Soviet pawn' and that its financial survival 'depended' on Moscow. The agency bravely faced a mounting and increasingly hostile media blitz. Then came the news that the United States government intended to seek the revocation of DCI's consultative status with the United Nations.

116

In the face of such intense and unremitting pressure, the agency issued a public statement hardly on the lines the Reagan Administration demanded.

> It is not easy to say, as the US authorities maintain, that what happened was simply an exercise in disinformation, designed to blacken the image of the United States. But it is ironic and disturbing that the US government should make use of intimidation and slander, when all DCI had wanted to do was to try and discover the truth about the traffic in children as donors for organ transplants.

Officially, the matter was left to rest. Privately, American government agencies continued to brace themselves for the day when the traffic would be confirmed. Meanwhile, Washington spokesmen continued to issue a standard denial on the matter: there was no proof so there was no more to be said.

After completing the call to Rivera O'Malley crossed out International Enterprises on the list of names on the pad on his desk. He next dialled a number in St Louis to terminate another sting. An agent had been running Computer Pen Pals Club, from Box 12290 in a suburban post office. The corporation was designed to trap more extreme deviants – men who sought 'amputee sex and necrophilia'. The Club offered to provide 'five pals of similar interest for $5'. The come-on had bagged a number of men.

But, once more, the NAMBLA *Bulletin* had alerted its readers that the Club was a Customs operated front. The journal of the North American Man/Boy Love Association regularly published details on undercover operations O'Malley devised. He had no real idea who tipped-off NAMBLA. Most likely it was a mole somewhere in the United States postal service. Despite such setbacks, O'Malley supervised stings which still continued to produce gratifying results. From offices in Cincinatti, Cleveland, Denver, Detroit, Kansas City, Minneapolis-St Paul and Indianapolis, his agents continued intercepting pornography from Sweden, Denmark and the Netherlands. Under the alias 'Harry White', an agent successfully operated Box 3603 out of Davenport, Indiana. 'John Prothe' had recently opened Box 683 in Grand Island, Nebraska. 'Roger Spencer' kept picking-up paedophiles who responded to his Box 126 at Sandstone in Minnesota. 'Jolene Edwards' – a macho male agent posing as a woman – still lured pornographers into his Box 1744 at the local post office in Council Bluffs in Indianapolis.

The agents worked within strict guidelines laid by the Department of Justice on how far they could go to entrap someone.

It was a delicate balancing line which O'Malley continuously monitored.

He listened on the phone to an agent in Phoenix reading back a letter he proposed to send, one which he hoped would bring him in contact with a child sex-ring he believed was operating in the area. The sting, like many of the others, was relatively uncomplicated: it requ.red no more than a small ad and a rented mail box.

Infinitely more complex was the operation involving Georgetown University. The Washington-based campus had long had an association with the CIA and other federal agencies; many of its teaching staff had worked in government service. Georgetown was a logical choice as a cover for yet another sting designed to try and penetrate chil l sex rings operating among academics in North America.

The agent running it placed advertisements in magazines under the heading:

> Seeking gays and paedophiles. A doctoral student conducting research in the area of male sexual preference, behaviour, fantasies and erotica for a PhD in Clinical Psychology. Confidentiality assured. This study may provide evidence which could clarify stereotyped notions, widely held by society. The results of this survey will serve as the basis for publication in the respected scientific journals and provide vital clinical information and knowledge in the field of sexology.

Those who responded to the advertisement were asked to complete a fifteen-page questionnaire. The questions included: 'Do you currently have an intimate relationship with another person?' 'What is the age of that person?''What was your first sexual experience?' 'Were photographs or films made of your experience?' 'Who took them?' 'Do you obtain and save erotic materials?' 'Do you produce your own sexual material?' The questionnaire asked for details of 'sexual preferences and fantasies', beginning with the age group 0–5 years. Finally, respondents were asked to give their names and addresses as well as those of others interested in participating in the study.

While he was keeping 'a fatherly eye from the Parish House on all that was going on', O'Malley was moving again on his own sting against Sturmer.

The German's passport photograph and other details about him had been circulated to some three hundred points of entry into the United States, and sent to the fourteen US embassies where Customs maintained agents overseas. They would add Sturmer to their list of names to watch out for.

Automatically, copies of Sturmer's photograph went to the seven

Regional Intelligence Officers in each of the fifty-five districts and areas into which the United States was divided by the Customs service. Its Intelligence Operations Center in Washington also received a print. There it was copied and forwarded to the FBI, DEA and the CIA. Those agencies would send it out to their field offices and stations. They would also institute an automatic computer search of their own files for any record of Sturmer. If one surfaced, it would be electronically transmitted to the Customs Intelligence Operations Center. From there it would be faxed to O'Malley.

A copy of the passport photo went to the National Obscenity Enforcement Unit at the Department of Justice in Washington. Founded in 1987, its brief was to interdict those importing pornography into the United States. The unit would copy the print to RICOS, the specialist force of lawyers and police officers who fought Racketeer-Influenced Criminal Organizations, and RAAP, the Religious Alliance Against Pornography, a group which lobbied the media and Congress about the perils of pornography.

The Gulf States Blue Lightning Operations Command, BLOC, based in Miami, and in the front-line in the fight against drugs, would receive a copy of the passport photo. BLOC computers, second only to those of the CIA in the secret data they contain, would be checked to see if Sturmer had any connections to drug traffickers.

A print would be forwarded to the National Narcotics Interdiction Service, and the Immigration and Naturalization Service. Those agencies would send it on to other law-enforcement agencies they worked closely with. Over forty separate law-enforcement agencies in North America and close to a hundred around the world would eventually be alerted about Sturmer.

'In theory,' growled O'Malley, during a call to his immediate superior, John Sullivan, in Washington, 'in theory, that sonavabitch should not be able to click a camera without us knowing.'

Sullivan sighed. 'Jack, you know about theories. I know about theories. Theories are for the FBI behaviour people. The guys at Langley. They deal in theories. We're still writing the rule book for fighting pornography.'

O'Malley grunted. Sullivan asked how he was getting along with his plans to find a sequel to Operation Borderline.

'The President still talks about it, Jack, every time the Commissioner goes to the White House. We need something new to keep him happy.'

Working with a small team of agents, O'Malley had created a bogus company, Produit Outaouais, with a box office address in Hull, Quebec. He reasoned that a company located out of the country would raise less suspicion. Produit's principal product were three-by-five photographs of children in pornographic poses; each print was mounted on cardboard as if they were a baseball card. O'Malley had supervised the selection of photographs, culling them from previously seized material and rephotographing them. He had consulted a paediatrician to verify that each child was under the age of eighteen, the statutory definition of a minor.

O'Malley designed a brochure advertising 'boys and girls in sex action'. A set of twelve prints costs fifteen dollars. He had borrowed the euphemistic language used by genuine pornographers.

The brochure began: 'Hullo Lolita Collector'. Lolita is the accepted international code among paedophiles for child pornography. The brochure listed the products available. Their 'foto sets' included 'Nymph Lovers', 'Incest', 'Loving Children', 'Mini Boys', and 'Joe and His Uncle'.

In March 1987, O'Malley sent one of his agents to Ottawa to mail 2,500 fliers to known paedophiles in the United States. There were over two hundred responses. Some requested child-porn movies. O'Malley quickly produced these from seized tapes. He also created a second brochure advertising them. Orders poured in.

Posing as messengers from DHL Worldwide Couriers, with the company's permission, the packets of pornography were delivered. After each drop, an agent would radio a team of federal and local police officers waiting nearby with a search warrant. One hundred and sixty searches had been executed in twenty-three states. Two suspects had killed themselves. A twenty-five-year-old Ohio student shot himself; a Wisconsin lawyer left a note saying he was 'cursed with a demon sexual preference'.

For O'Malley, the outcry those suicides caused in sections of the media was compensated for when agents entered a house in Conneaut, Ohio. It was the home of an unemployed Vietnam War veteran, David McNutt, his wife Marsha, and their three small children. The agents not only found a 'Loving Children' photo set, but pictures showing McNutt had forced his own children – two girls, aged seven and five, and a two-year-old boy – to perform acts of oral sex on him. He admitted he kept the children locked in their room, only allowing them out for meals and to satisfy his sexual needs. His wife confessed she was aware of the abuse, but was too cowed to protest. McNutt was now serving a ten- to twenty-five year jail sentence.

'Let those liberal reporters and lawyers who say I'm guilty of entrapment, read the McNutt case files,' O'Malley had told Sullivan.

Sullivan had said: 'Jack, don't waste your energy worrying about those guys. Just come up with another Borderline.'

Now a year later, O'Malley had an idea. He asked Sullivan to wait while he loped to his office door and closed it.

TEN

The Loss

In her mind's eye, Susan continued the drive with Sam Lombard. Two days had now passed since he drove into the desert, taking only his Bible which he always carried with him and a route map.

Sam had returned with a story which Susan listened to in total silence. If she had not known Sam so well, she would have dismissed it out-of-hand. Even so, she had to remind herself he *had* to be telling the truth. What he was saying was just too bizarre and fantastic for anyone to invent. And frightening.

Lee sat beside her on the bench, in charge of the bottle of wine. On the table were the cold remains of supper. Sam continued to prowl the kitchen, pausing to study or touch a piece of equipment or crockery. She thought he was behaving like a survivor, as if he wanted to remind himself of ordinary everyday things. He was behaving like someone with post-trauma stress.

Sam went on describing the drive.

He had taken the state highway, driving between fields of fruit and vegetables, the air shimmering from the whirling sprinklers, and pungent with the not unpleasant smell of thickly-spread farmyard manure. Then abruptly the scrub appeared, and with it the first of the high chain-link fences – the government protecting its secrets from the people, Susan had called it.

Sam had passed Sidewinder Mountain and continued along Route 395 to Four Corners. On his left was Edwards Air Force Base. Eating a quick lunch, he had watched the planes come and go, deciding their flight path was directly over the Ranch. He continued driving, passing one dried-out lake after another. In the distance was the darkness of the Scqudia National Forest and, towering over the trees, the peaks of the Sierra Nevada. He drove past the Tiefort Mountains, and then the Granite Mountain range which extends all the way to Death Valley. On his map many of the roads are marked 'Closed to the Public'. They lead to military test-firing ranges.

The drive marked the first anniversary of Marcia's disappearance. On that day she had been a leggy thirteen-year-old, with a toothy smile and plaits. Now, if she was still alive, God only knew what she looked like. Abuse, Susan knew, did terrible damage to a child's body in a short period. Marcia was Sam's only daughter, the elder of his two children.

The girl had vanished from a picnic spot after she went off to explore among the bushes; nearby were her mother, Trish, and her younger brother, Pete. It had taken an hour before they began searching and it had taken them almost another hour to mobilize the few other picnickers on hand to help. Trish finally called the police. About three hours after Marcia was last seen, the official hunt was under way. Police found tyre tracks some distance from the bushes. A detective told Trish Marcia could by then be a hundred miles away.

The other picnickers at the site were quickly eliminated from inquiries. The police concentrated closer to home.

Investigators had questioned Pete and his mother. Had they told anyone they were going to the picnic area? Had they heard Marcia tell anyone? Did they notice a vehicle behind the bushes? Had they heard an engine start up? Each time Trish and Pete had given the same answer – no.

The police next concentrated on Marcia's own behaviour. Had she made any telephone calls in the days before going on the picnic? Had she a 'special' boyfriend? Was she secretive? Had she recently seemed worried or nervous?

Once more there had been the same definite response from her mother. Trish was certain Marcia had made no phone calls – at least from home. Marcia was a girl who never seemed worried or anxious, and she was not one to keep secrets. She had no regular boyfriend, but was part of a local teenage group. Each member was interviewed and eliminated. Marcia's teachers, class mates and neighbours were seen. No one recalled Marcia behaving in any way untoward. The investigators told each other that that did not mean Marcia had not run away for some reason.

They spoke to Marcia's doctor. He told them some teenage girls develop phantom pregnancies or a phobia that they've an incurable cancer. Others become pregnant and are unable to tell their parents. Marcia, he said, was a virgin, and he could think of no medical reason for her wanting to leave home.

Hundreds of inquiries continued to draw a blank.

Initially, the detective in charge told Sam his money was on a kidnapping. Trish and the children had probably been followed to the picnic site, and the gang waited their moment to snatch the first child they could. Why, Sam had demanded, why his family? The detective raised two fingers. Sam could pay. Or raise a ransom through a loan. Probably a bunch of lousy kids trying to find money to satisfy their drug habits, the detective had added, lowering his fingers.

There had been no word from any kidnappers – only a number of crank calls. Each was checked. All were genuine crank calls.

After a week the detective said kidnapping no longer looked a good bet. Once more he put the same questions he had asked at the outset of Marcia's disappearance. Had she been happy at home? At school? Had she quarrelled with anyone? Could she have a 'secret' boyfriend? Had she taken any calls, from anyone, before she vanished? Had she made any?

Trish and Sam became angry and resentful. The detective explained, in that detached way they had come to dislike, that the repeated questioning was all part of the investigation.

The police called on Susan for help, checking the Center's list of paedophiles, child molesters and deviants against their own records. She mentioned the Ranch as a possibility of a place where Marcia could have been taken.

The detective in charge of the investigation said he would, obviously, follow-up every possibility. Sam had been present and, after the detective left, he had asked Susan where the Ranch was located. After some hesitation, she told him.

In those first frantic days after Marcia vanished, her photo appeared on every news bulletin on every TV station in the state. Each time it was screened there were more sightings. In the first forty-eight hours the police logged over three hundred. She was spotted as far north as Seattle, and south close to the Mexican border. Someone had seen her in Houston, almost two thousand miles away. People thought they spotted Marcia in the company of variously, a middle-aged woman, a smartly-dressed young man, and even a family.

The public were responding to a poster Sam produced which bore Marcia's photograph and essential information – her name, age and colouring. Copies were distributed locally, and then throughout California. It was then sent to police forces in other states. As well as the Center, Sam contacted every other local and national child-care organization. The National Center for Missing and Exploited Children arranged to include her photograph on milk cartons. The family hired a private detective. He worked for a week and then decided he would achieve nothing the police could not. All their inquiries produced not a single tangible lead.

Soon Marcia's name was superseded by other entries on the FBI computers in Washington, of children kidnapped by strangers or abducted by a parent, youngsters kicked out of home, and the runaways, gone for any one of the reasons youngsters leave home, such as curfews, arguments about clothes and music, or over friends, or a bad record card at school.

The FBI usually do not become involved in tracing them unless the agency is sure a child has been kidnapped and taken across state borders. Investigation into missing persons is left to local police forces. Often they have limited resources – and none to sustain a lengthy investigation.

After a week the number of new sightings of Marcia dropped. At the end of a month they numbered a handful. After three months they stopped. By then the posters of Marcia had either faded, were defaced beyond recognition, or been replaced in supermarkets, stores, and gas stations, by new posters of other missing children.

The detective in charge of Marcia's case early on told Susan that the family could do with counselling. She saw them almost daily in those first few weeks, showing them how they could support each other during a terrible time. She was there in those especially difficult days when, after a fortnight, the police took out their phones and recorders, folded their tables and left the house. The detective explained to Sam, his voice more detached than ever, that the department would continue to do what it could.

Trish had told Susan it was like being told that Marcia had gone forever.

After six months the last of the reporters stopped calling. The crank callers lasted a little longer. Susan continued to drop by the house at least once a week on the way home from work. Mostly, she saw Trish and Pete as Sam was away on business for weeks at a time.

He had been on one of his trips through Europe when Pete, coming up to be four, and just started at day-care centre, was discovered to have been sexually abused. Trish found out when the little boy started bleeding during bathtime. She had taken Pete to a paediatrician. After examining Pete, the doctor called the police.

Trish tried to reach Sam. He'd left Berlin, and she missed him in Warsaw. She finally caught up with him in Leningrad. It had taken Sam two days to fix a flight home. He had arrived white-faced, not only from exhaustion, but from that corrosive anger which sometimes accompanies guilt. He had not blamed anyone but himself for what had happened, saying he should have checked out the school and the man's background. He should have handled Pete's safety with the same care he handled a business venture. He had said it all in a calm voice and Trish had not begun to suspect the effort it had needed for Sam to keep the lid down.

When the police investigation had got into its stride, it turned out Pete was one of twenty boys and girls who had been molested by the day centre's principal. It also emerged the man was a Vietnam veteran who had confessed to the police that he had acquired a taste for small children in Saigon. He had even married a Vietnamese girl and persuaded her to go along with his paedophile desires and she photographed him abusing the children. She told the police GIs had molested her when she was a child in Saigon.

When Susan saw the photos, she was again struck by the helpless pleading in the children's eyes. After the police did their job and the press could find nothing new to say about the incident, she was among those who had tried to put back the pieces of shattered childhood.

The Center took a number of the molested children for counselling and Pete became one of her cases. Susan knew her best, perhaps only, hope of helping the boy was to deal again with the family as an entity. Once more, they had all been abused. The bastion of their life, the family itself, again cruelly breached.

For Susan it had been a tough time removing Pete's insecurity and fear, and the renewed guilt and shame of Trish and Sam. His anger had been all the harder to cope with, because Sam kept it well hidden. He was polite, smiled his controlled smile, and answered all her questions. But Susan knew it was there, buried and out of sight, but there.

She also knew Sam was entitled to his wellspring of anger. But handling it the way he did, bottling it up, was the worst thing he could do. She set out to make him understand he would destroy himself if he continued this way. He had gradually begun to respond, speaking increasingly openly about his feelings. One day his tears came, a great upsurge of emotion which engulfed him and then the entire family.

Susan now realized it masked the rage which finally drove him out to the desert.

Susan knew that almost fifty years earlier, the military had taken over the area as another internment camp for American citizens of Japanese origin after Pearl Harbour. They had fenced it with chain-link and posted warnings that anybody who approached would be shot. Twenty years later repatriated American prisoners-of-war who were brainwashed by the Chinese in North Korea were brought there to be de-brainwashed.

During the Sixties the area passed back to civilian hands and the land was bought and sold in rapid succession. The last speculator promoted its potential as a get-away-from-it-all resort, his investment brochure described it as the answer to Palm Springs. Not enough people believed the brochure and from the road the area remains as undeveloped as it had been at the Creation.

She continued listening to Sam describe his search for the turn-off to the Ranch.

'I took two wrong turn-offs. Drove a mile and three-quarters down the first one. Two-and-a-third miles along the second – each time the track petered out.'

Lee poured more wine into their glasses.

As Sam spoke, his nostrils flared, and the hand holding the glass shook almost imperceptibly. He was making a huge effort to remain calm and controlled.

'I took another wrong turn, and blew a tyre after a mile. By the time I changed the wheel I was sweating like I had worked-out for a week.'

Until then she had never imagined him actually being able to change a wheel.

Sam continued pacing and talking.

'I found the track at last. After about half-a-mile it dropped into a dried-up river bed.'

She knew it was important for Sam to take his own time. Shock often affected the thought process. The Germans had a word for it, *vorbeireden*, talking-past-the-point to delay coming to it.

Lee silently refilled their glasses.

'Four, five hundred yards, the track left the river bed and climbed. Got narrower. No place to turn. A real one-way to nowhere.'

Sam paused and sipped his wine.

'I'd gone about another mile when I reached what looked like an old guardhouse. Probably went back to the Japanese. No door. Windows gone. That's what made the sign look so incongruous. It was new. Or at least well maintained.'

Susan noticed Sam's staccato sentences and lengthening pauses. Stress victims often experience an increasing pressure as they relive their experiences.

'What did the sign say?' Lee kept his eyes on Sam.

'Just said "Private Land. Do Not Pass Beyond This Point". Or maybe the other way round. I can't remember now, exactly.'

Susan sensed his sudden irritation was a sign of the powerful inner forces battering him.

'It doesn't matter, Sam,' reassured Lee. 'So you drove on?'

Sam nodded, forcing down his anger. 'The sign didn't exactly indicate where the land became private. No fence. Not even a marker post. So right. I drove on.'

There was an even longer pause before Sam resumed.

'I drove on, maybe another quarter-mile. Another guardhouse. Like the first. And another sign.'

Lee nodded encouragement.

'Same words?'

'No. Just "Restricted Area". Yeah, that was it. "Restricted Area".'

'It could be an old military sign,' suggested Susan.

Sam shook his head. 'I got out of the car and took a look. Paint was new. I walked over to the guardhouse. Stank to high heaven. Animals probably use it in the winter.'

Sam stopped pacing and faced them. 'When I came out of the guardhouse, he was there.'

'Who was there, Sam?' Lee kept his voice steady. He was anchored, Susan thought. Thank God for Lee.

'Young fella. Twenty, twenty-five. Don't know where he came from. Dressed in fatigues. Like a soldier. With a gun. Pump-handle shot.'

'Did he threaten you?' asked Susan.

Sam shook his head, once more irritated. 'Just asked what I was doing on private land. Just that. What was I doing on private land? I told him I didn't see any fence. So where did it become private? He kept looking at me and said I'd gone past a warning sign. I was now on private land. I asked him if he was military. He stared at me in a funny way. Not actually menacing. More a look signalling if I asked more questions there'd be trouble. I said fine, okay, was there some place I could make a turn and get off his private land. He thought about it. Then said I should drive down the track and turn at the fence.'

Lee nodded equably. Susan watched Sam carefully. He finally broke another long silence.

'In the mirror I could see him watching. Then the next moment he was gone. Like he'd popped back into the ground. I thought I could have stumbled on some secret training base. Maybe Green Berets. But the military always post signs.'

Sam stared across the table, brooding, remembering. 'I just knew this wasn't military. FBI and Swat teams don't train out on the mesa. The CIA would've been all over me. Making sure I stay quiet. Not just this one guy with a pump shot. Not so much a point-man, more a look-out. Must have surprised him. Figure he probably hadn't known what to do. Just wanted me out of there as quick as possible.'

Susan asked a further question. 'Did he have a radio, a portable phone? Anyway he could have called for help?'

Sam shook his head. ''Bout another third of a mile was the fence. It seemed to run forever. About twelve, fifteen feet high. Beyond the fence the track ran over a ridge and out of sight. Like the guy said, there was a turning space. Big enough for a couple of cars. Also a gate. Guarded by a squawk box and remote camera. Like the entrance to some military facility. I thought just maybe this was one of those secret bases everybody says are out on the mesa.'

He closed his eyes, as if overcome with fatigue.

'Sam let me fix you something? A sandwich? You'll feel better,' said Susan.

He opened his eyes. 'Let me finish. I turned, facing back up the track, knowing the remote was watching. I thought the guys controlling the camera were holding Marcia. Something snapped, I guess, thinking that. I ran to the gate and yelled into the squawk box I have come to get her.'

Sam's hands spread on the table shook more perceptibly. Susan reached across and laid a hand on one. He appeared not to notice, caught up in the memory of what followed.

'Suddenly this jeep appears. Roaring over the rise. There's a guy standing up in the back with a gun. Only I don't know it's a gun until the first shot. That's when I said, that's it, Sam. Get the hell out of here. I jumped back in the car. There was a noise from a rock. You'd know that sound anywhere. Ricochet.'

Sam breathed more deeply. 'The Chevvy's no sports car and I had my hands full. She bounced over the rocks. All over the place. I couldn't hear anything above the engine going crazy. But I knew the guy in the jeep was still firing. Pieces of rock on either side were flying in the air. As the jeep approached, the gate swung open. They kept on coming. Then I had trouble ahead. The guy who'd stopped me was standing in the middle of the road like some traffic cop. I just aimed the car at him as he brought up his pump shot. I think I caught him as he dived. The jeep just kept on coming. I passed the second guardhouse in no time, keeping the Chevvy floored as far as I dare. It was like driving on ice. But she's a great roadholder. And to really give it a workout, I drove like a drunk. From side to side so as not to offer an easy target. The guy in the jeep was getting the range shot by shot. I reached the riverbed and skidded across it. I thought the Chevvy was going to turn over as it hit the track on the other side. I must have gone another quarter mile before I realized it was over. I figure the jeep must have stopped on the other side of the river. Probably too risky to keep firing close to the road.'

Sam exhaled. 'So, here I am.'

Lee asked what Sam intended to do now.

'Go to the police.'

Lee glanced at Susan. She continued staring at Sam, thinking there is something about the disappearance of a child which is like nothing else. There is no body to grieve over, no way for the healing process to be completed. There had been nowhere for Sam's carefully-hidden inner anger, his deep and consuming anger to go – until it had finally driven him to this reckless and foolhardy action.

'I'm going to the police,' Sam said again, not bothering to hide his anger.

Susan knew the next few moments were critical. She began to speak quietly and firmly.

'Sam, let's look at this from another way before you do that.'

No, Susan. No way! I want the police to go out there and tear the place apart.' Sam's voice had risen.

She leant across the table. 'Sam, we all want that. Me as much as you.'

'So come with me to the police!'

Never taking her eyes off him, keeping her voice level, she continued.

'You ignored signs this was private land. No one threatened you. You were just told to leave. Instead, you started yelling into the squawker. The guys in the jeep thought you were about to break through the gate and cause God only knows what damage. So they fired a few warning shots . . .'

'Susan!' Sam's face was working, the anger in his eyes burning.

She pressed harder on his hand, knowing she had to finish. 'Warning shots, Sam. That's all they were. Anyone is entitled to do that out there, where the police are not readily to hand. They just wanted to keep you off their land. If they wanted to stop you, they'd have shot out your tyres. If they had wanted to kill or injure you, Sam, they could have easily done so. But all they did was see you off. If anyone has committed a crime, you did!'

Sam leaped to his feet, his rage finally boiling over.

'What the hell you playing at, Susan? What are you trying to do . . . ?'

'Sit down, Sam.' She continued looking at him calmly. 'I'm doing what the police will do. What the lawyers for the Ranch will do.'

Sam finally sat down.

Susan continued. 'They'll put a different light on what happened. Assuming they'll even accept it did. Chances are they won't.'

There was once more a long silence in the kitchen.

Sam finally suggested calling in TV and the newspapers.

Lee looked at Susan. She once more shook her head, keeping her eyes on Sam. 'What are they going to report? That you drove out into the desert – because of *what*? What evidence do you have that Marcia is out there? You'd end up sounding like one more distraught parent. That wouldn't help you. It wouldn't help to get Marcia back. It won't help any of us.'

Sam stared, eyes blinking. She reached across the table and once more laid her hand on his.

'We can't go public on this. Sam, none of us know if Marcia is alive or not. A year is a long time. If she was taken to the Ranch, the chances are she's no longer there. After what you did, they will have moved her to some other place. They will have moved all the children just in case there *is* a raid. That's how they work. Children are moved all the time around the country. And in and out of it. It's a terrible, terrible thing, Sam. But it's going on. I wish there was some way I could say to you that we are going to get Marcia back. Get all the children back. I can't say that. Nor can the FBI. Or all the policemen in this country. No one can. That is the reality. To steal a child is always easier than to find one. This is a big country to police, Sam. Policemen are human. Even the good ones get tired of looking.'

In the silence she continued holding Sam's hand. After a while she felt his tears on the back of her own hand.

SOLUTIONS

There is a passage in Chekhov's *The Lady and the Dog* which is very apt. 'It seemed that the next minute they would discover a solution. Yet it was clear to both of them that the end was still far, far off, and that the hardest and most complicated part was only just beginning.' Well, I feel like that every day. We get a little closer to places like the Ranch, and it just seems even harder to do anything about it. Then, I think that one day we will win. Must win. There has to be a solution. There just has to be.

– Susan Davidson, Executive Director,
Adam Walsh Child Resource Center,
Orange, California; in conversation
with the author, 10 October 1989.

ELEVEN

A Detective's Dues

Sixth Street was a few blocks off the route Sanders chose on that Saturday evening in late October for the drive across the city in pursuit of another lead which might help him solve the murder of John Doe Sixty. In the weeks since he had left the necropsy suite the detective had seen and heard of things he never knew existed.

While it is true that most murder investigations involve sensitive and complex problems, and all depend on good communications and teamwork it is equally true, Sanders would add, that most killings are depressingly ordinary. They generally involve little passion or genuine evil – people kill during thievery, over domestic tensions, in bar fights, or for simple juvenile machismo. Occasionally a prostitute is stabbed in the city's Tenderloin district, or a headless pusher ends up being dumped in the Bay, and left to drift in the tidal race between the bridges and Alcatraz Island.

The fourteen investigators with the Homicide Detail do what they can, what is possible in the real world of cutbacks which has seen their strength reduced by a third in 1989.

Sanders knew most of the detectives worked, like he did, on their own time because there is no money to pay overtime. Sanders earns a basic salary of $43,000 a year; with overtime he grosses over $60,000. After all deductions, he takes home around $700 a week, often for working more than seventy hours in that week. Ten dollars an hour doesn't seem much of a return even for solving run-of-the-mill murders. It was a distinctly modest income for investigating the case of John Doe Sixty.

It had plunged Sanders and Hendrix into Satan's underworld. Gallant had pinpointed for them cult and coven members around the Bay area who were either potential suspects or informers. One by one suspects had been eliminated after the detectives tested alibis to absolute breaking point, when they knew they were touching raw nerve ends they would tweak a little more, waiting for the snap, for the story to come apart. When it didn't, they knew an alibi was genuine.

Cultists often told them they wanted to help because they were angry at seeing the entire Satan community branded as ritual sacrificers. As long as they kept feeding information, Sanders didn't much worry what motivated them.

Opposite the Baptist Church in which he had worshipped as a boy, he and Hendrix had sat with the high priest of a cult. The man was middle-aged and soberly dressed, as befitted a broker with one of the city's leading financial houses. From the front door of his palatial home, he led them past a shrine covered with what Sanders now recognized as Satanic objects – animal skulls, pieces of bone and amulets. The living room was darkened. In one corner stood a black-draped altar, with an inverted cross, an athame, the ritual knife, and also a silver bowl.

In a soft, cultured voice the man explained that the knife, with its black handle and foot-long gleaming blade, represented the Sword of Power. The cross was so positioned as to mock the death of Jesus, and illustrate Satan's power over Christ. The bowl was his Chalice of Ecstasy, from which he would drink to relax and intensify his emotions.

'What sort of stuff you drink?' Hendrix asked casually.

The man smiled quietly. 'Oh, animal blood. Always animal blood, Officer. I buy it from a butchery. Like the address?'

Hendrix shook his head. He doubted if the man would lie about such a simple, checkable fact.

The detectives stood before the altar staring at a carved wooden phallus. The man removed the phallus and demonstrated its purpose, shaking it so that water came out of a hole in its top.

'It's part of our communion,' he explained patiently.

Sanders pointed to a large black candle on one side of the altar, a smaller white wax one at the other.

The black candle, the man continued, was Lucifer's own light. He nodded towards the white stick. 'This represents the hypocrisy and failure of Christianity and other religions.'

Sanders crouched and peered at the severed head of a goat resting against the front of the altar.

Once more the man smiled. 'Plastic. But very lifelike, don't you think?'

Sanders straightened, chuckling. 'You really believe all this?'

The man nodded, deadly serious. 'Of course.'

He bowed to the altar, intoning: '*In nomine Dei nostri Satanas Luciferi Excelcis!*'

In a voice little more than a whisper, he explained the words

134

protected the gates of Hell, where dwell the Infernal Ones, from Abaddon to Yen-lo-Wang, the gods of the pit.

Hendrix sighed. 'I'm just old fashioned. I believe in this.' He tapped the slight bulge beneath his jacket concealing his gun.

The man led them to the opposite corner of the room to stand before a life-size statue of the Devil. Candles burned inside a circle drawn at the idol's feet. The man picked up a hand bell inside the circle and continued to explain.

'They represent the Flames of the Hole. If I ring the bell, the Forces of the Night will appear.'

Sanders chuckled softly. 'Don't you go ringing that bell. We got enough problems.'

The man carefully returned the bell to its position. Then, ignoring the detectives, he turned anti-clockwise, pausing at each of the four cardinal points of the compass to murmur further incantations.

Hendrix shook his head at Sanders and mouthed, 'Better than Hallowe'en.'

The man squatted before the statue, and in the sort of voice he might have used to advise on a tricky investment, continued to speak about the power of the Evil Eye, and how those who are possessed of it are capable of holding a person under its deadly glance.

He spoke about the great dragon of the Watery Abyss, and of the power possessed by Gorgo, Leki, Mormo and Thoth. His voice thickened and grew more excited, and he rocked back and forth. Finally he fell silent, lost in reverie before the statue. The detectives tiptoed from the room.

Outside, Hendrix let out a long slow breath, as Sanders chuckled. 'Mormo? Sure we don't need to see him?'

They had travelled over the Bay Bridge to Marin Country to talk to an old woman about the mystical power of magic. Wizened and wheezy, she spluttered and coughed her way through an explanation of practices which went back to the dawn of time. Nothing she said fitted with what they knew about John Doe Sixty's death. He hadn't been wrapped in an embroidered garment or sprinkled with herbs.

They went to Berkeley to meet a cultist who was a specialist on the athame. He showed them his collection of daggers, each with its triangular blade and a haft in the shape of a dorje, or thunderbolt. As they were about to leave, he suggested that the person or persons they were looking for could have come from Tibet. Sanders asked why. The man replied that Tibetans often travelled on the astral plane.

For a further hour they sat, transfixed, as he explained the astral plane is part of a 'super-physical world' where witches and warlocks are able to leave their earthly bodies and travel in 'spirit form' to all parts of the earth at 'the speed of light'. In a single night, explained the cultist, 'they can visit all five continents to carry out tasks which the Ancient Gods had set for them.'

Driving back into the city Sanders chuckled, 'California's in no danger of losing its reputation.'

In between such trips, they read about fallen angels and serpents and symbols. About the four Princes of Hell. And everything they could which related to the pentagram. Among much else they discovered that 'the Mark of the Devil' is placed upon a Satanist at the time of initiation. Sanders learned the mark is identified as an extra finger on one hand – or a third nipple on a woman. Anne Boleyn is supposed to have had a third nipple, which was why Henry VIII declared he had been seduced by witchcraft. The extra nipple or witch's teat, was specifically mentioned by the Act of Parliament against witchcraft introduced by King James.

Hendrix had grunted, 'I don't recall our John Doe had a third nipple. Nor did he look the sort of guy who'd end up on the statute books of England.'

Sanders chuckled, 'Maybe he got there by astral plane.'

They had gone to a cultist's house in the affluent suburb of Heywood, noting down the locations the man provided of local Esbats, the monthly meeting places of witches' covens, which are held when the moon is full. Each Esbat was checked out. They turned out to be gatherings where old magical legends are recited and songs sung. The most popular was 'Greensleeves' and 'The Coal-Black Mountain'. They were told the ballads had a traditional association with the moon and witches.

In a high-rise building on Grant Street, a middle-aged highly-educated woman began her lecture by telling them that it was not easy for outsiders to realize the importance of fertility rites and flagellation. She had cried out the name of Shemhamforash, the great harlot of Babylon, and then of pagan goddesses called Lilath and Hecate, asking each of them in turn to fulfil her lust. She was still doing so as they beat a hasty retreat.

Still nothing too far-fetched was overlooked. A local hypnotist was consulted who confirmed that hypnosis was one of the earliest techniques of magic. Then, it had been called 'enchantment'. But there was no way to say whether John Doe Sixty had been put in a trance. They looked into the magical use of incense, and continued to read all they could about initiation ceremonies, invocations, love charms, moon worship and the role of nudity in ritualism.

In the Old Testament Sanders discovered the prophets of Israel did their prophesying naked, and the Book of Job, believed to be the oldest in the Bible, testified to the religious antiquity of moon worship. Love potions, he found, are as ancient as Isolde and Tristan, and invocations go all the way back to the seers of ancient Babylon. Initiation ceremonies were long-established before Christ walked the earth.

But trying to link any of this to the actual murder of John Doe Sixty, he also found, was impossible.

What forcibly struck Sanders was that Satanic worship in all its forms is not something for the ignorant, impoverished and under-privileged – as John Doe Sixty most certainly had been. The cultists the detectives met were often highly educated, well-off and held important jobs in local and federal government, with the military, industry, commerce, even the caring professions. All continued to express themselves angry and repelled by the killing. 'It breaks every one of our ancient rules,' protested a doctor who admitted to worshipping the Devil.

He explained to them the rudiments of Enochian, the language used in Satanic rites and believed to be older than Sanskrit. It resembles Arabic in some sounds and Hebrew and Latin in others, they listened to its barbaric tonal qualities for several hours, familiarizing themselves with passages of the Keys, or Calls. The doctor explained they are known as 'the windows to the fourth dimension'. Sanders told Hendrix afterwards it sounded like hell on earth.

Gallant suggested the killer, or killers, could also be drug runners. Many cultists are financing their activities by selling coke and crack. But the Drug Squad had not come up with one potential suspect.

After another long day chasing leads, Sanders and Hendrix sat opposite each other in the Homicide Detail squad room.

'Nap, we're floundering,' said Sanders, no longer chuckling. 'Murder we understand. But this . . .'

Out there, in Whisper Land – on street corners, in the back booths of cafés, in all those places where only born detectives feel at home seeking information – they were being told that John Doe Sixty was just one of hundreds of young people taken by cultists for killing every year. The younger the better, ran the whisper.

Hendrix riffled through a pile of statements, selecting one.

'Guy here says babies and young children are the perfect candidates, and Satanists like to eat the joint fingers of kids. Index of the right in particular.'

Hendrix tossed the paper on to his desk and selected another.

'This woman says Satanists believe the right-hand side of the body represents the 'Jesus' side. Supposed to do with Christ sitting on the right-hand side of God in Heaven. Destroy the right side, she says, and you destroy the influence of Jesus.'

He dropped the sheet back on the pile.

'Think we can tie that into John Doe Sixty's losing his right testicle?' asked Hendrix, the frustration in his voice plain.

Sanders shrugged. 'I don't know what to think. Not any more.'

The stories sounded so incredible the detectives still had to constantly remind themselves that any bizarre killing always attracted its fantasists.

But the claims persisted there existed an underground system which transports people secretly back and forth across North America, and beyond. They were told some of the victims were brought out of Mexico, others from Canada. Some were for the sex-for-sale industry, but an increasing number were alleged to be sacrifices for ritual cannibalism.

Gallant told them she was hearing the same reports – and how it was not only Susan Davidson and her workers who were warning of this underground traffic. Experienced police officers were voicing their fears. One was detective Robert Simandle in Chicago. Gallant considered him one of the best investigators into Satanic practices in the country. Simandle had begun to describe an international network of Satanists which he thought could be behind some of the drug-dealing and much of the child pornography. Simandle was firmly convinced Satanic-related offences would be the crime of the '90s. Another respected investigator, Larry Jones of Boise, Idaho, was sure the network survived because Satanists were increasingly infiltrating the upper echelons of the criminal justice system.

Sanders considered calling them. Then he realized there was nothing Susan, Simandle or Jones could tell him Gallant had not. And nothing he had learned from her had brought him closer to discovering who had killed John Doe Sixty.

Now, on this Saturday evening, he was about to try once more.

Beyond Union Square the traffic thinned and the fog thickened as Sanders came closer to the shore. Out in the Bay a container ship headed for a pier, riding low in the water. He thought California had become one long assembly line for what was die-stamped on the other side of the Pacific. He drove towards a billboard facing out to sea – '*Welcome to San Francisco, USA*' – wondering what next would be swallowed by the invincible yen. The car headlights picked out indecipherable spray-painted characters on the steel pillars supporting the hoarding. Japanese or Chinese? He couldn't tell. All he knew was that the last time he'd driven this way the graffiti was not there. Suddenly and irrationally, he felt fiercely protective about this exhausted looking area still untouched by the money from Tokyo which elsewhere had transformed the city skyline.

He drove slowly. Behind, away to his left, he glimpsed the towers of midtown, so tightly packed they looked like one great mass. When he first came to live here he was conscious that many were built so close to the fault, or on refilled land, that when the next big tremor came, and come it would, they would probably tumble down. Now he never thought of that. It was enough to be here, to be able to do what millions all over the globe wanted to do, to live and work among those towers and walk the hilly streets. For him it was still a more exciting place than Rome or Paris or London, and infinitely more so than New York.

However, he suspected, few saw the other side of the city. Down here, near the waterfront, the vaporous mustard glow from the lights was further apart, and streets converged from odd angles. Without the reference point of the midtown towers rising above the fog, he would not have been able to tell he was still heading south. A figure loomed out of a doorway and stepped back again. Probably another derelict. Maybe John Doe Sixty had lived and died down here? Was that why Eddie had chosen this place to meet him? To show him where it had happened?

Maybe, thought Sanders, he was finally going to be lucky?

A crime like John Doe Sixty's, he had told Gallant, made a man wonder what the world was coming to. He didn't mind the overtime and the paperwork, if the long trail from the scene of murder eventually led to a witness box where he could give his evidence and lock the whole business away. But in John Doe Sixty's case, the chain of evidence was as slack as he could remember. Even the time of his death had not been established.

That was the essential starting point. All the crime scene measurements, the plastic bags of samples, scrapings and particles which had been on or around the body, Dr Ferrar's report, those from the labs, the street canvass and all the other inquiries: without a properly fixed time of death they meant a great deal less. His own skills and talent were hampered by the absence of that one compass point from which he could navigate the investigation. The variables were numberless without the time of death.

Without it, questions had multiplied: was John Doe Sixty dead or alive when dropped on Sixth Street? Why there? Was Sixth close to where he was drained of almost all his blood? Had that been done in one place? Or had John Doe Sixty been moved from place to place, and an amount at a time drained? Certainly not in the semi-trailer. The CSU team had picked it apart and found nothing.

If he had been bled to death at one time there would have been buckets of blood. Too much to drink all at once – unless a number of people were involved. But, several people sitting around drinking blood? That sort of thing got talked about – even on streets like Sixth. Yet the ACU teams had not picked up a whisper.

Forensic confirmed that storing blood in a fridge or freezer is possible. But anyone who did so ran the risk of urea poisoning. Blood, like anything else, has a limited life unless kept under proper conditions.

Yet the medical experts said John Doe Sixty's captors could have kept him alive for weeks, or even months, replacing his blood with fluids they made him drink. That led back to Sixth. When the last drop of blood was drained, had he been killed and dumped there because it was the nearest convenient spot? Or was Sixth chosen because it was as far away from the scene of the actual killing ground as it was possible to get?

John Doe Sixty could have been killed outside the city, brought in and dumped. His killer, or killers, could have come from anywhere, and gone back there. He, or they, could be a hundred miles away, or a thousand; he, or they, could be in Haiti, Africa, or any of those places Gallant had mentioned.

But why even bother to dump John Doe Sixty? Why not bury him some place? Out in the mountains? In the desert? There were hundreds – dammit thousands – of places out there where all the police forces in California together would never find a body. But suppose whoever killed John Doe Sixty wanted him found? Was that part of their fun? Having half the department run round like a headless chicken? Were those who had done it crazies who believed they could change into werewolves or vampires? That still sounded just too incredible. But, then, so was the whole business.

Sanders had always done some of his best thinking in a car, and on this Saturday evening he continued trying to fit together the pieces. Mostly, he posed questions. He soon had a number more bobbing around in his mind.

Was John Doe Sixty a one-off? Or part of a whole series of killings? Was he murdered primarily for sexual gratification? Or purely for sacrificial purposes? Were his killer, or killers, first-timers or repeaters? Were he or they white, black or yellow? Juveniles or adults?

Instinct told him John Doe Sixty's murder was a one-off. From his reading he knew that with a serial killing, there would have been other similarly-slain bodies by now. He also had a strong feeling that John Doe Sixty had been killed both for sexual pleasure and sacrificial purposes. Again, it was only instinct, but he was sure his killer or killers were adult and white. He didn't see a black or yellow person doing this to someone who was not their ethnic own. And, even allowing for the way kids have become savages, it would have needed years of exposure to brutality to have been able to do that to a person.

The labs had established that the criss-cross cuts on John Doe Sixty's back and buttocks were made by the skin being flayed by a chain. Gallant didn't think the Piquets or the Petro Society went in for that kind of crude sado-masochism.

A very hardened, callous and evil adult probably had killed John Doe Sixty.

140

But Nap was right. This looked like a forever, forever, forever. Until Eddie called.

There are over a million people in the city and county, and a surprising number are persons of goodwill who want to help the police. Eddie hadn't sounded like one of these.

Sanders paused at an intersection to check his bearings. From somewhere up ahead came the mournful blast of a ship's siren.

From experience he knew there is always at least one crazy who calls on every case, with the kind of details which only someone who was there when it happened could have known.

It is usually some small thing, the kind of stuff Public Affairs did not issue to the press: the type of stone in a ring; the make of a watch; the colour of an item of clothing. The detail is so correct that everything else the crazy says has to be checked. The crazy would be interviewed by one investigator, then another, and become the centre of respectful attention, and even the very pivot around which an investigation is revolving. Then, after one more lucky question too many, the whole thing would fall apart, and the crazy given hell for wasting police time and money. It is impossible to lock-up every crazy. Sanders had never figured out how a crazy could go on hitting the dime spot time and again by sheer chance.

Eddie, he reminded himself, hadn't sounded like a crazy. A crazy is usually calm and reasonable and authoritative. Eddie had mumbled and hesitated. Yet, and that was the damnest thing, while he had sounded like a sack of nuts, there was just something believable about what he'd said.

Sanders passed another block of abandoned-looking buildings, their loading bays steel-shuttered. Beyond was a row of yards, filled with semi-trailers, sheltering behind fences topped with coils of razor sharp wire. He made another turn.

So why had Eddie called? Tip money? A possibility. Some people would turn in their own bloodline for a few dollars, but usually they haggled beforehand, trying to settle a price before parting with information. Eddie hadn't mentioned money, so it had to be some other reason.

Sanders had phoned and checked the headquarters computer before leaving the apartment. Eddie wasn't listed, at least under the name he'd given, as either a convicted person, or someone wanted on suspicion of committing a crime. That left other possibilities. Eddie could have witnessed the crime and was scared. It happened; not often, but it happened. Yet why phone? Why not turn himself in to the nearest precinct? Instead he'd chosen to meet down here.

It could be, Sanders accepted, that Eddie was from out-of-town, on the run and wanted to trade what he knew for a good word in the ear of some other force. That also happened. But it would depend, of course, on what he was wanted for: murder, manslaughter, rape, any of the serious category offences, no way. But something smaller, stealing, brawling, that kind of thing – something might be worked out. The detective knew plea-bargaining is not just for lawyers.

Sanders looked at his watch: he was early. If Eddie was playing games, he'd chosen a good place to play. On a weekday morning Sanders would not have been able to move in this grid of streets without being in danger of being squeezed by a sixteen-wheeler or a rig. But this was Saturday evening, when a man could get ambushed down here among the wood-frame offices, low-roofed warehouses and truck yards, and no one would probably know until Monday morning.

Even on a weekday this would have been a good place to have kept John Doe Sixty. These meat warehouses had corners into which no one probably peered from one year to the next. And whoever had killed him could have kept the body in one of the freezer rooms. He'd heard they could hang more beef in just one of those caverns than John Wayne had herded in his entire screen career. With a little planning a body could be kept among the frozen steers without anybody knowing. Another possibility was that John Doe Sixty arrived in the city on board some out-of-town rig, already frozen, and was allowed to thaw out, before being taken to Sixth. But, he reminded himself, the labs had knocked down those theories, proving John Doe Sixty had not been frozen before or after death.

So far there was little to show except an overtime bill which would make somebody wince in the outer offices leading to the Chief. From that sanctum continued to come a repeated question. Any make on this guy? The Chief didn't want to get woken in the middle of the night by some reporter, and asked to comment about John Doe Sixty being the son of some politician, or born-again Christian preacher.

He had told the Chief that John Doe Sixty could be anybody, from anywhere. Thumbing rides on freeway ramps is still a rite of passage – it is cheap, it is easy. Those who did so do not stop to think it is dangerous. But not all of them fell prey to an underground network. Had John Doe Sixty done so?

Sanders drove another block. Ahead, came a snapping sound of wood. The car lights picked out a pile of fruit boxes and the men breaking them with their boots and across their knees. There were five or six, young and white. They fed the wood into an oil drum to keep a fire going. They stopped what they were doing to watch the car approach. He kept on driving down the middle of the street, maintaining his speed, easing by them. Out of the corner of his eye he saw one pick up a chunk of wood and move towards the car. Another said something and the man dropped the wood into the barrel. A moment later they were behind him, lost in the fog.

Being Saturday, he wore a brown sports jacket and light tan trousers, brown loafers and a cream casual shirt, open at the neck. His gun was holstered under the jacket. In an inner pocket, beside the wallet holding his gold star, was the slim, leather-bound edition of the New Testament he still carried.

The crime had viscerally engaged the entire detail. Detectives on other cases had shaken up their informers, and put the word out on the street that anyone sheltering the killer or killers would have to answer. Teams had worked the area around Sixty Street, listening in bars, cafés and on street corners. Forensic had lifted prints around John Doe Sixty's neck, buttocks and chest. The film was sent to the FBI Latent Print Laboratory in Washington, in the hope they matched any of those on its computer. It was a long shot, and no one really expected it to yield anything. It hadn't. John Doe Sixty's own fingerprints drew a similar blank. Whoever he was, he had no police record. A photograph of his face and his dental impressions was distributed, joining all the other anonymous faces and teeth in official circulation. There was no response.

The FBI Behavioral Science Unit at Quantico combed its records. The BSU teletyped detailed descriptions of slaughter and evisceration, cannibalization and ritual torture in the name of Voodoo gods and Gris-Gris idols. For good measure, it sent its own psycho-profiles of the types of person who committed such crimes. There were under-scored references to childhood rejection, impotency, introspection and poor adult associations. Most of it, Hendrix growled, could probably fit a sizable proportion of the population. A computer search showed none of the perpetrators BSU listed had any known links to the Bay area.

Pathology and Toxicology reported yielded the usual details. Those which interested Sanders were that John Doe Sixty was AB-Negative, and there were traces of heroin and cocaine in his blood and two types of semen in his anal canal, one of them animal. The hairs Hendrix removed were identified as coming from a dog, probably a German Shepherd. There was no way of telling how long the dead man had been an addict, or whether he had been drugged simply to make it easier to sodomize him.

Sanders and Hendrix had conducted a thorough canvass of Sixth Street, calling on everyone who could have noticed the blue van and its two occupants. No one had seen or heard anyone come or go in it. The original eye-witness was repeatedly questioned but the longer he was interviewed, the more uncertain he became. His description of the two men was circulated. It was vague enough, for it could fit any of thousands in the city.

More buildings loomed up out of the fog, their sides and fronts spray-painted. Here the graffiti was recognizable, the slogans of gangs and activist groups, Jesus freaks and devil followers.

Sanders continued to think about Eddie. Eddie hadn't sounded like a set-up, but he tried to recall who had recently come out of San Quentin, and was sufficiently vindictive to want revenge. No one came to Sanders' mind.

He drove past another silent block of warehousing, reminding himself that a vengeful ex-con was not the only problem he faced.

There was always a danger in chasing too many theories and listening to too many experts. He had long known no murder is the same, just as there is no such thing as 'the' criminal type. Yet scientists were fixated with such nonsense as the supposed brain temperature of killers. One week there was all this stuff in the journals about the XYY chromosome inclining someone towards violence. Next, it was shown that people with such chromosomes are actually less prone to crime. Every week there was a new theory. Currently, the talk was about the criminal being two types of personality, undercontrolled and overcontrolled. Reading that had given him a succession of chuckles.

He wasn't opposed to experts; he simply wished they knew their place. In the end, he believed, solving homicides is for professional homicide detectives.

And that meant interrupting his weekend to talk to Eddie.

Eddie had called Operations late that afternoon asking to speak to the officer in charge of the case. The operator was smart enough to have gotten Eddie's number and asked him to hang-on. He thought she'd judged her man well, because most informers at that point would probably have hung up.

He had been watching football on TV after a late lunch when her call came on one of the two telephones he maintained at home – one exclusively for police business: calls from colleagues and informers at all hours. The department made no contribution to the phone costs. Paying from his own pocket for the extra line was part of a pride in his work.

Espanola emerged from the kitchen and looked at him quizzically, he'd smiled across the room and gone on listening. Espanola returned to her cooking. When they had married he had promised he would try to keep work from intruding upon their lives but long ago they both accepted this isn't possible.

After taking down Eddie's number, Sanders gave the operator a couple of numbers for her to try if Hendrix was not at home. Then he called Eddie, keeping his approach low-key for formal.

'This is Inspector Earl Sanders of the Homicide Detail. How you doing, Eddie?'

'Fine, man.'

'Understand you want to help me with what happened down on Sixth?'

'Sure, man. Wunna help.'

'That's fine, Eddie.'

'Zaz okay, man.'

The voice sounded young.

'You know this guy, Eddie?'

A pause. 'Sor' of.'

'He got a name?'

The pause was longer. 'No name, man.'

'What did you call him, Eddie?'

A longer pause. 'No name, man.'

'Is that what you called him, Eddie? No Name?'

'Zaz right, man. No Name. Zaz his name. No Name. Eve'budy called him zat. No Name. Zaz his name.'

Sanders scribbled on a pad: No Name.

'How'd he get to be called No Name, Eddie?'

'Zaz what zey call him, man.'

'Who's they, Eddie?' He managed to keep his voice casual.

'Cliff, man. 'N Clin'. Like Eas'wood. Only mo' powe'ful.'

Sanders scribbled: Cliff and Clint.

'Where they live, Eddie?'

Another hesitation. 'No place spec'hul, man.'

'They got any other names?'

'Hey, man. Wa'u wunna know tha' for? Eve'budy know Cliff 'n Clint.'

He let it pass.

There are no hard and fast rules about asking questions. Listen to the last answer and take your time, he told his Crime Interview Class, and don't be afraid to go boldly in early on.

'Did they kill him, Eddie?'

'Who man?'

Could Eddie be this spaced?

'Cliff and Clint. They kill him?'

'Didn' kill him there, man. Happen' other place. Path of Agarthi.'

Eddie's words were followed by a sniffling sound. Was he overdue for his next fix?

''U there, man?'

'I'm here, Eddie.'

'Cliff 'n Clint only use it for spec'hul occasions.'

He made another note: Path of Agarthi. 'This Path of Agarthi, Eddie. Is this some sort of place? A club, maybe? Some special place where people meet?'

There was a sudden cackling sound in his ear.

145

'Zaz crazy, man. No club or place, man. Sor' of launchin' pad for souls. Unnerstan'?' Eddie's voice filled with irritation. 'Suppose' know these things, man. Eve'wun knows Agarthi. In the Calls.'

'Remind me,' Sanders replied trying to remember what the doctor had told him about the Enochian language.

Eddie's voice once more lapsed into sing-song. 'O man. *Odo Quava. Zodonga, lape zodiendo.* Unnerstan'?'

Sanders felt his entire nervous system quicken.

'Eddie, where'd you learn to talk like that?'

'Calls, man. 'U know? Calls? Keys? Same thin' man. Unnerstan'?'

'I heard of them.'

Eddie sighed once more in his ear. 'No Name was slave of Keys, man. Cliff say true believer of the flesh live forever. Unnerstan'? *Noco Mada!*'

'Eddie, can we talk?'

'Talkin', man.'

'I mean, meet and talk. Just you and me?'

Another unintelligible sing-song. '*Lape zodiac ionad.*'

'That mean we can meet?' ·

'Man, where 'u come from? That mean I am that live forever. Keys, man.' Eddie sounded aggrieved. 'Wuz poin' talkin', if 'u don' understan'? Wuz poin', man?'

'Maybe if we met, you can explain?'

The silence was broken by another sniffling sound. 'U kno' 'bout Otahia Gigaphe? Twelve Kingdoms, man. Ate wunna balls. For the Kingdoms, man.'

Eddie's voice once more broke into chant. 'Sleep 'n shall rise. That's wha' Cliff 'n Clint say, man. Sleep 'n shall rise. Balls good for zat, man.'

Sanders continued making notes and thinking hard. Eddie could have picked up news of the evisceration of John Doe Sixty in any one of a dozen places. Even down on Sixth it was bound to be a talking point, but the ACU teams had not reported any talk about the excised testicle.

'Eddie can I ask you one question that's been puzzling me?'

'Shoo' away, man.'

'Eddie, just tell me this.' Sanders used his best buddy-to-buddy voice to ask why John Doe Sixty's left testicle was removed.

Eddie sighed. 'Hey man. Wa'u playin' wi' me for? Wazzis right one. 'U know tha', man. Like hole in his neck wazzon righ' side. And wax wazzon righ' eye. Righ' all the way, man. 'U know wha' righ' means, man? *Bajile Madarida!*'

He wrote it phonetically. He hoped Gallant could make sense of it.

Eddie continued to talk. 'Ten'h Key, man. Big powa'. Understan'?'

146

'I'm not sure, Eddie.'

Eddie groaned. 'O, man. You really summin'.' Once more he lapsed into guttural language. '*Od ragaline maasibajile caosigi*. Means heads of scorpions, man, and live sulphu'. Big anti Him.'

He guessed before he asked. 'Who?'

'Him! Jesus, man! Him! Why 'u no' unnerstan'? Righ' side, Jesus side. Righ' side, failure side. Righ' ball away, weaken Jesus. Now 'u understan'?'

'I think so.'

Sanders recalled the explanation of how, for Satanists, the right-hand side of the body symbolized the hypocrisy and failure of Christianity and other religions.

'Eddie, how about it? Let's meet.'

Eddie finally said they could do so in a restaurant which stayed open all weekend for those who worked in the produce district.

During the drive, the police operator called on the radio to say she could not locate Hendrix. Sanders knew Nap could be anywhere at this hour, coming home from a ball game, or gone for an early dinner or movie. He asked her to keep trying.

Pausing at an intersection to check his bearings, he took another left turn. There were cars parked in the street and lights burning in a few of the wood-framed buildings. Clerks working overtime, balancing last week's books, writing up orders for the next.

Much of Eddie's call still made no sense. Cliff and Clint, the Path of Agarthi, were like something out of a low-budget horror movie, yet his references to the Keys and Calls certainly sounded authentic.

Fog swirled past the windscreen. Sanders turned up the heat, it was always colder down by the waterfront.

Eddie had translated some of the Calls into English. How had he learned to do that? From Cliff and Clint?

He looked at his watch. No point in being early. An early cop could look like a desperate cop, he'd tell a class. He reduced speed and continued to think. The business about Eddie knowing about the right testicle, the wax and the neck wound tied him in to the crime. But how? Was he a participant now trying to save his own skin? A willing bystander? Either way that would make him an accessory to the murder. Yet a man facing twenty-to-life didn't call up and want to help. Not usually.

Eddie *had* sounded weird – that was the only word he could think, weird. Was he so spaced-out he didn't realize he could be charged as an accomplice? Or just spaced-out? Another crazy, after all?

Ahead an engine started-up, and powerful lights suddenly cut twin paths across the street. Sanders passed through the beams, wondering who would be trucking on a Saturday night. He picked

147

up the radio and asked for a patrol car to check. Trailer-stealing was booming.

He drove into another street. Half-way down light spilled out of a window on to the street from the restaurant. He eased the car into the kerb, cut the engine and sat watching. He got out finally, closed the door quietly and locked it. Jacket buttoned to conceal the gun, he walked into the restaurant exactly to the minute he told Eddie he would be there.

A couple of middle-aged men sat in the front booth, eating and talking. The cook was listening to another customer at the counter.

Eddie was in the back booth. He'd have known him anywhere. He had seen that coiled, expectant look a hundred times when he turned up to meet someone.

Outside a car swished past. He glimpsed the patrol on its way to check on the truck.

He walked down the room, smiling. 'Hullo, Eddie,' he slid in opposite.

'Lo, man,' mumbled Eddie. His mouth remained half-open as he sat down. Sanders noted lank black hair, a moustache curved down around his lips, a slightly yellowish complexion and bad teeth. Eddie wore faded Levis and a long-sleeved blue sweatshirt. A red-knit hat was pulled tight on his skull. He put his age at about twenty. He kept moving his empty cup in a circle before him.

'Coffee, Eddie?'

Eddie nodded. Sanders called for the cook to bring two coffees. He turned back to Eddie.

'Where you from?'

'Roun' here, man.'

'You work round her, Eddie?' Once more the tone was relaxed, buddy-to-new-buddy.

'Of 'n' on.' Eddie shrugged.

The coffees arrived.

'What kind of work?'

Eddie moved his cup in a circle.

'Anythin', man. Loadin'. Unloadin'. Packin'. Every piece a bullshit pays a dolla'. Unnerstan'.'

'No Name work with you?'

Eddie smiled. 'He don't work, man. He kep' baby.' He rolled his eyes across the table. '*Zodacre lea od Zodameracu odo cicale Qua!*'

He hurled the word – *Qua!* – across the table.

'Take it easy, Eddie. Where'd you learn all this talk?'

'Cliff 'n Clint tol' me, man.'

'They have any other names?'

The traditional face of modern-day slavery. This little girl, Mati, is a slave in Ethiopia. She was bought in 1988 by a slaver for little more than the price of a can of dog food. Her eventual resale value to one of the brothel keepers in the Middle East will be around £100 – money Mati will be expected to earn in a long day and night of enforced prostitution. Ten years old when this photograph was taken, she can expect to live no longer than a year or two before disease kills her. *(UNICEF/ Claudio Edinger)*

The street children of Brazil. No one knows how many million there are. No one knows what happens to them. Few care. Note the way the woman holds her bag to avoid it being snatched. Many of the children are trained by modern-day Fagins to steal, beg or prostitute themselves. *(UNICEF/Claudio Edinger)*

This photograph was taken by an Anti-Slavery Society investigator. It shows boys and girls arriving from the northern provinces of Thailand – unsuspecting that their journey's end will be a life as sexual slaves, or working in one of Bangkok's sweat shops. *(Anti-Slavery Society)*

This mother and daughter are both chattel slaves in the Philippines in 1989. The woman works 14 hours a day breaking rocks. The little girl, six years old, spends the same time carving souvenirs like this mug for tourists. They are paid a pittance – and have few rights. They are told by their employer if they do not meet a certain work quota, they will receive no food or wages. *(UNICEF/Jack Ling)*

The children of slavery. Many of these boys and girls waiting to begin another long day outside a carpet factory in Morocco are as young as seven and eight years. They will work 10–12 hours a day, six days a week for the equivalent of a few shillings. *(Anti-Slavery Society)*

In El Salvador, as elsewhere in Latin America, the exploitation of children is rife. Now they face a new threat – of being stolen off the street and killed so that their organs can be used to meet the growing demand for human transplants. *(UNICEF/Peter Tacon)*

A month after this photograph was taken in Costa Rica, nine-year-old Carlo suddenly disappeared from his shoe-shine pitch. Police said he 'probably' had been stolen by a slave gang seeking new bodies for one of several sex rings that cater for wealthy paedophiles from the United States. *(UNICEF/Peter Tacon)*

Timi is eleven years old. He is a street porter in one of Bangkok's markets. For 12 hours a day, six days a week, he pushes loads of up to 100 pounds. He receives in return the equivalent of £1. To help eke out his income he also delivers mail – at a penny a letter. *(UNICEF/Marcus Halevia)*

Another face of modern-day slavery – construction workers on an Indian building site. These four Indian women have known no other life except to labour on a building site. They work from dawn to dusk, and receive a pittance for their hard labour. *(Anti-Slavery Society)*

A boy like Shambu. Note how the little jockey is tied to his mount with straps. *(Impact Photos/Alain le Garsmeur)*

US Customs agent John 'Jack' O'Malley – known as the Sting Master for his skills in tracking down child pornographers. One of his many specialities is writing letters to persuade traffickers to come to the United States – where he promptly arrests them. *(John O'Malley)*

The Mlacanang Palace in Manila – touts often wait here to entrap unsuspecting young Filipino women. *(Gordon Thomas)*

Police Officer Sandra Daly Gallant, pictured in front of a display of satanic graffiti in San Francisco and *(below)* in her office displaying a collection of satanic-linked music albums. *(Sharon Beals)*

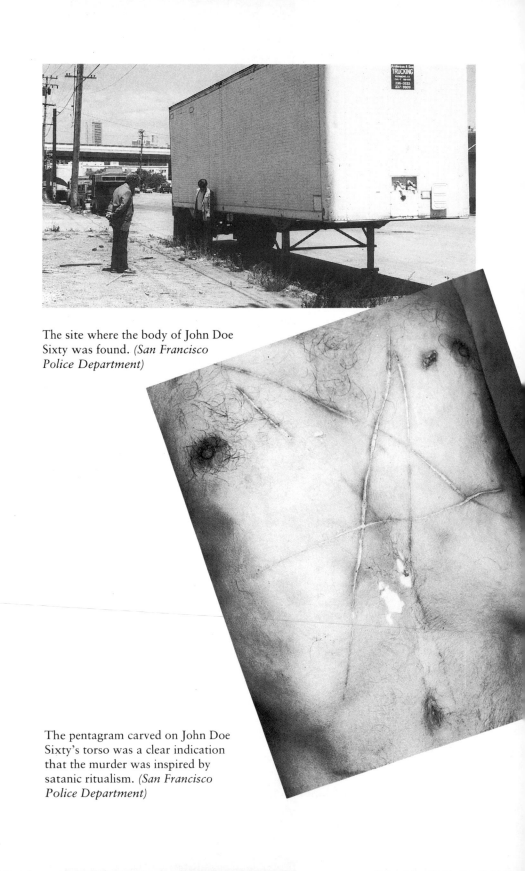

The site where the body of John Doe Sixty was found. *(San Francisco Police Department)*

The pentagram carved on John Doe Sixty's torso was a clear indication that the murder was inspired by satanic ritualism. *(San Francisco Police Department)*

Pamela Harris. *(P. Harris)*   Susan Davidson. *(S. Davidson)*

In their office at San Francisco Police Headquarters, Inspector Napoleon Hendrix *(left)* and Inspector Earl Sanders *(right)* photographed during their long investigation into the death of John Doe Sixty. Confronted by one of the most baffling and unspeakable crimes imaginable, they pitted their detective skills against what Sanders called 'the ultimate evil' – ritual murder. *(Earl Sanders)*

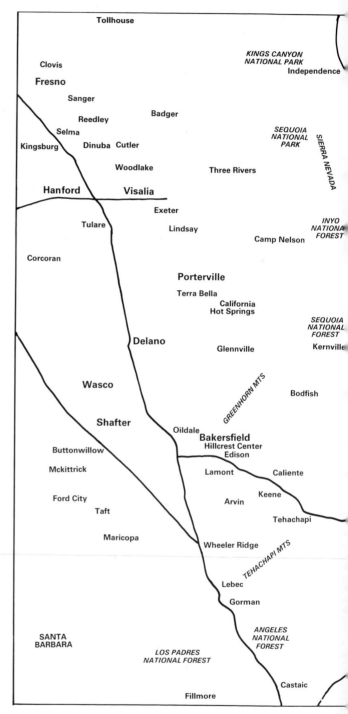

The map of the area where Susan Davidson has located the Ranch where she said her evidence showed children were still being abused in 1989.

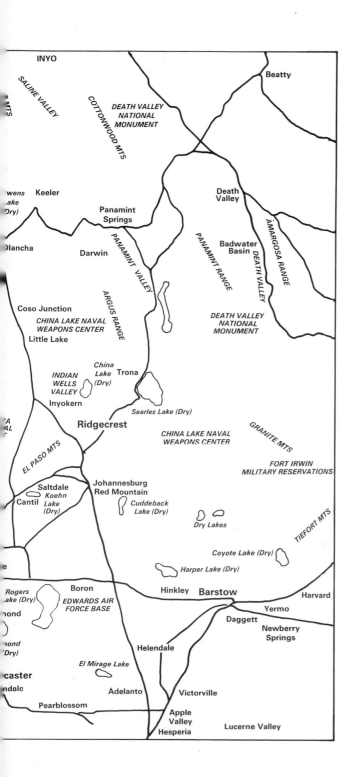

Missing

If you have any information on any of these children please call:

- LOOK CAREFULLY AT THESE PICTURES, THEY WERE TAKEN BEFORE THE CHILDREN WERE MISSING.
- THESE CHILDREN'S NAMES COULD BE CHANGED.
- ALL CALLS STRICTLY CONFIDENTIAL.

CHILDREN'S RIGHTS OF PA., INC.
P.O. BOX 4362
ALLENTOWN, PA. 18105
(215) 437-2971
MISSING CHILDREN NETWORK 1-800-235-3535
NATIONAL CENTER FOR MISSING AND EXPLOITED CHILDREN. 1-800-843-5678

ERIN RENEE McGUIRE
SHANA CORRINE McGUIRE
LT. BROWN HAIR — BROWN EYES
BROWN HAIR — BROWN EYES
BORN: 11-8-79 & 11-17-80
MISSING: 12/10/82
MISSING FROM: LUCARNE VALLEY, CA

CHRISTOPHER SMITH
CHARLES SMITH
BOTH - PALE BLONDE HAIR & BLUE-GREY EYES
BORN: 7-18-80 & 5-4-78
MISSING: 9/21/85
MISSING FROM: MADISONVILLE, TX

PAULA M. PALANCIA
DIRTY BLOND HAIR — DK. BROWN EYES
BORN: 11-25-81
MISSING: 9-8-85
MISSING FROM: MAMARONECK, NY

JOSEPH B. PALANCIA
BLOND HAIR — DK. BROWN EYES
BORN: 5-27-83
MISSING: 9-8-85
MISSING FROM: MAMARONECK, NY

BETH (Elizabeth Ann) MILLER
BLONDE HAIR — BLUE EYES
BORN: 7-27-69
MISSING: 8-16-83
MISSING FROM: IDAHO SPRINGS, CO

SARA PRYOR
(STRANGER ABDUCTION)
BORN: 1-13-76
MISSING: 10-9-85
MISSING FROM: WAYLAND, MA

MONACA RAE SLAWSON
BLONDE BROWN HAIR — BLUE EYES
BORN: 4-20-77
MISSING: 9-80
MISSING FROM: PARKLAND, OREGON

JAIME JEAN KUNKEL
BLONDE HAIR
BORN: 2-6-81
MISSING: 8-3-86
MISSING FROM: OVERLOOK PK., KANSAS

CHERRIE ANN MAHAN
BROWN HAIR — HAZEL EYES
BORN: 8-14-76
MISSING: 2-22-85
MISSING FROM: SAXONBURG, PA

JEREMY GRICE
BLONDE HAIR — HAZEL EYES
BORN: 1-12-81
MISSING: 11-22-85
MISSING FROM: N. ATLANTA, S.C.

KERRI LEE GREENIER
BROWN HAIR — BROWN EYES
BORN: 9-11-71
MISSING: 7-6-80
MISSING FROM: NEW BEDFORD, MA

ALLEN (Squeeky) BRISCOE, JR.
DARK HAIR — BROWN EYES
BORN: 12-5-69
MISSING: 12-13-85
MISSING FROM: PHILADELPHIA, PA

ANN GOTLIB
CURLEY AUBURN HAIR — GREY EYES
BORN: 5-5-70
MISSING: 6-1-83
MISSING FROM: LOUISVILLE, KY

PETER CASSIZZI
BROWN HAIR — BLUE EYES
BORN: 1-15-76
MISSING: 5-5-83
MISSING FROM: PHILADELPHIA, PA

KIMBERLY A. YATES
BLOND HAIR — GREEN EYES
BORN: 8-26-85
MISSING: 8-26-85
MISSING FROM: WARWICK, R.I.

LISA LYN CAUSEY
BROWN HAIR — BLUE EYES
BORN: 4-6-69
MISSING: 1-26-85
MISSING FROM: EASTON, PA
(TEETH NOT VERY STRAIGHT)

BRIAN R. GLEYL
BROWN HAIR — BROWN EYES
BORN: 12-2-68
MISSING: 2-28-81
MISSING FROM: PHOENIX, ARIZONA

LINDA MICHELE HICKS
HONEY BLONDE HAIR — BLUE EYES
BORN: 8-24-79
MISSING: 5-83
MISSING FROM: GILLETTE, PA

CLARK TOSHRO HANDA
BLACK HAIR — BROWN EYES
BORN: 12-5-80
MISSING: 5-82-84
MISSING FROM: FAIRFIELD, CA

KELLY YATES
BLONDISH HAIR — GREEN EYES
BORN: 10-26-84
MISSING: 8-26-85
MISSING FROM: WARWICK, RI

GWENDOLYN BENVIE
DK. BROWN HAIR — HAZEL EYES
BORN: 10-14-81
MISSING: 7-22-86
MISSING FROM: HOLBROOK, MASS.

NICOLE LOUISE MORIN
BROWN HAIR — BROWN EYES
BORN: 4-1-77
MISSING: 7-30-85
MISSING FROM: STOBICOKE (TORONTO) CANADA

LOUIS MACKERLEY
DIRTY BLONDE HAIR — BLUE EYES
BORN: 2-15-77
MISSING: 6-7-84
MISSING FROM: ALLENTOWN, PA

ALAN MAHER COLLINS
BROWNISH HAIR — GREENISH EYES
BORN: 3-22-84
MISSING: 9-84
MISSING FROM: HAYWARD, CA

SANDRA MARIE TODD
DONALD LEE TODD
BOTH HAVE DIRTY BLOND HAIR & BLUE EYES
BORN: 12-29-79 & 10-15-76
MISSING: 7-81
MISSING FROM: ALLENTOWN, PA

PLEASE POST THIS NOTICE
4th Edition

Mack TRUCKS Prepared Courtesy of Mack Trucks, Inc.

Posters like these appear every day in the United States. Few children are ever traced.

ADAM: HIS SONG CONTINUES

These children appeared on the roll call at the end of "Adam: His Song Continues"
September 29, 1986 9-11PM ET on the NBC Television Network

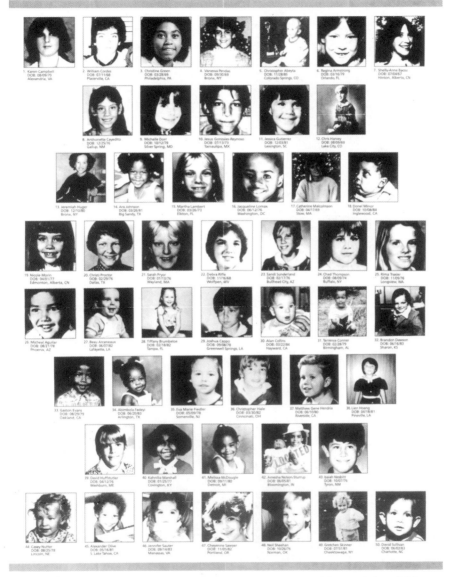

If you have any information that could lead to the recovery of these missing children,
call the toll-free Hotline: 1-800-843-5678 (United States and Canada). TDD line 800-826-7653.

For more information, write the National Center for Missing and Exploited Children,
1835 K Street NW, Suite 700, Washington, DC 20006

1-800-843-5678

Sister Margaret Healy, an Irish nun based in London, runs a unique rescue service for young Asian women who have either been used as domestic slaves or tricked into marriages of convenience. *(M. Healy)*

Alan Whittaker. He co-ordinates the world-wide investigations of the Anti-Slavery Society and produces reports for governments and the United Nations. *(Anti-Slavery Society)*

Maureen Alexander Sinclair, Deputy Director of the Anti-Slavery Society. In the twenty-five years she has worked for the oldest human rights organization in the world, she has seen little improvement in the situation. To date she estimates that there are 200 million slaves in the world, half of them women and children. *(Anti-Slavery Society)*

Eddie's slack-mouthed smile wavered. 'Yeah, man.'

Softly, matter-of-factly and completely without threats, Sanders asked again for the full names of Cliff and Clint.

Eddie gave the sigh he had heard on the phone. 'Wazza matta', man? I call t'help and now 'u hazzle me. Why 'u do tha' man? Huh?'

Sanders kept his voice at the same even tone. 'Eddie, when a man says he's going to help me, I want to know that man is telling me the truth. About everything.'

He was beginning to slowly increase the pressure. He had always been good at that.

'Tell 'u tru', man,' said Eddie, beginning to nod and smile.

Sanders deliberately eased the pressure. 'All right, Eddie. Now this *Qua* . . .'

'*Q-ua, man.*' Eddie enunciated the word. '*Q-ua.* Him big'n Jesus.'

Sanders smiled back. 'I never heard of *Qua*. All I know is that I got a guy you said you could help me over. So how about it, Eddie?'

The pressure was back on.

'He kep' baby, man.'

'What's that mean?'

'Kep' man. Kep' for Cliff 'n Clint, man.'

Sanders laid his hands flat on the table. 'How about telling me, how come you know so much about this guy? You help kill him?'

Eddie rolled his eyes. 'Wha'u saying, man? I don' kill No Name. I don' kill no one. You thin' I kill him and call 'u? You thin' tha'? Thin' I'm crazy, man?'

'Easy, Eddie. You want to talk here, fine. You want to go down-town? No problem.'

He allowed his jacket to fall open, showing a glimpse of holster. Eddie drained his coffee.

'Want something to eat, Eddie? Burger maybe?'

Eddie nodded. Sanders called the order to the cook. He turned back to Eddie. 'Who are they, Eddie? I want their full names, where they live. What each of them did to No Name. Where they did it, and when. I want to know everything you know.'

Eddie sighed. 'Firs' we eat.'

'Okay, Eddie. First you eat. Then I listen.'

After he had eaten, Eddie finally began to make sense.

Nevertheless he continually changed direction, introducing often startling new details, before once more back-or-side-tracking. Sanders would nudge him with only essential questions, wanting to hear the story for the first time in its raw form.

One minute Eddie was spilling precise details about where the cuts were made on John Doe Sixty. The next, he would reel off a list of names of men and women involved in this kind of ritualism. Suddenly, he would talk about a black box filled with ceremonial knives, candles and books. Then it was back to how John Doe Sixty's blood was drained while he was still alive. How he had been drugged and chained and kept totally nude inside a circle drawn on the floor. How he had been repeatedly raped by a German Shepherd, during which there was a lot of chanting by Cliff, who had done all the cuts as well as the final sacrifice. Before that Cliff had beaten John Doe Sixty with a chain on the buttocks, explaining it was to give a sacrifice more meaning. That's why he drank John Doe Sixty's blood and ate the testicle.

Absorbing Eddie's story, Sanders made other judgements. The youth would be a poor witness. More worrying, his testimony was hearsay. While it supported the known facts, Sanders' questioning revealed that Eddie's description was not based on first-hand testimony but had been passed to him by Cliff. Sanders saw serious problems if the case came to court. The prosecutor would try and argue that Cliff would not have lied to Eddie. That people just didn't admit to such things unless they are true. The defence would fight it all the way. Either Eddie was motivated by malice or just plain crazy; they would present him as a junkie, a street waif, the lowest. Cliff sounded like a man who could afford good lawyers.

Eddie identified Cliff and Clint as 'blood brothers' – Cliff and Clint St Joseph who lived in a Victorian house off Third Street which was only a few blocks from where John Doe Sixty's body was found.

He asked Eddie to describe them physically. Neither matched the eye-witness description of the two men seen at the crime scene. Did the St Josephs own or lease a blue van? Eddie shook his head.

Sanders next discovered a further problem with Eddie's evidence. He had never actually seen John Doe Sixty. Nor did Eddie know the man's real name, where he came from, how long he had known Cliff and Clint, and where and how he met them. The defence would have turkey-shoot picking holes in Eddie's testimony.

He asked how long Eddie knew Cliff and Clint, and what was his relationship to them.

Eddie had known Cliff since he was thirteen, when they began a homosexual relationship. The youth moved on to other lovers. He and Cliff resumed casual contact a few months before. One day Clint appeared. Cliff introduced him as his brother from Canada although Eddie had not known Cliff had a brother.

Sanders came to the point like a hound. Why had Cliff done that?

'Cliff tol' me because he was gonna let me take part in the next human sacrifice to welcome Clint.'

Sanders nodded. The gaps were closing. He stood up. 'Let's go, Eddie.'

Eddie looked alarmed, 'Man, Cliff sac'fice me if he fin' out.'

Sanders gave his most reassuring smile. 'You'll be OK, promise.'

Short of keeping the youth in custody, the detective had no clear idea how he was going to keep it. And would a prison cell be secure against the demonic revenge of the St Josephs?

TWELVE

Sting Master, Sting

On the morning of Hallowe'en, O'Malley checked the rented mail box in the post office at Oak Park. It was empty. However, he was confident it would only be a matter of days before it contained another envelope. Ten days ago, Sturmer had finally broken his weeks of silence.

His letter was filled with the pornographer's further crude descriptions of his sexual desires and how he hoped Sheila would soon satisfy them.

O'Malley read the letter several times, smiling his pirate's smile, thinking there is always a flatness of language and absence of emotion in pornography. He promptly responded with a carefully worded reply in Sheila's name, saying she would very much like Sturmer to visit her in Chicago. O'Malley was careful to give no direct response to Sturmer's sexual advances, not wishing to create a loophole for some defence lawyer to raise the old cry – entrapment.

Nevertheless, the tone of O'Malley's reply was friendly and encouraging. They would 'have a lot to discuss and explore, and some matters are always best spoken about personally'. It was the closest he dare sail to the legal wind.

He sprinkled Opium on the paper. After posting the letter, he returned to the eighth floor, feeling an old tug in the stomach, acutely aware of the cause. The onset of winter had coincided with an upsurge in operations. This is always a time of tension, of fine-tuning already honed instincts, to polish the invisible template in the brain called experience.

Walking down the corridors of the Parish House, he could feel the excitement of nervous systems receiving and feeding back signals. Like flakes of snow, no two cases are ever alike. Each has its distinctive qualities, often tiny but there. The art is to distinguish the signals. To know there is a factor beyond the obvious truth that must never be forgotten. For O'Malley this is an essential part of the intuition of faith which makes the Parish House hum at these times.

In a darkened office an agent was working his way through the latest seizures, a stack of videos which would shock even a hardened locker-room.

O'Malley watched the depravity unfolding on the screen. One child had acne scars. Another was plump in the wrong places. A third spoke obscenities in a voice still to break. They all seemed so pale, so filled with deadness around the eyes. Their skin was bruised and their private parts red as a sore. None of the children was more than twelve-years-old.

'When it can allow this to be done to kids, a society's in trouble,' said the agent.

'Amen,' murmured O'Malley, moving on.

In another office a seasoned investigator was explaining to a newcomer signs to watch for.

'It's like joining a secret sect. They've got their special codes. To establish identity. To warn of danger. Theirs is the fellowship of Orpheus without the music.'

O'Malley smiled. Orpheus' underworld – he'd use the phrase in his next lecture.

He continued to listen as the agent led the novice slowly and painstakingly through the basic rules of dealing with pornography.

'If ever you think, just for a moment, it's getting to you, don't panic. We all get to feel like that. Watching this stuff, anyone can feel vulnerable. It's the old thing about repetition corrupting. You see something a thousand times. And it loses its impact. That's when you touch your nose. Think of your family. Say this is no game. This is filth with a big, big F. Then you come and talk to me.'

The agent looked at O'Malley. 'Right, Jack?'

'Right on the money.'

O'Malley walked away, happy. An agent like that was beyond price. What he had said could be carved in stone over the entrance to the eighth floor. The words were the unadulterated truth of what special qualities were required to work there. It was not only that the newcomer had to commit himself to the betterment of his country, to assume whatever persona the moment required, to surrender all claims to a private life when work called. It was more. It was that special loyalty O'Malley demanded. Always.

Long ago the older agent had bound himself to O'Malley. Long ago they had come to terms with any temptation.

In another office two agents were absorbed with reading. Every day scores of magazines and newspapers reached this office, some obviously pornographic, others outwardly respectable. The agents concentrated upon the advertisements, looking for a word, a phrase

153

which at first glance seemed incongruous, but which upon closer scrutiny fitted perfectly. It was an art. The first step in any sting.

Sturmer had surfaced first in this room, his advert spotted by one of the pair poring over the printed columns.

'Got one,' an agent said. He used a felt pen to circle an ad in the latest issue of the NAMBLA journal.

O'Malley walked over.

'Can you beat that?' he said, laughing. 'We busted this guy two years ago. Now he's back with the same old pitch!'

He picked up the magazine, whistling as he went. He'd begun to plan a new sting while waiting for Sturmer to come to the boil.

He could not remember off-hand now how many pornographers had been convicted as a direct result of a careful study of publications like NAMBLA's, which promoted child sex, and acted as contact points for paedophiles and outlets for distributors of pornography. O'Malley reached a conference room. Around the table three agents, two men and a woman, were bouncing ideas off each other for new stings based on the porno magazines before them.

The woman had a copy of the NAMBLA journal in her hand. O'Malley saw she had ringed the ad he'd spotted.

'Sorry. Saw it first,' he smiled his pirate's smile.

'There you go,' she said – but it was all very friendly.

O'Malley drew up a chair. 'Bet there's at least another one in there if you look hard enough.'

He turned to the journal's editorial page and began to read aloud.

NAMBLA's newsletter had once more claimed that children and adults are entitled to 'satisfying emotional and sexual relationships, based on consent'; that physical intimacy should not be governed by society's present age limits, but minors should 'have the right' to select 'intimate adult companions'.

O'Malley read out the passages, not bothering to hide his anger and disquiet.

'This philosophy ignores that a child is almost never capable of fully understanding what is involved when he or she enters into a sexual relationship with a grown-up; that with the end of innocence often at such tender years, usually comes physical damage and lasting psychological impairment.'

One of the male agents – a beefy man, wide across the shoulders, thick-necked and endearing the way some strong men are – picked up another magazine.

'Try and tell Tetcher that.'

O'Malley was immediately interested. 'Something new?'

The agent shook his head. 'Same old stuff. Wrapped the same old way.'

Tetcher uses every opportunity to promote sex with 'consenting children' as acceptable.

He publishes *Wonderland*, the quarterly publication of the Lewis Carroll Collector's Guild. In *Wonderland* the 'delights' of 'transgenerational sex' pepper the pages. Operating out of Chicago, the Guild describes itself as a 'voluntary association of persons who believe nudist materials are a constitutionally protected expression and whose collecting interests include pre-teen nudes.'

Each issue contains drawings of very young children and the 'philosophical thoughts' of Tetcher. Between dwelling on what has become the paedophile's Bible, Vladimir Nabokov's *Lolita*, and the work of an English photographer who specializes in portraits of early-teenage girls, the publisher pontificates on the 'joy' of 'family fun', and 'the family that plays together stays together'. Those around the table knew that 'family fun' means sex within the nuclear family – or children introduced to sex with other like-minded families. 'The family that plays together stays together', a coded phrase for a sex ring.

The third agent, small, dark and wiry, spoke for the first time since O'Malley entered the room.

'Tetcher and the jerks at NAMBLA are just kid's stuff.'

He reached down for his briefcase. In the expectant silence he opened it and removed a sheaf of papers. He selected one and in an emotionless voice began to read.

It is best when beginning sex with a kid to do it as part of a game. Sometimes a kid will make the first move. Sometimes the adult. Sometimes the adult can create a situation where a kid can ask for sex or start sex if they want. Curiosity is a big factor. Exploring somebody and having them explore you is another good way to start off. This can be a kind of show and tell. Just about everything that adults can do together an adult and a kid can do together. It is best to go slowly the first time – and it's more exciting that way too. But, of course, you have to be sensitive to size differences. Kids enjoy non-penetrating sex the best. Most very young or small kids cannot and should not be penetrated by an adult. Having sex is having fun. If anyone is not able to relax, it won't be as enjoyable. Sex is play, not work. If you have sex with some that like it, they can tell those of their friends who may also be interested. Sometimes starting out sex is better if other kids are there doing it too. Group sex is a good way to experiment and experience all kinds of sex with all sorts of different partners. What better way to learn!

155

The agent carefully put the paper back in its place in the sheaf.

'Je-sus,' the woman said, breaking the silence. 'Je-sus Holy Christ.'

O'Malley addressed the wiry agent.

'Those guys still going?'

The agent nodded. 'And strong.'

Ten years before, the 'Howard Nichols Society' – named after the fictional character who attacked young girls in the television film, *Fallen Angel* – had attracted thousands of members with its underground pamphlet, *How to Have Sex With Kids*. The agent had recited its opening paragraph.

O'Malley came to a decision. 'As of now, they're yours. Use anything, anybody. Shove their filth down their gullets!'

He rose to his feet, his voice tight.

They're destroying the next generation. We all know that. Just as we know they destroy their young victims' basic resistance and inhibitions to sex by using alcohol and drugs. Show them dirty pictures. Say it's okay to behave like that. They bind their little victims – and we are talking about kids as young as three or four – to them. By rewards. By threats. We all know they photograph their helpless victims in compromising situations. Then threaten to expose them unless they continue to do as told. We all know they use already corrupted kids to recruit new victims.

He looked around the table. 'We all know all of this. Right?'

They nodded.

'Right. So let's go get them! Each of you plan to have a new operation ready for me to approve by the morning!'

He walked to the door, turned and gave his pirate's smile. Then he was gone.

Striding down the corridor O'Malley was conscious of his own feelings, as if some saving mechanism in his brain was telling him what to do. He knew there had been no need to remind the agents why they were there. He'd done it for himself. He did not ever want to forget, not for a moment, how disgusting the world was, in all its disgusting detail. By the time he reached his office he knew, of course, that he would never forget. It was burned into his memory so deeply that he could not imagine ever being rid of the details. He closed the office door.

No one saw O'Malley for the rest of the morning. For a while he sat behind his desk evaluating new operations. An agent sought approval to target a photo-lab in Detroit processing child porn videos from master tapes smuggled in from Amsterdam. Another to move

156

against a photographer in Pittsburg who specialized in making 'foto sets' of prepubescent girls. A third to investigate a sex ring operating in Akron, Ohio.

O'Malley knew the operations were interlinked. The photographer's work was processed in the Detroit lab, which supplied the Akron ring.

He initialled his approval, scribbling a note that the Akron operation was the most important; the other stings should take extra care not to jeopardize that one.

Destroying sex rings was always a top priority. Not only did a ring promote sexual acts between children and its members, but it often used children to produce pornography, which is sold to other rings. Many rings also trade children between themselves, transporting them considerable distances.

Detectives in Tulsa and Houston had recently broken a ring that dealt exclusively in girls aged between eight and eleven. They were driven around the mid-West to have sex with men in motels, these clients were often elderly, rich and influential within their communities. It turned out the tots were the younger sisters of girls who previously also had been traded until they became too 'old' – at puberty.

O'Malley knew some North American rings had been in existence for decades, creating new offenders out of each generation of victims.

The stings approved, he settled in his high-backed chair, hands behind his head, and did what he enjoyed: sitting quietly and thinking hard. Then he was at his most formidable, these times when he put everything else out of his mind and concentrated only upon a chosen topic.

This undivided focussing helped keep him in untroubled balance. It was part of the steadiness which comes from a good marriage and strong faith.

After sitting for a while, eyes half-closed, the tension around his mouth and eyes easing, he began by first thinking how the baby porn circuits are expanding.

Ten years ago the phenomenon was unheard of. Now, there is not a major city which does not have its circuit. They had begun to flourish in smaller cities and towns.

Nor did circuits any longer only operate within the anonymity of large urban conurbations. For years in the village of Waterville, Maine, children from four years upwards were offered for sex at $30 a time. The tiny victims were rented out by parents to help pay domestic bills. It had gone on until 1988. He had no doubt it was still going on elsewhere in places as idyllic as Waterville. The circuits are everywhere where there is a demand for sex

157

with children. And that, O'Malley reminded himself, is just about everywhere.

The kids were being started younger. There were rings stocked with five-year-olds. A two-year-old had turned up in one. When the children became too old – some rings have a ten-year limit, most have no further use for children when they reach puberty – the victims are often sold-on to pimps catering for street trade. Los Angeles police had sent word there were as many as 5,000 child prostitutes in the Big Orange, and that most started out on the baby porn circuits.

Similar reports came from police and social workers working in New York City's Times Square, Chicago's Uptown, Boston's Combat Zone, the Tenderloin in San Francisco, the Strip at Las Vegas and Miami's Biscayne Boulevard. Young hustlers gave the same account of being first corrupted by a baby porn circuit.

Without breaking his concentration, O'Malley reached for a booklet on his desk. It was about the size and thickness of one of the tracts evangelists for religious groups distribute at airports. The booklet had come in the morning mail, compliments of a West Coast police contact. He'd only had time to glance at it. Now he studied the instruction manual a Californian circuit had prepared on how to torture little children.

He read the way he always does at his desk, hunched over, head propped in his hands.

'The victim should be nude and helpless, tied or chained by the arms, legs, sometimes by the neck . . . '

As he read some unseen, involuntary hand made a fist in his stomach.

'. . . Tight ropes and chains should be used so that they sink into the flesh, causing pain. The victim should be spreadeagled, arms and legs stretched until he or she feel as if they are going to split apart.'

He forced himself not to think of his own children. He read to the last revolting instruction.

'. . . No matter where the torture is to take place, it should be in a concealed and secluded spot where the slave's screams cannot be heard. If in the home, the radio or TV can be turned up to drown out the noise . . . '

The manual offered no clue as to who had written and printed it on a home computer. Those who produced this evil almost never left a clue.

He placed the manual in the file for the Pittsburg sting. Photographers were being increasingly hired to film torture scenes and maybe the scum-ball in Pittsburg had done some of that work. He'd tell the agent running the sting to bear that in mind, it was still a very long shot, but better than nothing. O'Malley simply hated the feeling of being able to do nothing.

He settled back in his chair and thought some more about the way American photographers now produced kiddie porn which rivalled anything Sturmer was shipping into the country. Photographers like the man in Pittsburg were not using Asian children – but American toddlers. O'Malley had seen 'foto sets' of them performing sex with animals, with other kids, or with their parents, often their mother.

This, too, was on the increase – parents ready to exploit their children in this way. Like those in Waterville, many insist they are driven to this from economic necessity. He couldn't buy that. If a mother felt that peddling flesh was the only way to pay the rent, then it should be *her* flesh, not her children's, she should be selling.

There were persistent reports of mothers touting their children across country from one studio to another, renting them out for anything between $100 and $500 for a morning's work. A photographer could take up to 200 pictures in a session which could earn him a flat fee of $30,000 from a 'foto set' manufacturer. The eventual return from a morning's work could run to $1 million.

This explained another trend, how increasingly the traffic in child porn is in the hands of criminal syndicates. They have mailing lists and glossy brochures; their trade in filth promotes procuring, prostitution, the sex tourism industry, nude dancing and ultimately all forms of exploitation of minors. It's pure sexual slavery. And it's not happening in Bangkok or Manila. It's happening in our cities. O'Malley would make the point in his next lecture.

He swivelled to a side table and switched on the recorder on which he tapes all such thoughts. The comparison with Bangkok and Manila was put in the context of Orpheus and the underworld in our midst. He spoke clearly, directly and forcefully.

With some audiences he was careful: parent-teacher groups, church organizations. At those sort of meetings, there was no way of him knowing who was in the hall, no point in tipping off a pornographer on how things are done. But in a few days he would be talking to a group of police officers on how he ran his operations. Even then he intended to confine himself to only certain aspects. There are some secrets which would never leave the Parish House.

He swung back to the recorder, punched a button and began to formulate his thoughts for the police lecture.

In any survey of convicted paedophiles there is a significant number of accountants, doctors, dentists, bankers and judges. They are the ones who can afford the high prices pornography costs. Some of them spend hundreds, even thousands, of dollars a month adding to their collection of movies and magazines. When it comes to choosing an alias, I try and get close to an agent's real name, or an alias which doesn't sound too made-up or doesn't fit into the community. I wouldn't choose a Jewish name for a sting running out of a known Catholic neighbourhood. I wouldn't use a Polish name, or any other one that's going to stick out.

He paused. This was basic stuff. He'd tell them a pornographer could be as tricky as any of the criminals they chased.

A supplier will try and run as many checks as he can before replying to a test letter. He may write back and ask who was the contact who introduced him. Usually the name of another genuine pornographer is enough. Sometimes the recipient of a test letter will check the phone book for a listing of the writer. He might call the local banks in the area of the rented box and try and check. Experience has taught us to select post offices in suburban, middle-class areas as the ideal places to rent mail boxes. Suppliers know that is just the sort of neighbourhood where paedophiles live.

He paused to gather his thoughts. He didn't need to come on strong with cops. Just give them the plain facts.

For material we order, we always send cash to cut down the risk of being spotted. If a supplier is really cautious he will even keep watch on a rented box. An agent always visits a box at irregular hours and makes sure that it is not under observation. Once we receive a response, we place a test order. Once we receive that, we have established the crime of shipping pornography through the mails. The test order is not for real hard-core material. To order that at once could make a supplier suspicious. When the test order material is received, the agent will write back and ask for more. He is also trying to build up a relationship with the pornographer. He may throw in the names of other suppliers whom the pornographer will probably already know, or mention the name of a paedophile almost certainly being supplied by the pornographer. The agent is trying to establish trust as well as show he knows the score.

He pressed the pause button. In the beginning the relationship between a case agent and pornographer is always tricky. The agent is like a warlock joining a new sect. He knows the signs and incantations – but is not yet sure in which order to use them. One mistake and there is no going back. Orpheus will indeed have

160

slipped back into that loveless underworld without music. O'Malley released the buttons.

> When things are moving along nicely, the agent will begin to request the real horror stuff. Babies being violated. Little girls being raped. Little boys being sodomised. That sort of stuff removes any worries an agent, or I, have about going to the very edge of the law to get those supplying it. The sort of filth which is literally sickening to see. Strong-stomached agents have thrown-up after viewing some of that material. When those liberal lawyers yell 'entrapment', they should take a look at what has been trapped.

He stopped the tape, smiling his pirate's smile. That should get him a round of applause.

After lunch O'Malley began to attend to what he calls his 'foreign affairs'. He dictated requests for information from US Customs attachés in Europe and Asia, and dealt with correspondence from police forces in various parts of the world. In some countries – Denmark, Sweden, Thailand and the Philippines among them – the attitude of denying rather than attacking the issue of child exploitation made him feel he was 'trying to balance on a surf board while running against a tidal wave in a diver's suit'.

In some cases there was little that could be done; ancient cultural beliefs overrode all else. In India, sexual involvement with children is still given a religious respectability, as exemplified by the young female prostitutes of the temple. For thousands of years they had offered their bodies to supplicants; they would continue to do so. Among the Chinese, sex with children is still deemed to guarantee longevity.

The foreign mail, he knew, brought its spate of horror stories.

A Philippines child-care agency reported that over 75,000 children still prostituted themselves on the streets of Manila in the third year of President Aquino's regime. Thai social workers estimated 40,000 children a year are joining the ranks of pre-teen prostitutes in Bangkok. French social workers confirmed that the number of under-age prostitutes in Paris had grown to over 10,000 in 1988. In Amsterdam a six-year-old girl had been systematically drugged and forced into prostitution; she died of an overdose of cocaine. In Dhaka, India, an eleven-year-old girl had been tortured to death in a brothel when she tried to escape. In Phuket, Thailand, five child prostitutes were found dead handcuffed to their beds.

There was nothing in the reports to show anything was being done to end all this. The realization once more made O'Malley turn his attention to the thick file on his desk. It contained everything he knew about Sturmer.

He had read every line, reviewed every obscene picture more times than he could now remember. Yet each time he pondered over the file he looked for something new to further his knowledge.

At college he'd read Macauley's injunction that a perfect historian should possess an imagination of great power, yet be able to control it absolutely and to work only with the material to hand and to refrain from adding anything. Macauley would never have fitted into the Parish House. One of its cardinal rules is that it is precisely any deficiencies that an agent is expected to seize upon and speculate about. Another is that the art of informed conjecture is as important as an obvious truth. From the realm of surmise sometimes came a new fact which could open a fresh trail.

Sturmer's file was proof of that.

O'Malley began to read. From time to time he paused at something which caught his eye – a phrase, a sentence, a paragraph, at a full page.

He concentrated once more on Sturmer's letters to his clients in the United States. They had been uncovered through the technology O'Malley put such store by. At the outset of the operation, inspectors at all postal entry points to the country had been alerted to maintain an electronic supervision for all Sturmer's letters and packets. O'Malley had supplied a sample of his mail to Sheila. The computers had done the rest. Each time Sturmer's envelopes turned up, they were extracted from the system and the addresses noted before the mail was allowed on its way. Inspectors at the envelope's destination then placed the recipient's outgoing mail under surveillance.

The intercepts produced further proof of Sturmer's obsession with behaviour of an unusually sadistic nature involving children. To a man in Houston, he described 'adventures' with young boys. In correspondence with a paedophile in Kentucky he detailed his sexual relationship with prepubescent girls. To a client in Hawaii, he wrote about his fondness for sado-masochism with children.

There were doctors who, if called by defence attorneys, would argue that this is simply a further proof that men like Sturmer are clinically disturbed, needing hospital treatment not a prison cell. They were the clinicians who spoke in dulcet tones about the 'problem' of medically classifying pornography, sometimes adding it was no more than the inevitable result of a response to all the other sensual freedoms on offer in the movies, the media and advertising industry. He'd seen those doctors in the witness box, deftly turning a prosecutor's questions to ask their own. Was reportedly showing a child explicit photographs – those doctors never called them pornography – likely to have a long-term effect? Was witnessing or even taking part in sexual by-play – again, never molestation – really harmful in the long term?

Then, in their grave professional voices, the doctors would quote Freud, and any other sexologist they could muster, Kinsey was almost always trundled out – that now notorious passage from his study of human sexual behaviour in which he argued: 'it is difficult to understand why a child, except for its cultural conditioning, should be disturbed at having its genitalia touched, or disturbed at seeing the genitalia of other persons, or disturbed at even more specific sexual contact'.

The prosecution would try to show Kinsey's views are long discredited. The defence doctors would smile indulgently, murmuring that was only a point of view. No matter how fierce the questioning, it would seldom shake the erudite, all-knowing attitude of the expert on the stand. All too often the jury was influenced by such calm authority and gave the defendant the benefit.

O'Malley wished those doctors could read just a portion of the Sturmer file. That would shake their complacency.

The section marked 'Jeanie Copeland' gives no clue to what follows. Yet from the very first intercept O'Malley had shuddered with disgust. Reading it all again, he asked himself: how can any woman behave like this? Let alone a mother do this to her children?

Copeland surfaced when one of Sturmer's packets was intercepted on its way to her place of work – a respected business school in Santa Barbara, California. In a letter ordering more child porn, Copeland had scribbled on the top of the order form, 'for some reason US postal inspectors have an unusually high respect for official titles and evidence of higher education'. She signed herself Professor of Business Studies and she once more instructed Sturmer to always address her by her formal title and always to the school.

O'Malley's inquiries revealed she was indeed a senior academic, thirty-six-years-old and mother of two girls, one aged thirteen, the other fifteen. She was married to a wealthy property dealer. A photograph she sent Sturmer revealed a pleasant-faced woman, with intelligent eyes and a friendly smile. The photo was accompanied by a neatly typed letter. The contents matched Sturmer's explicit demands.

That had been enough for O'Malley. Copeland became a prime target.

Now, reading her intercepts, he was again struck by how the female role as pornographer remained largely unrecognized because of the traditional resistance to the idea of women as child exploiters. Copeland's letters to Sturmer provided valuable insights.

In one, after ordering a number of videos with such titles as *Mother*

& Daughter, School Children Sex Orgy, and *Lolitas and Animals*, she appended a postscript.

'As you know, my husband and me have trained and taught our daughters to join us in sexual delights. As a healthy, sexual male I am sure you will be very pleased with them both. My daughters are very excited at the prospect of meeting you.'

Her sexual invitations were interspersed with shrewd advice. She told Sturmer to space out his packets of pornography with real-estate brochures and European business magazines, explaining why.

> This will allow the postal inspectors at point of entry into US (usually either New York City or Newark, New Jersey for mail coming from your area), to become accustomed to my name and address and to the fact that I am getting considerable mail from you in Germany. They may check two or three items you send me so it is important that you send at least seven or eight non-pornographic items to me in the next two or three weeks. They will be satisfied you are running a normal business conversation thru the mails, and will become lax and deficient in their checks and then when you send porn to me it will sail right thru.

He had promptly alerted the postal inspectors of Copeland's ruse.

Copeland displayed a similar flair for handling payment.

> I suggest I make payment to you by International Money Orders on my personal bank account at the Santa Barbara Bank and Trust Corp. If you sell me $500 worth of material, you will get that amount in money orders of smaller amounts ($100 or $200). I do not want to alert US Federal income tax agents by sending you large dollar value money orders!

The IRS had been tipped-off. They had agreed not to move until O'Malley was ready to pounce, when he finally had Sturmer in his sights.

He read on, noting a pencilled observation he'd made on one of her letters – 'G.U.' – remembering this was the time the Georgetown sting had begun to pay-off.

Academics had responded to the questionnaire sent from the campus by the agent posing as a researcher, revealing not only their obsession with unformed bodies, but some were also using their universities as a postal cover for receiving hard-core child porno.

O'Malley continued his review of a correspondence which was a bizarre mixture of hard-headed business acumen and filth.

Copeland's letter contained warnings that European-made video tapes do not work well in American-made equipment; and 'for security's sake' Sturmer should send items in small lightweight packages. Interspaced with the exhortations were increasingly erotic suggestions. She craved 'for your body', and 'my husband has said again I must make intimate plans for you and me', or 'my lovely daughters want and need you and I shall allow it under discreet and private conditions'. After quoting the dollar rate – 'which will serve as the basis for all payments' – she wrote: 'my daughters will enjoy what you send, and it will increase their desires. They enjoy good sex both in quantity and quality'.

In another letter, after once more reminding Sturmer he must quote a price for each item of porn before shipping, Copeland revealed she had established contact with a German couple in Los Angeles, Hans and Lotte Schreiber.

> They are like us, open and frank about what they want. Right now they are trying to make a little extra to pay for a vacation home. They are marketing a film and foto sets of a little girl. I have seen them and they are very good quality. They say she is twelve, but she looks younger.

The Schreibers had told her that the child, Charlene, had been procured by a pimp in Montreal, called Steve. 'As I understand it, Steve actually purchased her in exchange for a used car.'

She said Charlene had been brought by train across the Canadian border into the United States – 'there are almost no checks on Amtrack.'

There was another pencilled annotation of O'Malley's in the margin to see how the loophole could be closed. He'd fired off memos to Immigration and back had come the promise to tighten surveillance. He didn't blame anyone for not spotting the loophole. There was always a loophole.

He turned another page, the knotted feeling again in his stomach. No matter how many times he read it, it still revolted him.

Charlene and her pimp had left the train at Boston. Lotte Schreiber's crude words did nothing to diminish the horror Copeland described to Sturmer.

> Steve told Lotte that at first the girl gave him a lot of crap and refused to do what he wanted, even after he had broken her in, so to speak. So he just set her up in a room with four guys. The way Lotte tells it, it must have been one big scene. While it was going on Steve videoed the whole event.

As simple and brutally as that the little girl's nightmare began. Schreiber wrote how the pimp

worked Charlene across the country. They travelled by Greyhound or Amtrack. Steve was referred on from one city to another by the street people. For a piece of the action they made it safe for him to operate. When he and the girl arrived in a town, the word went out to key people like bartenders, hotel doormen and cab drivers. Steve and the girl usually set up in a motel out on a freeway where supervision was poor. Sometimes he paid the desk clerk to look the other way. Sometimes he offered sex with the girl as a bonus. That way he made sure the right people kept quiet. The girl worked from the motel room for a few days and she would earn Steve maybe $100, $200 a trick, whatever the market would bear. She could easily do ten tricks a night. After a day or two, Steve would move on to another motel on the opposite side of the city. That way the local vice squad never got close. By the time they reached California, the girl must have earned Steve close to a quarter of a million dollars, even after he'd paid off everyone. Steve also made a number of tapes with her in action. Which is how he came to pal up with Lotte. Would you like to buy them for your European clients?

Sturmer declined the offer, explaining 'nothing you have over there can be as good as what we have here.'

Copeland made another proposition. She wrote that she had shown some of Sturmer's pornography to Ramone Bauk, 'a good friend of mine who has enjoyed the delights of my daughters'. Bauk said Sturmer's material 'could be good for his business'.

Bauk is a Colombian, and had operated as a pimp in the Los Angeles area in the early 1980s. He was charged with procuring a minor, but the week before the case came to trial, the girl was found dead in an alley with a needle in her arm. The police wrote it off as another street kid overdosing.

Bauk went free. Subsequently, he turned up in various West Coast cities. He worked out of rented mail boxes, changing their locations frequently.

O'Malley now knew why. Copeland had written that Bauk catered exclusively for a wealthy clientele.

Big Hollywood names, lawyers. Power people. He provides them with children. He handles special requests, such as mother-daughter, or kids for group sex. An evening with an eleven or twelve year-old costs as much as $2,000. Even more if she's guaranteed free of disease. Top money goes for a virgin, naturally. I hear a ten-year old fetched $3,000 in San Francisco the other night. A commemorative video of such an encounter cost a customer another $200.

Bauk was now another prime target. But catching him would be a real problem, as another of Copeland's letters explained.

Those willing to pay Ramone's fees know the kids are superior to those available on the street. He is able to set his own market price because demand far exceeds supply, and because his clients know they are safe. Parents get big $$$ for their kids. So they are not going to talk. If a kid did, who would believe her? It's about as foolproof as it can be.

The terrible, terrible thing is that it was.

Sturmer had written to Copeland saying how he would very much like to meet Bauk, adding that could be sooner than he had thought.

On the same day he had broken his silence to Sheila with a note which once more brought the pirate's smile to O'Malley's lips.

He closed the file and settled back in his chair. Thinking. He looked like a man at peace with the world. These are the moments when no one really knew what was going through his mind.

Abruptly he rose to his feet and gathered papers into his briefcase.

He strode down the corridor, waving his goodnights and, from the seventh floor downwards, rode in an elevator with those who were too preoccupied with their own problems to ask how he was managing. He would never have told them, anyway.

An hour later O'Malley was back at the mail box. He opened it. Inside was an envelope covered with airmail stickers and German stamps. The address was neatly typed: 'Sheila, PO Box 2455, USA-Oak Park, IL 60302.'

O'Malley removed the letter and locked the box. He walked to his car. Inside, he carefully opened the envelope and read the neatly typed letter.

Dear Sheila! Many thanks for your nice letter. I think it is possible for me to travel to the USA for one or two weeks. But my financial situation is not good for the moment. I have debts by the government and by my bank. Could you loan me the money for the ticket and organize a room for sleeping?

167

A crudely descriptive passage followed of what Sturmer planned to do to Sheila. The letter ended with the hope the enclosed photograph would give her 'some idea of my size, and will you please send me a foto of yourself.' Sturmer signed himself with 'a hot kiss'.

The photograph showed him naked and smiling into the camera.

O'Malley put the letter and photograph in the envelope and placed it in his briefcase. Pulling out into the heavy traffic he began to whistle an Irish ditty. He always does this when he feels he is on a winning streak.

THIRTEEN

The Exorcism

Shortly before three o'clock on a Monday afternoon, under a hazy sky, Susan and Pamela drove to the church in Orange County. It is an imposing brick structure, opening on to the street, its front appropriately solemn and its entrance cool and inviting. They had come to witness the exorcism of Charlie. Susan carried a blank video tape she had bought on the way.

The walked down the central aisle of the sanctuary, its windows sparkling in the diffused light, giving the Christ on the stained glass above the altar the appearance of being crucified against a purple sky tinged with red, darker than blood. The body was luminous, hanging limply from hands nailed through the palms, the knees bent and weakened, the hair dark and wet, the face resolute despite its pain. Christ's wounds glowed.

Once more Susan was reminded of the unique torture of the Cross. Jesus had endured all that torment so that others would know God's grace. It reinforced her belief in what was about to happen to Charlie.

Near the altar a television monitor screen was set-up to relay proceedings from the sacristy where the exorcism would take place. Only those directly involved would be allowed to be present during the spiritual reversal: Charlie, the Reverend Ed Sempstrott and his two assistants, theologians from the Pacific Church College. The trio had worked together on previous exorcisms.

Watching the scene in the sacristy from their pew were Charlie's parents and another pastor. He read passages from a Bible on his knees. As Susan approached she recognized the words from the First Epistle of the Apostle Peter. 'Your adversary, the devil, is a roaring lion, walking about, seeking whom he may devour.'

Charlie's parents murmured their 'amens'.

Their eyes never left the screen. Charlie sat on a chair to one side, solemn-eyed, his hair for once neatly combed. He wore a white shirt and grey shorts. The Reverend Sempstrott ordered his assistant to move the video camera to various positions. Through the screen came the pastor's final decision to post it in one corner of the sacristy. It would provide the widest possible view of the room.

He leaned into the camera and smiled. 'Almost ready.'

The pastor began to recite another familiar passage of scripture. Pamela slid past him to sit between Charlie's parents. She would provide any further support the couple would need during exorcism.

From the screen, Reverend Sempstrott's voice boomed. 'Susan here, yet?'

'Coming,' called Susan, before realizing there was no way he could hear her. She smiled at Charlie's parents. 'He'll be okay.'

She walked through a door beside the altar, thinking what else do you say at a moment like this. Beyond the door the light was murky.

When she reached the sacristy, the Reverend Sempstrott waved at her, then continued the business of supervising the positioning and testing of mikes. His eyes were ever moving, ever alert. They seemed to be endlessly charged. Susan watched him, reassured.

Charlie had the look of someone caged up in the midst of a private ritual. He was being primed for confession, but had no idea what was his crime.

Susan walked into the room and handed over the tape to the pastor. She turned to Charlie.

'How are you, Charlie?'

''Kay,' mumbled Charlie. He shifted his weight.

'Nearly ready, Charlie,' said the Reverend Sempstrott.

Charlie nodded, unimpressed.

'Here take a look,' the pastor moved a monitor so the boy could see. Charlie stared fixedly at his image.

'Can you say a few words, just to make sure everyone can hear you?' asked the pastor.

'Don' know what to say,' mumbled the boy.

Susan put her hand on Charlie's shoulder. This was no day at the beach for him.

'Pam's out there. With your Mom and Dad. Want to say a few words to them?' she asked.

After a while he spoke, 'Hi, Mom, Pam and Dad.' His voice was soft and barely audible.

'How about a little louder, Charlie?' asked one of the assistants.

'How about bringing a mike closer,' suggested Susan quickly.

The Reverend Sempstrott nodded and moved a microphone closer to Charlie.

Susan smiled down at Charlie. 'Want to tell everybody you feel fine?' She stroked his hair.

'Feel fine, Mom,' Charlie managed a smile. 'Can I have an ice after this?'

'You can have all the ices you like,' promised Susan.

The Reverend Sempstrott looked up from the recorder beside the camera. 'All set.'

Susan knelt beside the chair, looking into Charlie's eyes.

'I'll be just across the way, Charlie. Pam too. We'll be with you as if we were here.'

She reached forward and kissed him on the forehead. The skin felt hot and dry.

'Be okay, Susan? Promise?'

'Promise, Charlie. God is here with you. With all of us.'

She rose and walked from the sacristy to a large airy room across the hall. A number of people sat in a semi-circle before another screen relaying the scene from the sacristy. They were deacons and church elders, men and women in dark suits and dresses.

Near the screen was a tank filled with tropical fish. The water filtration system bubbled noisily. Some of the watchers leaned forward to better hear what was going on in the sacristy.

The Reverend Sempstrott and his assistants stood with their heads bowed in prayer while Charlie stared fixedly into the camera. The image was haunting enough to make Susan feel a lump in her throat.

She remained, for the moment, standing by the door, watching the screen and thinking she could not remember now how many times in these past weeks she, too, had prayed for the little boy to be freed from the effects of the abuse he had received. She had also regularly prayed for Sam, Trish and Pete, and especially for Marcia. She had prayed for all the children out there at the Ranch. Now, once more, she asked God to not only keep Charlie, but go on looking after all children in trouble.

Her faith, like everything else about her, is unswervingly direct. It sustains her when she knows people doubt her claims. They are the kind of people, she tells herself, who probably reject the accounts of Jesus walking on the Sea of Galilee, feeding the multitude with a handful of fish and loaves and making the blind see. It needs faith to believe all that happened – the same kind of faith which persuaded her that Charlie's exorcism is necessary.

It could also provide the evidence which would, at long last, make people believe her statements about the Ranch. That was why she wanted the exorcism videoed.

Her prayer over, Susan took her place in the semi-circle. Even now she could not quite believe the spiritual reversal was really about to happen. The journey to this room had been a slow and often difficult one, of sorting out the misunderstandings, festering hostilities and

171

frozen affections which all too often lie just beneath the surface of families in turmoil.

After Pamela had spoken to Charlie's mother, Lili, Susan and her deputy had together seen both his parents to explain how spiritual reversal had helped several other victims of ritual abuse. Pamela described how the Devil sometimes uses a priest or minister because it means he has managed to subvert another of Christ's specially appointed ambassadors on earth. She added the power of those corrupted ministers could only be overcome by a pastor who has the spirit of Jesus dwelling in him.

Charlie's father had rounded on them. 'How'd we know this is gonna work? That Sempstrott has the power?'

Watching him, a once-strong man who'd shed his strength before her eyes in the past months, Susan thought it was understandable for him to believe nothing would work. She knew what a constant struggle it is not to get skewed by the daily struggle against evil.

'It'll be okay. Pam and Susan have said so,' said Lili, reaching for her husband's hand. He pushed her away.

Susan realized again that in a crisis some families pull-together, nurture and love. This was now no longer one of them. In the end, what had happened to Charlie had finally affected his parents. They each loved him still, but themselves no longer had the strength to help each other lift the burden of guilt.

Susan was convinced their only hope of surviving as a family unit was for the exorcism to succeed.

She explained once more that Charlie had been turned into a weapon, an instrument of evil, abused and damaged, yet not beyond redemption. But only if God was allowed to do His work.

Charlie's father had sat there, the dark shadows round his eyes deepening. Once more Lili reached for his hand. This time he did not resist.

'How'd we know it'll work?'

Susan watched his massive frame shift on the chair. Charlie must have gotten the reflex from him. She told the boy's parents the truth.

'The evil in Charlie will fight hard to retain its hold. The powers of Satan can only be overcome by the greater power of Jesus Christ. There is no magic involved in what the Reverend Sempstrott will do for Charlie. He will only expose your son to the power of prayer. This should lead to healing.'

'Supposing it goes wrong?' asked Charlie's father.

Pamela shook her hand. 'Nothing can go wrong with prayer.'

He would not let go. 'Supposing it don't work?'

Susan smiled quickly. 'Supposing we wait and see?'

Charlie's father finally gave a brief nod.

Susan breathed out slowly, hoping her power to reassure would not desert her. She told Charlie's parents they should not expect the spiritual reversal to be a sudden and dramatic experience. Often what followed was a slow and gentle process. That was the best kind, the one which almost always produced a lasting result.

'To help Charlie you have to prepare. That means praying. Asking God to help,' Pamela explained.

Charlie's father once more looked defeated. 'Neither Lili or me were ever very strong on going to church. Since this happened, our faith's all but shot.'

Susan embraced them in turn. Then she stood before them, smiling, and shaking her head.

'Getting it back's easy. Just tell God you want him back in your life.'

They had looked at her, uncertain.

Susan reminded them of the passage in Luke describing how Jesus promised those who ask will receive, those who seek will find, to those who knock it will be opened.

Lili's 'amen' was heartfelt. Her husband's response, when it finally came, as fervent.

Susan smiled at Pamela.

Together they spoke to Charlie. In the Center's interview room they all sat together on the floor and leafed through a children's illustrated Bible. Susan let Pamela explain how Jesus has the power to take away all the hurt and pain Charlie had experienced, and how to help him do this, Jesus had chosen a very special person, the Reverend Sempstrott.

At a mention of the title, Charlie flinched.

'He's not like the other pastor, Charlie. He's a good man,' said Susan.

Charlie clung to Pamela, saying nothing, burying his face in her arms. Finally he whispered he would only go if Pamela would come with him. She had said that not only would she come, but so would Susan.

The visit to the Reverend Sempstrott was a lengthy one. First he questioned Charlie's parents about their beliefs. Next he prayed over them. Finally he gave them a selection of Scripture passages, telling them they must read them every day, explaining they would help ward-off the tremendous struggle Satan would undoubtedly wage to keep Charlie in bondage.

Old doubts once more surfaced in Charlie's father. 'How can us praying help our boy?'

The Reverend Sempstrott repeated Pamela's assurance to him that prayers helped everyone.

The boy's father had not spoken again during the rest of the interview.

The Reverend Sempstrott turned to Charlie. The boy stared at the floor, sucking his thumb. The pastor led him over to a sofa.

'Sorry this is taking so long, Charlie.'

The boy did not answer. The pastor continued.

'Charlie, to help you I have to know a few things. OK?'

Charlie finally gave a nod.

Susan liked the way the Reverend Sempstrott continued in his matter-of-fact, non-threatening way.

'I know you've heard a lot of bad things. Seen a lot of bad things. Had a lot of bad things done to you. We're going to stop all that. God's asked me to stop it. There's no one more powerful than God and His son, Jesus, Charlie. You believe that, don't you?'

Charlie finally raised his eyes to look at the Reverend Sempstrott. The little boy told the pastor that the Devil was more powerful than Jesus.

The Reverend Sempstrott leaned forward and gently held the boy's face between his hands. In a voice suddenly deep and resonant, he repeated that no one was more powerful than Jesus.

For almost an hour the pastor explained the true meaning of faith to the child.

Driving back to the Center, Susan told Pamela she had rarely been so deeply moved by the restatement of hallowed beliefs.

Now, weeks later, she watched the screen as once more the pastor reached forward to cup the boy's face, and repeat Jesus was about to demonstrate His power and authority over the forces of darkness. Charlie stared fixedly into the camera.

One of the pastors seated near Susan rose and stood before the group. Clasping his hands he asked them to remember the words of St Matthew. In a voice as powerful as the Reverend Sempstrott's, he intoned: 'And Jesus said, suffer little children, and forbid them not to come unto me, for such is the kingdom of heaven.'

In the passage of Scripture, Susan found an echo of the past weeks, a coming together of so many strands, a reminder of so many truths. Watching the three silent figures grouped around Charlie, bowed in prayer, she thought again of all the other children who were turning to her for help.

The number receiving treatment at the Center had reached unprecedented levels. It was not the result of a sudden upsurge in ritual abuse, but because those in therapy elsewhere often had made little progress. They were either finally referred by their doctors to the Center or brought there by parents, who displayed their bitterness and anger that it was impossible to obtain suitable psychotherapy elsewhere.

Susan sympathized with their feelings. While directories in Southern California listed thousands of therapists offering a lexicon of treatments, only a few are qualified to deal with child victims of sexual abuse, and almost none with its mutation: the victimization of children by Satanic cults.

Skilled therapy all too often still lags well behind the horror stories Susan and her staff unravel every day. They are increasingly convinced what they hear is only the tip of an immensely evil and powerful movement, one which certainly goes all the way back to the Pilgrim Fathers. Some of the country's founders had brought secret and sadistic practices from Europe to the New World, ensuring that child-murdering Satanic cults became embedded in American society. In the past, such activities had rarely surfaced: Salem, Massachusetts, 1692, a famous example.

Since the late Seventies, there has been a wave of Satanic related crimes. The public response was one of horror – and growing disbelief this was simply too awful to be happening – therefore it could not be happening.

The first therapists who began to ponder how their clinical skills could be adapted to deal with the survivors of such abuse, initially had little understanding of what was involved. Most knew little more than that the number 666 identified Satan as the mark of the Beast in the Book of Revelation. But that number, written by children in their colouring books, slowly convinced some therapists that they were going to have to treat a strange and frightening condition. Its symptoms, they learned, also include repeated references by small victims to animal and human mutilation, the devouring of the newly dead and preoccupation with faeces and urine. All too often, the children described such incidents in the same trembling voices they used to insist that television characters are real people.

The possibility the children were fantasizing still found a ready response among police, overwhelmingly they said the children's stories were purely imagination. Matters were not helped by the way the issue was commercially exploited.

A company marketed 'Kiddie Alert', a radio transmitter which could be attached to a child and would trigger an alarm if he or she went out of a pre-set range. At $129.95 it was a steady seller. Another manufacturer produced 'Kiddie-Kufs', nylon bracelets which handcuffed a child to an adult. They cost $7 a pair. The company said they could also double as dog-leads. Dentists charged between $50 and $150 to implant the name and address of a child on a tooth.

Scandal had joined cynicism over such methods when, in Florida, a company was set up called 'Child Search Inc'. Its stated aim was to seek 'solutions to the problem of lost and missing children'. The company turned out to be the brainchild of a group of paedophiles.

Dr Benjamin Spock denounced not only such commercial crassness, but attacked the claims and counter claims about how and why children went missing, 'The issue is creating a nation of morbidly frightened youngsters.' His colleague, psychologist Lee Salk, spoke for many policemen, 'America is breeding a nation of children too afraid to talk to strangers.'

From the outset, Susan viewed such criticisms calmly, prepared to accept the evidence in her own case files. For her, a more urgent matter had been to create workable therapies. These took into account that in children there *are* well-developed fantasies, while at the same time it is important to recognize they are not automatically lying when they describe instruments stuck into bodies and the use of narcotics and sedatives. The therapies reinforced her belief that children do not invent stories of weird songs and chants, or learn by themselves to write letters backwards, the Devil's alphabet. Children are shown and taught all these things by adults. Believing this remained a vital part of her approach.

She knew that faced with often hostile medical colleagues, the number of therapists prepared to devote their careers to treating victims of ritual abuse remains small. In the United States there were still less than 350. Yet, Dr Al Carlisle, a psychologist at the Utah State Men's Prison publicly stated in 1988 that his own investigations into cult-related crimes showed the number of human sacrifices in North America annually ran to 'several thousand'. He stressed that to be a conservative estimate. They were mostly John and Jane Does, the flotsam of society no one missed. Dr Carlisle was ridiculed by his peers in medicine and law enforcement.

Their attitude was reflected elsewhere. Fifteen years after the Child Abuse Prevention and Treatment Act was introduced, its funding remained pitifully inadequate. In 1988 the annual federal grant to research the entire field of child abuse was under $30 million – less than half the amount of foreign aid Congress voted each year to support a regime like Haiti's. Yet if the root cause of such abuse is ever to be properly understood, Susan believed it essential to study victims for the rest of their lives, to observe them as they grow up, become teenagers, marry and have children of their own. Such long-term studies, she is convinced, will provide valuable pointers to what so often turns the abused into abusers.

She hoped one day the Center would have sufficient funds to conduct such studies. But at present every penny was used to meet running costs – and no longer could she call upon the fund-raising efforts of Allen Simmons.

He had walked into her office and stood awkwardly before her desk. She motioned him to a chair and asked what was on his mind. He said he wanted to resign. She asked why, and he'd smiled and said it was time for him to 'move on'. He offered no other explanation and she had not sought one. Privately though, she wondered whether he found it difficult to make an adjustment from a life of priestly celibacy to being the only man on the Center's staff. He asked if he could leave at once, and she agreed. He had gone, in many ways as little known as when he arrived. She supposed a sense of mystery is something a priest never shakes off. She had plunged herself back into work.

On the screen, she watched the Reverend Sempstrott begin to use God's power to help Charlie.

Flanked by his two assistants, the pastor stood before Charlie. Each man held a Bible in his hand. The adults formed a protective shield around Charlie as the Reverend Sempstrott began to speak.

'Let us do what the Apostle Paul instructed the Ephesians. "Put on the whole armour of God that we may be able to stand against the wiles of the Devil".'

From either side of Susan came a murmured response: 'Amen.'

The Reverend Sempstrott's resonant voice rose above the gurgle of the fish tank as the pastor reminded the boy of the passage from the Book of Exodus where God spoke to Moses on Mount Sinai. 'Thou shalt have no other gods but Me.'

Once more from around Susan came fervent responses. She saw Charlie glance uneasily towards the door.

In the sacristy the Reverend Sempstrott told the boy he was here, 'to make Christ the Lord the Master of the life.' Then, his voice deepening still further he uttered a caution.

'After you have accepted Jesus, Charlie, it will not mean that Satan will leave you alone. He is clever. He will go on and try and tempt you. He will want to see how weak you are. So every day you will have to ask Jesus to remain in your life. Every minute of every hour of every day, you will have to ask Jesus to be there.'

Susan saw Charlie's lip begin to tremble. She had never seen him close to tears before. Was it relief – or fear? She concentrated on the screen.

In the sanctuary Pamela slipped her hand into Lili's, squeezing reassurance. The pastor beside Charlie's father murmured in unison the words from Paul's Epistle to the Ephesians being read out in the sacristy.

The Reverend Sempstrott stepped back from Charlie and riffled through the pages of his Bible. In a thunderous voice that startled some of the elders around Susan, the pastor read from the Acts of the Apostles, walking around the sacristy as he did so.

'"And many that believed came and confessed, and showed their deeds. Many of them who had used curious arts brought their books together and burned them before all men. So mightily grew the word of God and prevailed".'

Pausing in the middle of the room, the pastor spoke almost conversationally. 'You hear that Satan? We don't have any of your books. But we know they are still with us. So while we can't burn them, we are going to burn you with the power of Jesus.'

He resumed his measured pacing, Bible closed and held to his chest. He stopped before Charlie, motioning for him to stand. The two assistants moved to either side, holding Charlie.

Dwarfed by the black-suited men, Charlie looked like a tiny prisoner, Susan thought. From the screen came once more the loud resounding voice of the Reverend Sempstrott.

'Lord hear us. We are here today to bring out the evil spirit in Charlie. We are here to proclaim his rejection of all the secret and shameful practices and activities this little boy has been forced to do. We are here to return him to the Lord Jesus!'

There was silence in the sacristy. Around Susan the responses were mere whispers. All eyes concentrated on the screen.

Charlie had suddenly stiffened, his lips moved uncontrollably. No words reached those beyond the sacristy.

Lili half-rose from her seat, hands reaching towards the screen. Pamela pulled her down. Charlie's father lowered his head. The pastor placed an arm around his shoulder. Once more they all watched the screen.

In the sacristy the Reverend Sempstrott, in the same powerful voice, began to ask questions.

'Charlie, are you ready to receive Jesus? Now!'

Charlie's mouth continued its strange silent chattering.

The assistants held Charlie more firmly.

'Now, Charlie! *Now!* Are you ready now, just as you stand here, to come to Jesus?' thundered the Reverend Sempstrott.

Charlie suddenly broke free and ran to a corner opposite the camera. He cowered there, trembling violently all over, his lips in rictus, eyes large and glaring.

Susan tensed, trying to decide whether to intercede. Several of the elders had buried their faces in their hands. She continued to watch the Reverend Sempstrott.

He walked slowly towards Charlie, a crucifix in his hand. He stopped before the boy, extending the cross towards him.

'Jesus wants you, Charlie,' said the Reverend Sempstrott in a normal voice.

Charlie recoiled, the rictus more pronounced.

178

The pastor inched the crucifix closer to the boy, his voice once more loud and certain.

'Paul says, give no place to the Devil. John said, the Son of God agreed to destroy the Devil's work. Paul told the Colossians that God delivered us from the power of darkness and brought us into the kingdom of his dear Son.'

Susan realized the pastor was directing the words not so much at Charlie but at some other force. She suddenly felt the way she had that morning she discovered the presence of evil in the Center. Now, as then, she sought refuge in silently reciting the Lord's Prayer.

The Reverend Sempstrott moved a step closer to Charlie, the cross held unwaveringly.

'God is telling us, Charlie, *you*, Charlie, that Satan's power and authority are taken away by the Cross. Do you understand that, Charlie? Do you?'

Charlie shrank further into the corner, the rictus beginning to make his whole body shake.

In the sanctuary, Lili was sobbing loudly, her face buried in her husband's shoulder. He pulled her closer to him, his tears mingling with hers.

Susan watched the Reverend Sempstrott close his eyes, both hands gripping the cross, fingers wrapped around the carved figure in His agony.

Charlie's tremble increased, his eyes burning as if with some fearful fever, but still no sound came from the boy.

The Reverend Sempstrott opened his eyes. Once more in his normal voice he began to question Charlie.

'Was Satan your friend?'

Charlie's lips worked back and forth.

'Admit it, Charlie. You must first admit that Satan was your friend. We must hear you say that.'

The pastor's voice had again begun to deepen. Susan watched Charlie's lips struggling to frame something.

'Was Satan your *friend*, Charlie?'

Charlie's lips continued their unstoppable movement.

The pastor continued to press.

'Was he, Charlie? Was he *your* pal? Is that what he was, Charlie – *your best pal*?'

Susan willed Charlie to shout. *Say yes, Charlie. Everything will begin with that. Just – yes. Say it Charlie!*

Lili wept loudly, clinging closer to her husband, her sobbing once more broken by the powerful voice of the Reverend Sempstrott.

He began to recite further passages of Scripture – the words of Isaiah urging the Israelites to put the past forever behind them. The reminder of Matthew that Jesus promised 'Heaven and earth shall

179

pass away, but My words shall not.' St Paul's declaration to the Galatians that Christ has made us all free.

Towering over Charlie, the pastor demanded to know whether he wanted to be free of Satan.

'No!'

Charlie's scream pierced the air. Susan leapt to her feet and was halfway to the door when the commanding voice of the Reverend Semptstrott stopped her.

'Yes, Charlie! Yes, you want to be free! Yes, you will be free! Satan has no further claim on you! Satan has nothing in common with you! Nothing of you belongs to Satan! Satan has no power over you!'

Susan watched, transfixed, at what was happening on the screen. Charlie was on his feet, lips bared, screaming in that same piercing voice.

'Satan is in me! Satan is me! Satan is in me! Satan is me!'

The Reverend Sempstrott raised one hand high in the air, holding the crucifix aloft.

Their two voices fought each other, one thundering holy writ, the other obscenities.

'The Lord will make you strong and protect you!'

'No! Satan will!'

'You are safe in Jesus – Jesus will protect you!'

'No! Only Satan!' screamed Charlie.

The pastor never wavered. 'Jesus loves you. He died for you. And he is saying now that he wants you to come to him.'

'No! Hate Jesus! Love Satan! Hate Jesus!'

The pastor held the crucifix closer to the boy.

'Now, Charlie! *Now!* Come to Him, Charlie. Jesus is waiting!'

Charlie was no longer coherent. Spittle dribbled faster from his mouth.

The pastor edged closer, shielded behind the cross, reciting the words of the Apostle John.

'Jesus said I am the bread of life. He that cometh to Me shall never hunger. He that believeth in Me shall never thirst. Jesus is talking to you, Charlie. Listen to Him!'

Charlie screamed as if physically hurt. His hands were up to ward-off the cross as he retreated into the corner.

Susan remained rooted where she stood, watching the struggle going on in the sacristy. It was one so powerful that its force seemed to be coming out of the screen. She could feel evil fighting good. God and the Devil engaged in mortal combat for the soul of Charlie.

The Reverend Sempstrott continued his slow, steady forward movement towards Charlie, shielded behind the cross.

'Look at Him, Charlie. Jesus died for you. To free you.'

Charlie was backed against the wall, body shaking, hands flailing. 'No! No! No!' He screamed a torrent of abuse.

The Reverend Sempstrott moved the cross closer, saying nothing. His two assistants moved close to him, forming a further protective shield – and blocking off any way Charlie could escape.

In the sanctuary Pamela and the pastor put their arms around Charlie's parents.

Susan silently repeated the Lord's Prayer, her eyes never leaving the screen.

Charlie lunged, trying to knock the crucifix to the floor. The Reverend Sempstrott side-stepped the attempt and thrust the cross directly into Charlie's face, so that its figure brushed the boy's forehead.

Charlie screamed as if he had been burnt.

Once more the Reverend Sempstrott touched him with the cross.

'Receive Jesus, Charlie. Tell Satan to be gone. Only you can do that. You must tell Jesus that you want no part of the Devil.'

Another unearthly scream came from Charlie.

The Reverend Sempstrott stood only inches from the boy. The crucifix cast its shadow over them.

'Tell him now, Charlie! *Now!* Say after me, Charlie. "In the name of Jesus I command Satan to get out of me!" Say *it*, Charlie!'

Still Charlie resisted.

'No! No! Satan is me!'

Around Susan the pastors and elders were on their feet, reciting the Lord's Prayer. In the sanctuary, Lili moaned, no longer able to watch the screen. The pastor placed the Bible in the hands of Charlie's father, and laid his own hand on the cover. Together they began to recite the Lord's Prayer. Pamela joined them, directing the words at Lili.

With a sudden sense of hope Susan watched the Reverend Sempstrott take Charlie's hand and place it on the cross. Taken by surprise, the boy did not resist the pastor.

'Feel the power of the word of Jesus, Charlie! Feel it! That is why Jesus wants you to say you command Satan to leave you. Say it just once, Charlie. Just once – and it will be over. Just say "in the name of Jesus, I command Satan to get out of me!" Say it – *now!*'

Susan whispered to herself. 'Sweet Jesus. Help Charlie. Help him.'

In the sacristy Charlie crumpled to the floor. The two assistants bent forward and lifted him to his feet. The boy hung between them, eyes closed and lifeless.

Around Susan, people rose, stricken-faced. She steeled herself to continue watching the screen. Charlie gave a sudden animal-like sound. Once more he slumped, only stopped from falling by the grip in which he was held. Susan felt something was dying inside Charlie. Her sense of hope grew.

181

In a voice she had never heard him use before, Charlie spoke.
'In the name of Jesus, I command Satan to get out of me.'
There was total silence in the sacristy, sanctuary and hall.
The Reverend Sempstrott crouched before Charlie.
'Say it again. One more time. Let there be no doubt.'
Charlie repeated the words.
The pastor hugged him. 'We've won, Charlie, Won! The Devil will never again be able to touch you. Jesus will see to that.'
The words were choked with emotion.
Lili looked wonderingly at her husband and Pamela. They began to smile at each other, their eyes fixed on the screen.
All the pain and anger and hurt had gone from Charlie's face. He was looking around him, and smiling like any other child. It was the most wonderful smile Susan had ever seen.
She started to run towards the sacristy. From the sanctuary Charlie's parents emerged, supporting each other wordlessly. Behind them came Pamela and the pastor, smiling.
In a group they entered the sacristy. Charlie ran towards his mother. She hugged him. Then his father hugged them both. Then they turned to Susan and Pamela and hugged them. Soon the sacristy was filled with people embracing each other.
The Reverend Sempstrott walked to the recorder and rewound the tape. Susan walked over and thanked him.
'It was God, not me,' said the pastor. 'I was just a conduit.' He sounded exhausted.
He handed her the tape.

It had taken a while for Susan and Pamela to detach themselves from the celebrations. Finally they led Charlie and his parents to an ice-cream parlour. Charlie had looked shyly at Pamela.
'Can I still come and play games with you?'
Pamela nodded happily.
Charlie turned to Susan. 'And will you still read stories to me?'
She smiled at Lili. 'Your mom can borrow the books. Then she can read them any time you want.'
Susan knew that in the end the family must find themselves.
She and Pamela hugged them each one more time. As they left, Charlie was already absorbed in deciding what combination of ices to have.
It was dusk when Susan parked the car and walked with Pamela into the building.
When they reached the Center, its door was locked, the staff gone for the night.
Susan was glad. She did not want anyone except Pamela to see the tape. There were moments she wished neither of them would

have to look at again. Locking the suite door behind them, they went to the conference room. While Pamela sprawled in a seat, Susan walked to the video player, holding the tape which had not left her hand since the Reverend Sempstrott gave it to her.

She had bought the cassette shortly before the exorcism at a Radio Shack, choosing it herself from the store shelf. She had remained in the sacristy until the Reverend Sempstrott said the equipment was ready to record.

Susan placed the tape in the machine and pressed the play button.

She stood to one side so that Pamela could see.

The screen was filled with shadowy wraith-like images. The sound track had a loud constant hum, interspersed with the gurgle of the fish tank.

Susan let the tape play to the end. Picture and sound remained totally unintelligible.

'Could be a fault with the player?' said Pamela. The words rang hollow.

Susan removed the tape and chose one from the rack beside the player. She inserted it. It played perfectly. Susan switched-off the video.

Pamela's eyes narrowed, 'They did it again.'

She sounded neither angry nor surprised.

'But we got Charlie back,' Susan's voice was suddenly fierce.

They sat in silence for a while. When Susan next spoke she was once more calm and determined.

'We are going to go on winning back the children. All of them. They can try what they like. But in the end we'll win. Like we won back Charlie. Like I'll win back Danny.'

Pamela nodded. 'They better believe it.'

Together they walked out of the door, reinforced in their absolute commitment to continue fighting.

FOURTEEN

Beyond All Reasonable Doubt

One hundred and fifty-seven days after Sanders and Hendrix had first driven into Sixth Street to begin their investigation into the murder of John Doe Sixty, they were back. A mild Pacific air current continued to sweep in from the Bay. It was hard to credit, Sanders remarked as they had set off for Headquarters, him at the wheel, that this was a day in early February; it was balmy like April. In keeping with the weather, he wore a medium-weight tan suit, a cream shirt and check necktie. He looked like an investment broker from the financial district. Hendrix wore a dark blue worsted, a two-button, single-breasted suit, white shirt and striped tie. He still looked a cop.

Hendrix said the weather would not last; the morning TV forecast had predicted a cold snap heading down from Alaska. The subject exhausted, they rode in silence. Neither wanted to speculate whether they were finally about to solve the case. The prospect made neither man tense nor set the adrenalin pumping, there was time enough yet to engage reactions and emotions, to bring nerves to the highest pitch of response, be ready to act on the balls of their well-shod feet. In those past five months they had done so more than once, only to see their hopes dashed.

On this mid-morning in mid-week the silence they shared was not the contemplative kind. Long ago they both realized self-examination is not helpful in their kind of work. What they do, they do. What they did, is in the past. But they remained within the rules. *Always.*

Sixth Street still appeared to have strayed from Beirut. The semi-trailer had gone. Weeds grew a foot high at the spot where the detectives had crouched over the body and made their first deductions. Otherwise it was the same. People leaned against graffiti-covered walls, arms folded, knees slack, faces closed but missing nothing. They talked softly among themselves, following the progress of the car down the street, eyes glancing it on from one group to another. The day shift of small-time smack and heroin dealers. The pimps. The early hookers setting off up-town, young girls in Madonna tank tops who hit hard on their heels as they strutted, their breasts bouncing under the fabric. The old and the unfirm. The addicts and the dying. None missed the progress of the car. Its occupants missed not one of their looks.

From inside a building ahead came raised voices. A man emerged on the pavement, shoving his vest into his trousers, weaving uncertainly. Sanders registered him as white, five-six, in his early twenties, with the kind of muscles pumping iron produced, behind came a woman: five-zero, mid-twenties, dark face, blonde frizzy hair, baby-doll pyjamas, shouting, staggering. The man continued his unsteady way. The woman yelled he wasn't fit to be anyone's husband, let alone hers. She stumbled after him.

Hendrix grinned as Sanders slowed the car to watch developments. Family disputes are a no-go area unless a threat to life. The only danger here was which of the pair would fall down first. They moved like the seriously drunk, the woman showering abuse, the man intent only on escape.

The onlookers began to cheer as the woman closed the gap. The man looked over his shoulder, lost his footing, and tumbled into a pile of trash. The woman flopped on top of him. The cheers increased. The man rolled her aside and staggered on. She crawled after him on all fours. Urged on by the crowd, she somehow rose to her feet and, head down, charged the man in the back. They both sank to the ground. The woman began to wail she wanted him to stay with her. The man rose to his feet and lurched away, not looking back.

The excitement over, the onlookers went back to what they had been doing. Sanders picked up speed as he wondered what made a marriage end.

Gallant said hers had just come to a quiet dead stop. She said so a few days ago, quickly and without any relevance to what they were speaking about. Sanders asked if she wanted to talk, and she shook her head, and said thanks, but there was nothing to talk about. She smiled to soften the word, leaving him thinking how gracious some people could be in not wanting to give offence in the midst of their own misery. Gallant sounded as if her marriage had been dead for a long time.

Hendrix laughed and pointed. A man was helping the woman off the ground and she had her arms around his neck and was kissing him. Wrapped around each other, they staggered back into the building.

A block further on a cyclist appeared out of a side street, jinking and zig-zagging in front of the car, his skinny body pumping away at

185

the pedals of a BMX. Probably bought from the proceeds of drugs, Hendrix said. Dealers used cyclists to messenger supplies. On another day they would have pulled the youth over, but not today.

Sanders swung past the cyclist, Eddie had said Cliff St Joseph had promised him a bicycle. He mentioned it on the drive to Headquarters on that Saturday night after he had led the youth from the café to the car.

Driving out of the produce district, Sanders deliberately chose to go down Sixth Street. He wanted to see how Eddie reacted when passing the crime scene. It might jog him into remembering something important. Eddie said nothing as they drove slowly past the spot. The youth continued to slump in the passenger seat, knitted hat pulled down low on his forehead, eyes darting from one side of the street to another.

The youth was badly frightened – and Sanders had no doubt Cliff St Joseph and his brother, Clint, were the cause. What they had done to John Doe Sixty was enough to terrify anybody. Eddie must have realized the next sacrifice – to mark Cliff's return from Canada – would be just as horrific, and he was going to have to take part. Had Eddie felt his only way out was to go to the police? Sanders had not asked, preferring to leave the youth with his thoughts. Riding in silence in a police car, Sanders knew, often has a powerful effect in concentrating the mind.

He continued to review what Eddie had already said. The descriptions of John Doe Sixty's wounds were accurate, down to the cut on the lip and flaying his buttocks with a heavy metal chain. The problem was how to make Eddie's testimony believable, so that he could obtain a warrant to search St Joseph's apartment. He'd have his work cut out to do so, given Eddie had about as much credibility as any street kid.

The important thing was to convey a sense of optimism. Give Eddie the impression that, with or without his testimony, the case was solved. Therefore he had nothing to fear from Cliff and Clint St Joseph. That way Eddie could come up with someone to support his story. Even two street waifs would be better than one.

Turning off Sixth, a cyclist swept across their path, forcing Sanders to brake sharply. It was then that Eddie said Cliff had promised him a bike.

Sanders chuckled. 'He's going to be away for so long Eddie, when he gets out, bikes will have rockets.'

'He say no prison can hol' him, man.'

Another chuckle. 'We got prisons that can hold the Devil.'

Eddie continued to stare uneasily out of the car. Sanders parked in front of Headquarters and led Eddie into the building. They rode up to the fourth floor. The detective took Eddie to the interview room, sat the youth down, fetched him a coffee, and left him alone. It was Sanders' way of reinforcing control of the situation.

Hendrix arrived soon afterwards. Operations had finally tracked him down and the detective had abandoned his plans for a night out. Sanders briefed him. Together they went to the interview room, Sanders bringing fresh coffee, Hendrix a tape recorder.

For the next two hours they questioned Eddie. He repeated what he told Sanders, including the long list of names of those he claimed were involved with Cliff St Joseph in Satanic practices. Hendrix began to press Eddie.

'You see any of these people with him?'

Eddie sighed. 'No, man. Jus' tol' me their names.'

'And you just remembered them? How come you remember all these names?' Hendrix deliberately sounded sharp and suspicious.

'Hey, man. You thin' I make 'em up? Zaz it, man?'

Sanders was conciliatory, telling Eddie no one was doubting him. The roles of the detectives were being established. Hendrix would assume the aggressor; Sanders would remain non-threatening.

Eddie rolled his eyes at Sanders, leaving his mouth slack. Sanders smiled back at him.

'Who's next on Cliff's list, Eddie?' he asked.

'Ricki.'

'Ricki – what?' fired Hendrix. 'Ricki, man? Ricki, woman? Ricki, the goddamed dog? Come on!'

Eddie's eyes continued to roll at Sanders.

'Ricki Hunter. A guy. Gay.' After a long pause. 'Like me.'

'Where's he now?' salvoed Hendrix.

'Hidin' out.'

'Where's he hiding, Eddie?' interposed Sanders gently.

'Gays Against Violence.'

Hendrix nodded quickly. 'The group run a rape crisis centre near Market.'

Eddie nodded, smiling gratefully as Sanders poured him more coffee.

The detectives returned to their prime interest – John Doe Sixty. Repeatedly pressed by Hendrix, Eddie still could provide no background.

'Nev' met him?'

Hendrix shrugged, disbelieving.

'This No Name. He worked the street – right? Everybody knows everybody on the street. So how come you suddenly can't remember?'

Eddie slurped coffee, staring bug-eyed at Sanders.

187

'Hey, man. 'U forget. No Name kept by Cliff 'n Clint. Don' work no street. Tol' you that, man.'

Hendrix interrupted. He wasn't interested in what Eddie said before. He wanted to hear what he had to say now.

Eddie continued to roll his eyes and smile his crazed smile and repeat he hadn't even met John Doe Sixty. He only knew what Cliff had told him.

Hendrix continued to try and force Eddie into a mistake. Eddie was lying to save his own skin. He had taken part in the killing.

Eddie held firm. He had never met No Name. He only knew what Cliff had said.

Sanders was encouraged. If Eddie could survive Nap's interrogation, it further reinforced his belief that Eddie was telling the truth.

The two detectives left the interview room. They would question Ricki Hunter later. Right now they had to try and establish the veracity of what Eddie said.

A Clifford St Joseph was listed at the address Eddie gave. Hendrix pulled a file from Records. It listed a man of that name as having convictions for sexual offences against young men. A medical report described St Joseph as capable of sudden rages and obsessed with rituals.

Sanders chuckled. 'Good old psychiatry. Never fails.'

Hendrix held up the file photo. 'Maybe he got started because he didn't want to be Miss Universe.'

The photograph showed a white cadaverous face, lank hair and a mouth caught in a half-sneer. The eyes struck Sanders. Even allowing for the stark police lighting, there was something deeply frightening about them.

Sanders took the photo to the interview room. He laid it on the table, asking Eddie to take his time. He replied at once.

'Zaz him, man. Only olda now. Clint yung'r.'

Sanders scooped up the print, chuckling, 'When they get their next pictures taken, it will be their last.'

Despite his breezy confidence, Sanders knew that St Joseph's previous convictions were not going to be conclusive in linking him to the death of John Doe Sixty. Even a tyro defence lawyer could probably successfully appeal St Joseph's record as inadmissible.

As it turned out, Eddie's identification was the detectives' last piece of luck for a while. Hendrix called the doctor who wrote the report. He now lived up on Nob Hill. A butler answered the phone and, in his best butler's voice, asked if the call was really important. Hendrix said pleasantly that if the butler didn't fetch his master he would send a patrol car to bring him downtown. The butler told him to wait and, after a while, the doctor came on the phone. Hendrix explained the purpose of his call. The doctor replied, still and formal, that he could not recall the case. He bid the detective goodnight in a tone that Hendrix thought could probably have cracked open the San Andreas Fault.

Records had no file for a Clint St Joseph. The section in Clifford St Joseph's file reserved for family details was blank. For some reason he had not listed his brother.

'He don't have to be a blood relative. This Cliff is weird enough to make anyone a brother who'll play his game.' Hendrix pursed his lips.

'A bad situation,' sighed Sanders.

They returned to the interview room. Sanders asked Eddie if he had ever heard Cliff call Clint by any other name.

Eddie thought hard. After a while he said he had heard Cliff call Clint 'Morris'.

'Maybe he changed his name in Canada,' Sanders suggested to Hendrix as they left the room. Further searches yielded nothing on the FBI computer. There was no Morris listed at the St Joseph address.

They went back to studying his file.

They began to check addresses for the names Eddie had given. A number lived in fashionable areas of the city. Several had unlisted numbers. Sanders felt there was probably no other way Eddie could have learned the names unless he had been given them by Clifford St Joseph. His instinct that Eddie was telling the truth grew. He told Hendrix St Joseph had probably done that to impress Eddie.

'Fits your friendly shrink's bit in his report about St Joseph's boasting and showing-off.'

Hendrix hunched his shoulders and narrowed his eyes, like a bar fighter. 'Guy makes more money in a week than I do in a year coming up with stuff like that. Maybe I should take up psychiatry.'

'I hear gynaecology's more fun.'

They both laughed and continued checking addresses.

These provided further confirmation that people involved in Satanic practices are often men and women who would know how to shelter behind expensive lawyers. When the time came they would have to be approached with care. Even then, there would probably be no way of linking them to the actual killing of John Doe Sixty. People like that always took care to have good alibis.

They compared the words Eddie said he had been taught by Clifford St Joseph, with a list Gallant had provided. They matched.

Sanders called Gallant at home and asked whether she would recognize any of the names Eddie had provided. He read them to her over the phone. From time to time she said she did.

Close to midnight Sanders and Hendrix returned to the interview

189

room, Sanders carrying more coffee. Hendrix the recorder. Eddie sat as they had left him, hunched over the table, moving his empty cup in a circle. Sanders placed a coffee before him and settled down in the chair opposite. Hendrix placed the recorder on the table and leaned against the door.

'More questions, Eddie,' said Sanders pleasantly.

'Zaz okay, man.' The youth drank noisily.

Hendrix asked Eddie how Ricki came to be chosen as the next sacrifice. Eddie looked at Sanders. Sanders nodded encouragingly. The youth sighed.

'He replacemen' fo' No Name.'

Hendrix moved in, 'They know each other?'

Eddie shrugged. 'On d' street eve'budy kno' eve'budy, and nobudy kno' nobudy. Unnerstan'?'

Hendrix glared at him.

Sanders tried a smile. 'Okay, Eddie. Here's what you do. Tell us exactly what happened from the time Ricki met Cliff.'

Eddie began to describe how they met. A few days after John Doe Sixty's murder, St Joseph picked up Ricki on Market and persuaded him to come home. Eddie was there and saw what happened.

'Clint pours Ricki a drink. Is spiked, man.'

Hendrix pounced, 'How'd you know the drink was spiked?'

Eddie smiled his crazy smile. 'One sip 'n he's gone. Just fell over, man. They take his clothes off and wrap him in chains then drag him to Agarthi . . .'

The location of the mysterious Path of Agarthi turned out to be the apartment's main living room. The two men had rolled back the carpet and positioned Ricki in the middle of a circle chalked on the boards. They had then squatted on its circumference chatting. Eddie had been forced to sit between them.

'At some point Ricki comes-to. When he fine's chains, he starts to yell. Man does he yell. Cliff puts on some heavy rock metal music and turns up the sound. He crawls into the circle and balls him every imaginable way. Goes on all night.'

In between sodomizing Ricki, Cliff made him drink more of the spiked wine.

After more coffee, Eddie continued.

Next morning Cliff had turned the German Shepherd loose on Ricki. The dog raped the youth, just as it had raped John Doe Sixty. Eddie said it made him shake just to watch.

This had gone on for about a week, day and night.

'Then Cliff say he's gonna have a party to welcum Clin'. That we gonna sacrifice Ricki. When Cliff said he's gonna take out Ricki's right ball, Ricki just wen' crazy. Cliff turn up the music and says he's gonna make a hole in Ricki's neck. To drain blood. Cliff is

190

really getting-off on Ricki, and lookin' at me, kinda funny. Like I was next. Wuz real scary. When Cliff and Clin' gone to get guests f'o the party, I got Ricki out of d' house.'

Hendrix joined Sanders in trying to persuade Eddie to accept protective custody. The youth refused, insisting Cliff would reach him in prison. The detectives finally obtained his agreement to remain in a cell in Headquarters. They knew it could only be a temporary arrangement, but hopefully, it would give them time to try and come up with something.

The detectives drove to the rape crisis centre. Ricki was still very shocked, but able to confirm all Eddie had said. They persuaded Ricki to come to headquarters to make a statement and he was allowed to see Eddie in the holding pen after he signed his affidavit. The detectives sat at their desks and studied it. Ricki could provide no details about the killing of John Doe Sixty.

Sanders looked at Hendrix. 'From what they say, it's very possible John Doe Sixty was murdered in St Joseph's apartment, taken to Sixth and dumped. The spot's only a few minutes away. He could have been dumped in the middle of the night and nobody would have been aware. The body was wrapped so that it looked like an old carpet or some bedding. People are dumping stuff down there all the time.'

Hendrix grunted. 'But not bodies. To make it work we have to get physical evidence. Connect the body to the apartment. We need a search warrant. To get it we have to come up with some more substantial witnesses than Eddie and Ricki.'

For a while they sat and stared at each other. Sanders rose to his feet.

'I'll go talk to them again.'

When he entered Eddie's cell, both youths insisted they wanted to leave. Sanders did his best to change their minds. He failed. Eddie and Ricki left, promising to call-in regularly. The first deadline was for six p.m. that evening. When seven came and they had not telephoned, Sanders put out an all-cars alert. He checked the rape crisis centre. Ricki had not returned. By midnight there was still no word from either youth.

Over the next four months Sanders and Hendrix conducted a relentless pursuit for their two witnesses. They flipped open their shields at doors, and walked in and out of lobbies south of Market which either smelled of spices or urine and always stale overheated air. They staked-out houses, apartment blocks, movie theatres, bars — all those places Eddie and Ricki might be, and never were.

They conducted a canvas of the area between Second and Third Streets, to include the area where St Joseph lived. The detectives went from door to door asking the same polite questions. In that closed community, people mostly shook their heads and said they couldn't help, and made it plain they didn't wish to.

They reached Clifford St Joseph's apartment one mid-afternoon, and rang the bell several times before it opened. Even before he identified himself, they recognized him. He was more cadaverous than in his photo. Sanders noted the eyes were the same, deep set, blazing not just with suppressed anger, but something else. St Joseph wore a vest and shorts, was unshaved and smelled of wine.

They went through their routine. Sanders describing Eddie. Hendrix, Ricki. Each asked the same questions. Had he seen them? In the street? At a bar, a store, any place at all? They watched him carefully. His eyes glared at them. Finally he shrugged. He didn't recognize the descriptions.

They stood there staring at each other. Sanders asked was there anyone else in the apartment who might be able to help? St Joseph shook his head.

From inside the apartment came the sound of a phone ringing. St Joseph abruptly excused himself and closed the door. Coming out of the building, Hendrix spoke.

'A real hard nose.'

Sanders chuckled.

'Yes. But too sure of himself. Always a good sign.'

In the following weeks the detectives spoke to many of the people Eddie had named. Many lived in palatial apartments and houses. Sanders and Hendrix were received at front doors by manservants, and invited to sip coffee served by maids in frilly aprons and starched caps. Interviewees invariably had their lawyers present. Sometimes, the detectives were asked to come to the equally luxurious offices of the attorneys of those they wished to question. Wherever they met them, those men and women listened intently to each question and looked to their advisers before answering. In well-bred voices, they said they had never heard of, let alone met, either Eddie or Ricki, St Joseph or his brother. They had never gone to an apartment south of Market. That said, they said no more.

Driving away from one law firm, Hendrix sighed that money still could buy anything.

Sanders chuckled. 'Except peace of mind, Nap. They know we know. So behind all those tight little smiles, they'll go on sweating. And all the deodorant in the world won't help them.'

As the weeks passed, they kept telling each other that people are not good at disappearing; that they always left a trail of paper: credit card slips, cashed welfare payments, a contact number scribbled on the back of an envelope. People did that because they believed they were not going to get found. Then – one piece of paper and it was all over.

It was Hendrix' decision to take a few days vacation with relatives in the Los Angeles area which led to Eddie's discovery. On the last day, driving down a street he had never been to before, the detective saw him.

Eddie was thinner, his skin pulled like a drumhead over his cheekbones and jaw. But Hendrix would have recognized that knitted hat anywhere. The youth was coming at a shambling run down the street, panting and covered with sweat. The detective edged the rented car into the kerb and opened the nearside door. He took in the street with one quick look. Some kids playing and several elderly couples coming and going before they once more retreated behind the doors of their genteel poverty.

As Eddie came closer, Hendrix pushed the car door open wider, easing himself on to the pavement, moving slowly so as not to attract attention. The sun was behind him. Judging the moment, the detective moved to the middle of the pavement, arms by his side, relaxed and confident, jacket open, gun and cuffs to hand. He hoped he would not need them. Eddie was close enough now for him to hear the noise of his breathing, a raw rasping sound. Hendrix stepped into his path, smiling.

'Hi, Eddie.'

The youth stumbled into the detective, mouth working, saying nothing. Hendrix steadied him and held on to his arm.

'Man, whadya doin' here,' Eddie finally said.

'Just driving around. How you been, Eddie?'

Eddie shook his head, ''U sum'thin' else, man.' He looked at him.

Hendrix gently increased the pressure of his grip. 'No point running, Eddie. I'll find you. I'll always find you.'

Eddie sighed and nodded, ''U real sum'thin', man.'

That afternoon Hendrix and Eddie flew to San Francisco. Sanders was waiting at the airport and they drove to Headquarters. Both detectives spoke to Eddie late into the evening, reassuring him and trying to persuade Eddie to find Ricki. Finally, he asked to use the phone and they left him to make his calls.

An hour later Ricki was at Headquarters. He had been hiding in a gay's apartment.

The next break came a few days later. A report reached their desks that a Morris Bork had been arrested for kidnapping and robbery in the city. He was described as a Canadian citizen wanted by the RCMP for breaking out of the jail where he was serving a sentence for robbery. Bork's address was given as St Joseph's apartment. The mystery of Cliff's brother had been resolved.

*

With the arrest and conviction of Bork, the investigation of John Doe Sixty's murder took on new momentum – largely propelled forward by Bork. From his maximum security cell at Fulson, 120 miles from San Francisco, he sent a message he wanted to see Sanders and Hendrix.

Bork had just started a life term for the kidnapping and robbery. If he survived that, he would be deported to Canada to complete another long sentence there. Bork could expect to spend the remainder of his years behind bars.

'So what's he hoping to get?' growled Hendrix as they entered the prison.

'Maybe he just likes visitors,' chuckled Sanders.

The Canadian turned out to be an unprepossessing figure, small-boned with reddish skin and coarse hair. He had watery eyes which were slightly bulbous and a weak chin which began to recede almost below his lower lip. His file gave his age as twenty-nine; he looked a decade older. However he had a pleasant voice, low and surprisingly gentle for someone who had made his living holding up stores and post offices in Canada.

He sat across the table from the detectives in the interview room. Its top was bare except for the tape recorder Hendrix had brought. He switched it on.

Sanders asked Bork why he wanted to see them. Bork said he could help solve the case of John Doe Sixty. Sanders asked how. Bork replied he had 'clinching information'. Sanders asked what it was. Bork said before imparting it, he wanted an 'arrangement'. Sanders sighed and asked what kind. The Canadian looked at both detectives. Then, in the same pleasing voice, he explained he wanted to serve his sentence outside the California penal system. If that could be arranged, he would testify against Clifford St Joseph.

The detectives knew any such deal was not only probably unique, but would require approval from the highest prison authority, probably even the state attorney general. There would also be the matter of persuading some other state to accept Bork into its penal system. The Canadian's record for jail-breaking made him a formidable prisoner.

For the moment the detectives did not press Bork why he wished to move.

Instead, Sanders asked him to explain how he had met Clifford St Joseph. It was the familiar story of a casual pick-up. Having fled his Canadian cell, Bork arrived in San Francisco virtually penniless. He had gone to a gay bar and waited to be accosted. St Joseph bought him dinner and took him home, then St Joseph had invited him to stay on. Within a week he was introducing Bork

194

to Eddie and others in the city's gay community as his brother from Canada.

After a few weeks, St Joseph renamed Bork, Clint – after his screen hero, Clint Eastwood. He had done so after ritually cutting Bork's arm with a dagger and sucking on the blood.

St Joseph then showed Bork his 'family jewels'. These were a collection of Satanic books and artifacts stored in a black painted box in St Joseph's bedroom. He explained to Bork he could use them to summon the Devil to protect them.

St Joseph bought a German Shepherd. He kept the dog locked up for most of the time in a back room, feeding it raw scraps. Twice a day he and Bork walked the dog, lovers strolling hand-in-hand, like any other gay couple. On one walk, St Joseph confided that Lucifer had 'answered his prayer', by bringing Bork into his life.

'I had a bed, three meals a day. So I didn't think too much about this Devil stuff,' Bork added.

However, he soon became concerned at St Joseph's fantasies. He told Bork all his life he had dreamed of having total power over anyone he desired. He would be commanding and virile – his victims helpless and at his mercy. He described the sadistic things he had already done to other youths.

However, St Joseph assured Bork that he would never harm him, because he was 'a gift' from Satan.

Bork admitted to the detectives he had been 'a little excited at all this', especially when St Joseph read to him from the Satanic books, and explained the meaning of each artifact in his collection.

One day St Joseph announced that, 'in gratitude to the Highest One,' for bringing him, Bork, the time had come for a human sacrifice. St Joseph had gone in search of a suitable victim and hours later he returned with John Doe Sixty.

At this point Bork once more told the detectives that, in return for his testimony, he wanted a guarantee he would serve his sentence in a prison outside California.

They had looked at him, curious.

'Why so, Morris? People reckon our prisons are the best in the country,' said Hendrix.

Bork sat breathing noisily through his nostrils, hands pressed hard on the table top. Sanders realized it was not anger but fear he was trying to control.

'St Joseph has friends all the way to the top. I get this bad feeling he has already got a contract on me. The way I see it, the only way I can stay alive is to testify against St Joseph, on condition you move me out. I don't care where you send me, or how hard it'll be, just as long as no one knows who or where I am. You do that and I'll testify.'

Sanders asked if Bork had directly participated in the killing of John Doe Sixty?

Bork shook his head. 'I'm no murderer.'

Sanders glanced at Hendrix. They both sensed Bork was telling the truth.

Sanders said that while he could make no promises, he would strongly recommend Bork's transfer if his testimony could convict St Joseph. They would only know that when he told them the complete story.

Bork was silent, only his loud breathing pointed to his inner debate.

After a few more deep breaths, Bork began to describe the ritual sacrifice of John Doe Sixty. Like Ricki, he was given a spiked drink. St Joseph had then bound him with chains and dragged him to the centre of the circle on the floor of the living room. There he raped the half-senseless man. Afterwards, he made his first cut on John Doe Sixty's body, a knife wound in the chest. Crouching over the body, he had sucked noisily at the opening. St Joseph had fetched the dog and helped the animal to rape John Doe Sixty.

For the first few days, St Joseph repeated the ritual. In between he fed John Doe Sixty, and continued drugging him. Before and after each assault, St Joseph chanted from the Satanic books.

Bork refused to take part in the abuse. But he had obeyed St Joseph's order to increase the volume of the music while he made further knife openings in John Doe Sixty's body. One evening, St Joseph carved the pentagram. Afterwards, he made the lip cut. Then he lay beside the moaning man and sucked for hours at the cut.

St Joseph regularly smeared the blood on his skin, daubing his chest and groin in strange shapes. He told Bork they were the marks of Satan.

One night St Joseph squatted beside John Doe Sixty and cradled his head. He used a small dagger to make the neck wound, taking care to avoid the jugular. He allowed the blood to spurt over him. When there was a steady flow, he filled one of the bowls he kept in his box. He drank from the bowl and allowed the dog to lick it clean. Blood continued to spume on to the carpet. St Joseph placed a second bowl beneath the neck wound. When he filled several bowls, he staunched the hole with a wadded cloth. He placed the bowls of blood in the refrigerator.

St Joseph then spoonfed John Doe Sixty a mixture of steak, liver and a sheep's heart, which he blended in a food mixer. He explained to Bork that in one of his books there were precise instructions on how to replenish the blood of a sacrifice.

One day after he was fed and made to swallow his drugged drink, John Doe Sixty was allowed to sleep uninterrupted, the carpet casually thrown over his body. St Joseph busied himself on the telephone, making cryptic calls, often speaking in the same guttural language he used before assaulting John Doe Sixty.

When darkness came, the first visitor arrived at the apartment. She was a smartly dressed woman, young and well-spoken. Bork had never seen her before. St Joseph introduced him as his blood brother. He did not say who the woman was. St Joseph fetched a bowl of refrigerated blood. The woman drank a quantity, in between chanting. Afterwards she followed Bork to where John Doe Sixty lay. Hoisting her skirt, the woman squatted over the chained figure and urinated. While she did so, she chanted continuously. Then she left the apartment.

Throughout the night there was a steady procession of callers. Well dressed men and women who spoke in refined voices which coarsened when they too, uttered pagan words between drinking John Doe Sixty's blood. Some of the men lashed his buttocks with a chain. One of the women, middle-aged, her fingers covered with rings, knelt inside the circle and licked the congealed blood around the gaping neck wound.

That had remained the pattern of the last days of life for John Doe Sixty. To Bork it was plain that, despite the food and drink being spooned into him, the man was dying.

Bork looked at the detectives.

'I was real scared of Cliff. He was like the Devil himself. He never slept. His eyes seemed to glow. His teeth were stained with blood. He was like a werewolf.'

The recorder continued to tape his story.

One evening, after the last visitor left, St Joseph began to refill the bowls with fresh blood. Suddenly John Doe Sixty whimpered like an animal, rolling his eyes. St Joseph knelt over him. He took a knife and gouged-out John Doe Sixty's right testicle. He cut it in half and ate it. Next he lit a black candle and dripped the hot wax into John Doe Sixty's right eye. As he performed these acts, St Joseph chanted continuously.

He did not notice Bork leave the apartment. For several hours Bork walked the streets. Too frightened and unable to go to the police, in the early hours of the morning he finally returned. St Joseph was crouched beside the body, still chanting. John Doe Sixty was no longer chained.

'I remember he just kept saying "He has gone to Lucifer! Praise Satan!",' recalled Bork.

He also remembered that from the back room came the sniffing sounds of the dog.

St Joseph told Bork to fetch a blanket from the animal's bed. He rolled the body in its shroud. Then he covered the blanket with a large trash bag. St Joseph carried the corpse to his car. The two men drove to Sixth Street and dumped it by the trailer.

When Bork finished, there was a long silence. It was broken by Sanders.

'Why Sixth Street?'

Bork shrugged. 'No special reason. Cliff just said he was tired, and didn't want to go too far to dump the body. He said that anyway he was protected by the Devil. It didn't matter where he left the body. No one would harm him. When we returned to the apartment, he told me to clear up the blood and mess while he went to sleep.'

Bork had thrown-out the carpet from the ritual room, and tried to remove as much as he could of the blood stains on the floor boards. He dumped the cleaning utensils.

Sanders asked a final question. Who is John Doe Sixty?

Bork shook his head. 'Just a street guy. No name. No one knew where he came from. I guess no one ever will.'

In the weeks following, Bork's revelations were studied by the District Attorney and senior members of the California Penal Department. Finally, the state attorney general and the state governor approved the transfer of Bork to a prison in another state. On the day he left California, he signed his affidavit.

Now, hours later, Sanders and Hendrix drove down Sixth Street to arrest Clifford St Joseph and to search his apartment. Behind came patrol cars and a Crime Scene Unit truck.

A little before noon, Sanders parked outside the apartment building. From force of habit he touched the pocket holding his New Testament. Around him the patrol cars were emptying. Across the street people began to gather.

The two detectives walked into the building. They took the stairs to St Joseph's apartment, followed by the patrolmen and CSU technicians. From behind doors came the sounds of TV and music. Sanders knocked firmly on St Joseph's apartment door. After a while it opened, St Joseph stood there, dressed as before, only in vest and shorts.

The detectives displayed their badges and search warrant. St Joseph gave a half-smile but said nothing. Sanders told St Joseph he was arresting him for the murder of a still unidentified male Caucasian. St Joseph nodded slightly. Sanders read out his Miranda rights. St Joseph continued to remain silent. Hendrix told two patrolmen to escort the prisoner to Headquarters. Still unprotesting, St Joseph was led away.

The detectives entered the apartment, accompanied by the technicians. A patrolman remained guard at the door.

Sanders and Hendrix went to the ritual room – Eddie's Path of

Agarthi. The cheap carpet was new. They rolled it back. On the floor beneath was the still visible outline of a circle, inside its circumference there were in places dark patches. Sanders didn't need a technician's murmured 'blood' to know what had caused the staining. The police photographer began to take pictures.

In a cabinet Hendrix found Satanic books and music tapes. There was no trace of the black-painted box Bork had described. There was no sign of the German Shepherd, but in a back room they found animal faeces.

The detectives watched the technicians dusting and brushing, carefully gathering evidence, labelling each item. They used tweezers to pick up dog hairs from inside the circle. Sanders knew the hairs would turn out to match those found on John Doe Sixty's body.

He also knew it was finally all over. The only unresolved question was: who had John Doe Sixty been in life? The detective did not expect now to ever find the answer. Leaving the apartment, Hendrix asked how was it possible that someone could have been held like this, and nobody lift a hand to help him? It said, he added, a lot about society.

Sanders chuckled. Only he was not laughing.

FIFTEEN

A Matter of Conviction

The furniture had gone by truck, the garage sale over, the white-framed house empty.

Susan waited for Sam to remove the nameplate attached to the mail box - *Lombard*. Trish and Pete were already in the battered old station wagon. In a few days time they would be a couple of thousand miles away, out in the mid-west, trying to begin a new life.

In the end it had been Trish's idea to move. It was her only hope, she told Susan, of putting behind her the guilt she had over Marcia. Susan agreed. If salvation existed Trish and Sam must find it themselves. First in each other. Then for each other.

Susan walked over to the car.

'You come and see us Susan?' said Sam.

Susan nodded. She hated the banalities of farewell. She leaned into the car and gave Pete a hug. She kissed Sam and Trish on the cheek.

Susan stepped back on to the sidewalk. Sam eased the station wagon into traffic. As it turned a corner, Trish and Pete gave a final wave. Susan waved back.

As she walked to her car she understood why none of them had mentioned Marcia. Time healed in all sorts of ways.

But there was more good work to be done. Driving to the Center, Susan began to think of Danny.

She had arranged for the boy's mother to get a job managing a family-oriented complex. She and Lee had helped move them into the spacious new staff apartment. When Danny stood in the doorway of his bedroom he had asked if it was just for him. His mother had nodded, not trusting herself to speak.

Lee had taken Danny on a tour of the complex, showing him the baseball diamond, the football field and pool. Standing by its edge Danny looked longingly at the other children in the water. With a magician's flourish, Lee produced a pair of trunks still in their wrapping and presented them to Danny as a gift from Susan and himself.

Later when Lee returned with Susan to say goodbye, Danny was in the centre of a group playing splash-and-duck. He waved to them and plunged back under the water.

In the following weeks Danny had lost his pallor, put on weight and slowly gained confidence. Each time she brought him to the Center, his mother reported further improvement. Danny's night-mares had stopped.

Reaching the Center Susan knew it would still require all her skills to have Danny come to terms with what his father had done.

Already the boy had described matters of real horror. How his father had forced him to urinate on the Holy Bible and over a cru-cifix. How pages from the Bible had been rubbed against the boy's genitalia by men dressed in robes and cowls. How he had been made to stand before an altar in one of the Ranch's outbuildings to watch his father copulate with a woman in front of a crucifix. Danny had seen other children made to defecate on the national flag and burn photos of their families in a camp bonfire at the Ranch.

Susan knew self-participation is one of the most effective ways Satanists have of controlling a child – and especially when it involved the destruction of a child's natural belief in God, family and country. What happened to Danny had been a preparation for witnessing the sacrifice and being forced to eat that unknown infant.

At this morning's session she intended to explore another incident Danny had seen.

She led the boy into the interview room. Now there was no need for checkers to help Danny relax. He was ready to answer her questions at once. She switched on the recorder.

'Tell me what happened after you were all awoken in the bunk house,' she prompted.

Danny began to describe how he and the other children were, in the dead of night, taken to a cemetery. Waiting there were robed and cowled adults holding flaming torches. In the light Danny saw a freshly dug grave. Nearby was an open coffin. The torch-bearers circled the children and chanted. From out of the darkness more hooded men appeared escorting a naked young girl.

Susan had gently and deliberately slowed him down with her questions.

'How old was she, hon?'

'Dunno. Mebbe my age.'

It was no relief for Susan to know the girl was too young to be Marcia.

'Did she do or say anything?'

Danny shook his head. 'But her eyes were open.'

201

'What happened then, hon?'

'They all started saying those words again.'

'Do you remember what they were, Danny?'

The boy nodded. '"Dust to dust. Earth to earth. Back to Satan where she came. Dust to dust. Earth to earth. Back to Satan where she came."'

Danny described what happened next. The torch bearers held aloft their burning branches and the chanting deepened. Then it suddenly stopped. The silence was broken by an animal-like sound from the girl. The men holding her placed her into the casket and nailed down the lid. The chanting restarted as the coffin was lowered into the grave. The men took it in turn to shovel earth until the hole was filled.

Susan held Danny for a long time when he finished.

She knew the problem with the story was the old one – who would believe it? Satanists never leave a sacrifice buried. Firstly, it increases the risk of detection, and any human sacrifice is too 'sacred' to leave in the ground.

Susan was certain the coffin would have been dug up after Danny and the other children were taken back to the bunkhouse. The suffocated victim would have been dismembered and eaten, her bones burned. Even if the police bothered to check, all they would discover was newly disturbed earth.

Danny's story was another reminder for Susan that when a detective who has spent his time investigating homicides or drugs, where his suspects are adults, finds himself facing a small child who describes ritual murder, almost always he feels out of his depth.

Consequently children are not believed because the police do not know how to believe them.

But somehow she would make them believe. Maybe not today. Maybe not tomorrow. She now accepted it would take more time than she first had thought. But one day. Most certainly one day.

Danny's story was one more link in the chain she was forging. Part of that long chain of misery that extended all the way to that tiny village on the Indian sub-continent.

Another report had reached her that Shambu's father had sold-off another child to replace the income from Samina. The girl had recently died in one of the brothels of Heera Mundi. She was not yet fifteen, Marcia's age.

Shambu and Danny; Samina and Marcia. How many more? She did not know. All Susan knew was that she would fight until the day came when it really should not hurt to be a child.

She continued to hold Danny securely.

*

202

O'Malley strode through the international arrivals concourse at Chicago's O'Hare Airport. He had come to arrest Sturmer.

O'Malley's eyes flicked to every flight information screen he passed, as he continued to remind himself that logically nothing could now go wrong, short of the plane actually crashing. The American Airlines flight was a non-stop one from Frankfurt, chosen by him for that very reason. He did not want Sturmer to have the opportunity to change his mind in mid-journey and deplane at a stop-over. Not that the pornographer would probably be having second thoughts. O'Malley had done everything possible to take care of that.

From the moment Sturmer arrived at Frankfurt Airport, he had been shadowed by German Customs agents. One had even followed Sturmer on to the jetliner to ensure he took his assigned seat – 47C – in coach. Once the plane was airborne, a confirming teletype had been sent to O'Malley. Now, nine hours later, the flight was on its final approach to O'Hare.

O'Malley could visualize how, during the long flight, Sturmer would have re-read Sheila's letters, no doubt trying to stoke his fantasies from O'Malley's carefully chosen words. Perhaps he had fed them further by looking at the photograph O'Malley had sent.

Sturmer's request for a picture of Sheila had taxed even O'Malley's ingenuity. He ruled out selecting one of the photographs of women in the 'chamber of horrors', the locked room on the eighth floor, where he kept seized 'foto sets', many thousands of videos and pornographic magazines used to bait further stings.

Time and again in seizures, the same faces turned up – especially in pornography shipped from Sweden, the Netherlands and West Germany. While European Customs and police officials now argued that many of the photographs printed in their countries were actually taken in the United States and Canada, O'Malley believed there is a coterie of several hundred women in Amsterdam, Frankfurt, Stockholm and London who are regularly photographed for pornographic purposes. Sturmer would very likely be familiar with their faces.

Many of the women in the photographs showed signs of gross abuse. That did not fit the persona he had created for Sheila, as someone who knew all about wild sex but was still fresh. He had rejected the idea of obtaining a photograph from a professional model agency. While he would have had no problem concocting a story why he needed one, the potential legal risks of using an unsuspecting girl were too great. If the truth leaked out, the government could be sued for millions.

In the end he chose an Illinois police officer who specialized in infiltrating call-girl rings. The woman provided a picture of herself posing in a low-cut dress and gazing provocatively into the camera.

O'Malley had smiled his pirate's smile and said she looked the sort of woman who knew how to use Opium.

Along with the photograph, O'Malley wrote to explain that Sheila perfectly understood Sturmer's inability to pay for the fare to Chicago. But it so happened she had an American Airlines bonus miles coupon. She would send it to him. The cost of the ticket would be paid out of O'Malley's sting fund.

Sturmer gave various dates he could fly. Again, remaining in character for Sheila, O'Malley had not chosen the first date, but the second. He wanted Sturmer to do the running. Now that he was hot, he wanted to keep him on the boil by remaining cool.

Maintaining his long-legged stride through the concourse, O'Malley felt further satisfaction. Police in Santa Barbara were about to interview the Copelands. He was confident they had enough evidence to ensure the woman and her husband would no longer be able to exploit their daughters.

In his last letter O'Malley enquired whether Sturmer was bringing the 'latest hot action' from Europe. He hoped to arrest him actually in possession of child pornography. Sturmer responded with more crude expressions of what he was going to do to Sheila.

Even if Sturmer did not bring any samples, O'Malley had ample proof to arrest him. In the past hours, Customs agents had raided the homes of eleven of Sturmer's American customers and seized a total of ninety-three pounds of child porno. Some of the paedophiles would be charged under recently revised statutes which increased penalties for possession of such materials tenfold. Upon conviction a person could be fined up to $200,000 and jailed for up to fifteen years. O'Malley doubted if such penalties would ever be imposed. Courts still did not always recognize the damage this stuff does. Some judges seemed to think collecting the material as harmless as swapping baseball cards.

O'Malley wondered whether they would feel differently if one of their children was inveigled or coerced into the kind of depravity in which Sturmer traded.

There were also loopholes in the new legislation. It only applied to 'visual depiction', not written child pornography. But often that was extremely violent and specific in its detail. The manual on how to torture a child had shown that.

The law also only covered interstate trafficking in child pornography. Private possession of child pornography remained legal in all but six states. Many constitutional scholars believed the Supreme Court would uphold the rights of such possession.

Civil libertines still argued there is no 'proven link' between pornography and sexual behaviour – and even in sex crimes against children. O'Malley wondered if those social scientists ever stopped to think that for every depicted act of child pornography it *was* necessary to sexually abuse a child? He had made this point to a commission appointed by President Reagan to investigate whether viewing violent pornography contributed to violent sexual behaviour. He liked to think his argument helped to convince the commission into finding it did. He would go on advancing his claims in the face of all those psychologists and liberal-minded lawyers who argue otherwise.

Imbued with such determination, O'Malley reached the Customs area. An airport security officer and a uniformed patrol from the city's police force were on hand to lend assistance; he told them they should not interfere unless he signalled. He wanted the satisfaction of taking Sturmer alone.

A screen showed his flight had landed. O'Malley began to watch the lines of passengers being processed by Immigration and Customs.

How many of them, he wondered, would be sympathetic to what he was going to do? Would they shrug and say it was nothing to do with them? Would they even be shocked if he told them the number of cases of reported child abuse in the United States had risen from 150,000 in 1963 to almost two million in 1988? That those are only the known cases? How many more had gone undetected because of the reluctance of people to report those they suspect of child abuse?

In particular he could see no excuse for doctors who failed to report incidents. Yet every year only 14 per cent of such cases came to light in the US as a result of complaints by physicians. Only in 1988 had the American Board of Paediatrics insisted that doctors who worked in hospitals should have a basic training in identifying sexual abuse. Yet its vastly complex medical symptomatology was still not a specific subject for board qualification examinations in paediatrics, psychiatry or other medical child-care fields. Not one of America's medical schools taught a specific course on child abuse. It was the same in Britain and Europe. As far as O'Malley knew, it was the same everywhere.

In one of the learned journals that reached his desk a professor of psychiatry had argued that the subject could not be treated because there was no standard etiology. In the ensuing correspondence a urologist had called the concept of sexual abuse more of an intellectual one than a medical problem.

O'Malley had wondered how many times had that doctor, confronted with a child who is a chronic bedwetter, paused to consider whether the cause could be sexual abuse? Even paediatricians, while querying bruises, usually did not take throat or anal cultures to test for the presence of sperm.

Twenty years after an American doctor gave the world the term 'Battered Child Syndrome', and identified it, in part, as 'the child who has been taught not to cry when hurt', the great majority of physicians still refuse to accept there is widespread sexual abuse. Instead of diagnosing a vaginal discharge as one of the venereal diseases, they often suggest it is caused by a child's underwear chafing or that a bubble bath is unsuitable. Abdominal pains, headaches and symptoms of withdrawal are all too often dismissed as part of 'growing up'.

These failures of society had made it that much easier for Sturmer to operate.

O'Malley fished out the passport photograph, looked at it, then returned it to his pocket. He walked slowly towards the row of Immigration booths.

O'Malley began to stroll behind the booths, his eyes scanning faces, smiling his pirate's smile.

When he saw Sturmer he was momentarily surprised. He was shorter and somehow shabbier than he imagined. Sturmer wore levis and had a shambling gait. With his spectacles and lank hair he looked like a mature student.

O'Malley moved closer to the booth. He wanted to hear Sturmer's voice, the one on that video of the Thai child.

The inspector took Sturmer's passport and checked it against a thick book of listings for terrorists, drug dealers and criminals of all kinds. Sturmer was still clean. Perhaps that was why he wore a vacuous smile.

'What's the purpose of your visit, Herr Sturmer?' asked the inspector.

'Pleasure, sir. I come for pleasure.'

'What business you in?'

'*Bitte?*'

The inspector sighed. 'What's your job?'

Sturmer nodded, understanding. 'Ah. I make photos.' He gave a passable imitation of a photographer using a camera.

The inspector smiled. 'Enjoy your stay.'

He stamped and handed back Sturmer's passport and waved him into the United States.

O'Malley stepped forward.

Sturmer made to go round him, still smiling.

'Looking for Sheila?'

Sturmer stared, blinking owlishly.

'*Bitte?*'

The smile was fast fading, realization coming as quickly.

'You . . . are . . . Sheila!'

'And you just have to be Sturmer,' said O'Malley, going on to introduce himself by his full name and rank.

O'Malley held him firmly by the arm. In his most formal voice, he told Sturmer he was under arrest and why.

In silence they made their way from the Customs Hall.

Few gave them a second look.

In the end, it came to this: Sturmer admitted exporting pornography from Germany to the United States. He was formally charged and pleaded guilty to three separate counts. He refused to answer questions about any of his activities elsewhere. Without proof of Sturmer's trafficking in the Middle East and Asia, there was nothing O'Malley could do.

Sturmer was sentenced to four months imprisonment. Upon release he paid his own fare back to Germany.

Long before then O'Malley had begun to turn his mind to new stings. He continued to remind himself that beyond the misery of sexual trafficking there had to be a potential to reshape the future. Without that belief there is no future for all those who remain enslaved.

FOR THE MOMENT

There is such a thing as the pornography of silence. When we keep quiet we help to destroy what we are. Instead we refuse to believe, as we should believe, that pornography endangers our culture. Too often the bizarre *fantasy* of pornography becomes the bizarre *act* of pornography. In the end, of course, every act of pornography *is* a sadistic act.

> Excerpt from author's interview with Superintendent Iain Donaldson, then Head of the Obscene Publications Squad, New Scotland Yard, London; 12 April, 1988.

When I see the obsession of the pornographer with the unformed body of a child, I think of my daughter, going on seven. When I read another report of a child kidnapped into sexual slavery, I think of her. When I see all the terrible, terrible things which are done to other children I think of my little girl. In her I see again my own wholeness. But when I see another child's body turned into a pornographic object, I feel I am looking once more at the death of hope. Then I look again at my daughter and say to myself that I don't want her to grow up in the kind of world I see every day. Some of the people around here say I'm being an idealist. If I wasn't, I suppose I could not do this kind of work. To do it properly, everyone, in my opinion, needs a personal goal. Mine is my daughter. When I think of her, I always remember that enslavement is more than a terrible violence to the bodies of women and children. It is violence to their souls - to all our souls.

> Excerpt from author's interview with Darylene Foster, Woman Constable Investigator, Joint Forces Project 'P', Special Investigations Branch, Toronto, Canada; 8 June, 1988.

SIXTEEN

The Culture of Pornography

In 1990 the enslaved continue to be the victims of an alliance of criminal conglomerates reaching into every corner of the world.

Jean Fernand-Laurent, Special Rapporteur on Slavery, to the United Nations, has described their activities as growing daily.

> There are a number of inter-related networks involved in the traffic: one flowing from Latin America to Puerto Rico and beyond, to southern Europe and to the Middle East; one flowing from South-east Asia to the Middle East and central and northern Europe; a regional European market, in part supplied by Latin America and exporting women to Luxembourg and the Federal Republic of Germany; one supplying North America. The traffic is often carried out under cover of what purport to be marriage bureaux or advertisements for jobs in touring stage shows. There is evidence of procuring networks supplying Geneva from Paris; Switzerland and West Germany from Bangkok; Singapore from Malaysia and the Philippines; Spain from France. South American prostitutes are shipped from Argentina to Melbourne, young Hawaiian and Californian women to Japan and Swedish women to the Middle and Far East. The networks frequently interlink. Much as airlines interlink baggage, so the separate slave networks hand on their human cargoes, one from another. The networks are well-disguised and almost all involve the secret traffic of poor women towards rich men in all directions. It is only now that we are even beginning to see its full ramifications.

A stock-in-trade of the slavers has been identified by Maureen Alexander-Sinclair of the Anti-Slavery Society.

At Bangkok's main railway stations, for between £70 and £100, you can buy a child who will be yours to do with as you will. Every year some 6,000 children are estimated to be sold at these stations. These are aged from three years upwards. They are generally bought by agents for the fastest growing industry in the world, the pornography industry.

The industry cannot survive without its endless supply of child slaves. They are used for every kind of porno experience, including child-sex murder, and snuff movies. The terror the child displays heightens the sexual gratification of those who watch such films.

There are tens of thousands of slaves today in Asia and Latin America forming heroin and cocaine into convenient-sized shapes for smuggling into the United States and Europe. Other children, themselves drug victims, are used to courier the materials, say US Drug Enforcement Agency investigators. The children are often forced to swallow sachets of drugs which they later excrete. Some have become expert at regurgitating the packets and some have been simply killed and disembowelled to retrieve the drugs. They are all victims of what can properly be called the culture of pornography.

The image of women and children being somehow *less* is the dominant theme of this culture. They are presented as: less strong, less intelligent, less creative and less spiritual. Therefore, they are also seen as being less worthy of basic respect. Within that culture they do not exist for themselves; they depend on the existence of man. So nothing is too unspeakable for them to have to endure as they are made to bend to the whim of man.

Jean Fernand-Laurent has identified some of the pressures to which women and children are routinely subjected. 'Drugs which facilitate kidnapping and sequestration, beatings, torture, blackmail and threats of mutilation and murder.'

These remain among the tried and trusted weapons and techniques which the slavers use on a daily basis as they go about their business of stealing, buying and selling human flesh. Over 150 years after its abolition, and with no fewer than 300 international agreements specifically designed to ensure that it stays abolished, slavery in 1990 remains an endemic evil. According to the Anti-Slavery Society, there are an estimated 200 million slaves in the world. Some 100 million of them are children.

Other organizations concerned with combatting slavery, such as the United Nations Centre for Social Development and Humanitarian Affairs, the Defence for Children International, and the International Abolitionist Federation, all suggest the figures could be larger. No one really knows. Unlike the days when slaves were actually counted and registered, no records exist of those now held in enforced servitude.

The Anti-Slavery Society which is the oldest of the reporting and monitoring agencies (all told there are no fewer than thirty working directly within the United Nations system or are affiliated to that organization) defines five types of slavery. The first is chattel slavery; the second, debt bondage; the third, serfdom; the fourth, child slavery; the fifth, the enslavement of women.

Chattel slavery is the oldest; this is where one person *totally* owns another. It is the slavery of the Book of Exodus, the Pharaohs, the Greeks and the Romans; the slavery that Jesus and St Paul preached against, and later, St Gregory of Nyssa. Their words fell on stony ground, and continue to do so in those lands where slavery remains an integral part of the ancient social pattern.

Today, in the Gulf and throughout the vast emptiness of the Arabian Peninsula, the ownership of slaves remains a status symbol. There is not a sheikh worth his harem who does not have his quota of eunuch slaves; there is not a prince of the desert who is not surrounded by his slave guards, pledged to die for him in return for board and lodging. In a world where Western values still have little or no place, slaves remain part of a religious tradition which has always held that some men shall control totally the lives of others. So it was written in the Koran; so it has remained.

Islam's sacred teachings have been used in Iran to create a new form of sexual slavery called *sigheh*. The late Ayatollah Khomeini's *Tozihatol Massa'el* – 'Instructions for Problems' – forces Iranian women to rent their bodies for 'a certain time and fee'. This prostitution continues to be sanctified by the mullahs. They have dissembled Islamic holy writ to create a new category of 'temporary' marriage which allows a man to take 'as many women as he can afford'. The women are sexual slaves, chattels who have no say over who uses their bodies, and who can be discarded at will – cast out of their master's bed at the slightest whim.

Khomeini's legacy is that, swept to power, in part, with his pledge to end the country's endemic prostitution under the Shah, he expanded its scope under the guise of religion. In 1990 there are more prostitutes in the country than at any time since the death of the Prophet Mohammed in 632 AD. With Iran's economy steadily worsening, the number of women driven to this form of sexual exploitation – often simply to obtain enough to eat – has reached an estimated two million.

Chattel slavery remains an essential part of the structure of African life. On the edge of the Sahara there are today close to one million slaves among the nomadic tribes. In Mauritania and Chad, two of the poorest of African states to have emerged from the colonial era,

212

slavery remains rife. It thrives, too, in South America, in Brazil, Paraguay and Chile.

The second category – debt bondage – is where a slave is in such debt to his employer that there is no escape. In India alone there are today an estimated five million bonded labourers. They live and work like slaves and are bought and sold as such. Often their initial debt can be as little as £1.

Illiterate themselves, the slaves are made to put their thumb prints on the documents which bond them for life. Their masters simply add extra noughts to the debt sum and charge interest of up to one thousand per cent. Frequently, a man will be enslaved not only for life; he will also pledge the work of his wife and children – and sometimes their unborn children. All too often the debt is passed down through generations of people who have only their labour to mortgage and own nothing but their loincloths. In 1976 Mrs Indira Ghandi, the Prime Minister of India, outlawed debt bondage. Fifteen years later it remains rife.

Serfdom is the enslavement of migrant workers into forced labour. In the Caribbean, South America, Asia, the Middle East, Africa and the Mediterranean basin, the exploitation of labour is on the increase. Powerful global economic trends have created an environment where the poor must work for a pittance to avoid starvation.

These forms of slavery have long been there. And it is indeed shocking to know that slavery, which is itself far older than many of the nations who are pledged to suppress it, remains among the largest single source of labour in the world. There are more slaves than the entire workforce of North America, or that of all Western Europe.

There is something more shocking: for every adult male slave, there is twice the number of female and child slaves. The great majority are bought and sold for sexual exploitation. Some people insist it cannot be otherwise – when there is still disagreement on what is a child. The anti-slavery treaties generally define anyone under the age of eighteen as a child. The International Labour Organization said that fifteen years should be the division between childhood and an adult when it came to work practices. Most Third World countries have a Minimum Age Convention which makes twelve years an acceptable age to end childhood.

All too often they are still regarded as disposable assets. Members of an unregulated and officially non-existent slave labour force, supplying alike industrial corporations and clandestine workshops. The children are held in a thrall of fear, knowing it is more than their lives are worth to divulge the appalling conditions under which they toil.

Children are forced to endure a life of slave labour as the only way

213

for their families to stave off the shame of the begging bowl. Those children grow up fast and die young: at ten they are little adults, old at twenty, and dead usually by thirty. They are broken by the strength-sapping tasks of their mindless treadmill of slave labour.

Such labour is the traditional face of enslavement. It is rooted in cultures older than Judaism, though for centuries it was also widely practised under Mosaic Law. The Greek and Roman Empires practised slavery, so did the great colonial powers of Europe, of France and Spain, and later, the British Empire. It was not until 1965 that the Roman Catholic Church formally disassociated itself from slavery; it still widely continues where the faith is practised.

Attempts to introduce birth control are still vigorously opposed by Rome. Exasperated child-care workers say the Pope, despite his commitment to human rights, is actually encouraging the growth of the number of those denied such basic freedoms through his unswerving opposition to contraception. Families encouraged to have more children are assured God will somehow provide for their needs. All too often they believe it is also part of a Divine Plan for their children to be sold off. In the name of religion, as well as economic family need, the children are consigned to live in darkness, the victims of a cruel adult world, where the voices of the advocates for children's rights are never heard, and where the ancient cultural needs that create slavery still survive intact.

In India, where the Church is engaged in the ceaseless struggle for souls, an estimated 400,000 more children were sold by their parents in 1989. The Defence for Children International, the Geneva-based human rights organization, reported that most were destined to replenish the ranks of a child slave-labour force of around 44 million on the sub-continent. Despite recent constitutional guarantees to protect children, 90 per cent of this force is employed in places and under conditions effectively beyond the law.

Legislation still only applies to factories above a certain size. There are also ambiguities which allow employers to defy the law without directly contravening it. Minimum working ages differ from state to state and it is common practice to adjust ages to meet the needs of employers. A boy of six will be shown to be twelve to make him eligible to work; while one of fourteen given as twelve to avoid paying him the full minimum wage.

Employers usually fail to keep work registers. The few that do, rarely gave a true picture of the number of children employed – and never indicate which have been bought.

In 1989, the number of factory inspectors for the whole of India was little more than one hundred – about one for each 400,000 working children. When an inspector did stumble across a back street factory filled with child slaves, he was either offered a bribe to overlook the violation, or allowed himself to be persuaded that the children are still marginally better-off than enduring the grinding poverty and near-starvation of life at home. Tragically that is often true. Nevertheless, the children work for a pittance and under appalling conditions.

One in five children, aged between three and thirteen, according to Defence for Children International, toil up to seventeen hours a day, six days a week, for an average salary of thirty English pence a *day*. That is less than the price of a can of dog food in a supermarket of the Western world. They work cramped in pits, inside mud or wooden carpet-weaving sheds which are without light or adequate ventilation, and where the air is laden with dust which produces a variety of chest ailments.

In back street *bidis*, factories which produce cheap hand-rolled cigarettes, the children are also automatically exposed to lung diseases, including cancer. They work in brick works, coal mines or at the crude open furnaces of glass factories, spending their long days handling molten glass heated to 1500 degrees Fahrenheit. All those jobs were illegal for children under 14-years-old. In a statement to the Indian Parliament the Minister of Health reported that throughout the entire sub-continent the number of pre-teen children recovered from slavery during one year amounted to *ninety-one*.

Conditions in India in 1990 continue to be only part of a global shame. The pool of potential child slave labourers has doubled in the past two decades throughout the Third World. There are now some 1.2 billion children aged between five and twelve years. Many will be denied the right to play, to learn, to enjoy a normal childhood. Ironically, where modern medicine allows more children to survive the first critical year of life in underdeveloped countries, there has been virtually no clinical investigation into how slave labour affects their health in subsequent years.

No one knows if pesticides are more dangerous to the Mexican migrant children who pick crops in the United States than to adults. No one knows the level of emotional stress in children who labour at rock quarries, on road gangs and construction sites under the searing African sun. No one knows what it is like to be a five-year-old in Kenya and made to work six days a week as a kitchen help in one of the country's tourist hotels. No one knows what the lasting effects are of making a six-year-old in Cairo rise at dawn every day to work in a garment factory. No one knows what the emotional shock was for the more than 2,000 children, aged from five to twelve, who were sold in 1988 by their parents in Nigeria to work on plantations. Slavers paid either a head of tobacco or the equal of ten US dollars per child. No one knows the extent of the psychological damage to the tea plantation children in Sri Lanka, many as young as four years, who receive *two* US cents a day, in local currency, to work for ten hours spraying pesticides. No one knows what a seven-year-old feels as he spends his days tapping rubber trees in Malaysia, working in jungle-like conditions which rot the soles of his feet, and leave his hands blistered and bleeding – all for the equal of *one* American dollar for a 60-hour week. No one knows very much about the daily lives of tens of millions of little boys and girls who have never been to school, and whose only lesson in 1990 is that their lives will probably never change.

They are victims of slavery's worldwide network. Its members include taxi drivers in Guatemala City, who drive through the streets at night kidnapping children sleeping in doorways, selling them to small factories or, increasingly, to brothels. Touts in the Philippines buy children in Manila to work in the commercial vegetable farms in the country's remote hilly region. In Brazil recruiters simply steal children off the streets in Saô Paulo and sell them to the tea estates in the Riberia Valley. Two-thirds of the valley's workers in 1989 remain under fourteen years, many as young as five. They work in toxic conditions and when they become ill they are sent back to Saô Paulo, left to die on its streets – from where their replacements are once more taken. It is an endless cycle of abuse.

The little victims are regularly transported not only the length and breadth of North America, but in and out of Europe, and to and from Asia and Africa. The routes and methods remain as varied as the use of slaves limitless.

In the Bahr el Ghazel province of Sudan, young girls, members of the Dinka tribe, are still being sold in 1990 for US $75 each. That is twice the price of a sack of black-market rice in the famine-stricken region. In one week, Arab slavers bought over 500 from the soldiers of the Government of the Democratic Republic of Sudan. The previous year as many as 10,000 Dinka tribesmen, women and children were sold-off into slavery by the Marxist regime. Their fate remains unknown.

Elsewhere the old slave trails teem, again mostly with women and children who have been bought and sold, and whose lives depend totally on the whim of their masters.

From out of Africa continue to come newly-castrated eunuchs for the harems of Arabia. From northern Europe girls destined for the brothels of the Middle East. From Spain, Italy and Greece, that other prized commodity, boys. All are moved secretly through the Eastern Mediterranean, down through the Gulf of Aden and on through the Gulf of Oman. Brought from such cities and ports as Amsterdam, Paris, Rome, Naples and Athens, they are destined for Damascus, Cairo, Baghdad and Jeddah. In all those

216

places white flesh still has a high market value as it has been for centuries.

Slaves also remain part of the daily life of Asia, part of a world of fast deals in arms, drugs and shady transactions of all kinds. In Bangkok, off Yaowart Road, between a money changer and an incense-seller, children, as young as two or three-years-old, were regularly sold, in 1989, for as little as $20. The traffickers were an old woman and a leathery-faced man who operated from a fruit stall. They asked no questions. When they ran out of children, they returned to selling mangoes, papayas and tiny bananas over a charcoal fire. The fruits came from the same source as the children – Thailand's impoverished northern provinces. The fruits were paid for; the children often stolen. Bangkok remains one of Asia's principal slave junctions.

In Bangladesh, Chad, Columbia, the Dominican Republic, Haiti, Sri Lanka, in countries peopled with characters from the writings of Kipling and Maugham: there, too, slavery exists in 1990. Again, the slaves are mostly young, reflecting the fact that in these developing countries, the high birthrate often means that 40 per cent of the population is aged under fourteen. Many, far too many, are the children of darkness, denied from birth their innocence, condemned only to suffering. They are a reminder of the missing moral cog in societies which do not stop their children from being forcibly taken into slavery, or whose economies drive parents to sell their young to new masters who sacrifice them for greater profits.

Along its long-established routes, today's slaves travel far further. Often children or teenagers, usually girls, bought for the paedophile sex rings of Europe, to provide fresh bodies for the booming sex trade of West Germany, Holland and Scandinavia, with its outpouring of explicit videos, magazines and photo albums.

Often slaves, many of them also young, and all helpless, are herded along the jungle trails of Latin America, and up and over the permafrost of the Andes, and eventually to Mexico. From there, they are smuggled into the United States to toil, and sometimes, die, in the brothels, massage parlours or escort services of Los Angeles, Chicago, New York, San Francisco, and a hundred and more other North American cities and towns.

The number of children who are sexually exploited continues to grow dramatically. Some human rights workers say that by the mid-1990s the number of children used in the commercialized sex industries will outstrip that in the traditional child slave-labour market. Technology will finally modernize the looms of India, its glass-making furnaces and all the other industries which now still use children. The micro-chip will make it more profitable than having

217

to feed and house the little slaves. New markets will be found for new bodies coming on the market.

In a pioneering study in 1988, two American sociologists, Daniel Cambagna and Donald Poffenberger, reported that the

> hazards and risks of trafficking encourage exploiters to experiment with innovative methods. The advent of electronic bulletin boards, for instance, eased the burden of communications among paedophiles owning computers. Someone, somewhere is always testing new ways to guarantee the supply of children. The various market entrepreneurs operate on the premise that demand, though it may be restricted periodically by law-enforcement, will never disappear. When exploiters are hard pressed by vigorous law enforcement, two things happen. The price of child sex goes up. Exploiters become harder to identify.

A year later in Britain, Childwatch, the anti-child abuse group, was the first to alert Scotland Yard's understaffed and overworked child-porn squad that hard-core pornographic pictures were being viewed by children with home computers. By typing in a simple code which gave them access to one of hundreds of electronic bulletin boards around the country, children could receive on their screens close-up photographs of couples having intercourse and demonstrations of oral sex.

The vivid pictorial displays were possible because of advances in technology, which have made computer images as realistic as television. The bulletin boards offer thousands of selections, with such titles as *Raw Sex* and *Madam Fifi's Whore House Adventures*.

The material available in Britain is reinforced by imported hard porn from Europe. In 1989 a popular game on offer by a bulletin board based in the quiet West Country town of Ilminster was a German creation called *Pervert*. The game involved moving couples into increasingly obscene sexual positions and actions. It was readily available to any child with the fifty pence needed to obtain the access code to the bulletin board.

Hard-core pornography remains on offer to computer enthusiasts *of all ages* by mail order. A pioneer in the field is Event Horizons Inc, a company based in Portland, Oregon. From its modest offices in the north-west of the United States, the company offers 400 explicit colour pictures on floppy discs at $10 – a sum well within the pocket money range of many children. The company admits it has no idea who its customers are, let alone their ages.

Computer-linked sex clubs across Europe are marketing an ever-varied range of images showing often quite young children being sexually abused by adults, or involved with sex with animals. Some are depicted in scenes of even more extreme violence.

In 1990 bulletin boards in Amsterdam, Frankfurt and Stockholm continue to offer 'snuff pictures' – illustrations of people, including children, being murdered. Whether or not these are genuine killings, is surely not the point. The damage such images can do to young and impressionable minds, is incalculable.

It is deeply shameful.

SEVENTEEN

Towards Tomorrow

As Europe prepares for 1992, its year of unification, there is increasing anxiety among those trying to combat slavery. They fear that the removal of border controls within the community, will see it surge – particularly in the traffic of women and children.

There is growing evidence to support such concern. The number of *argati* – Yugoslavian gipsy children either stolen or sold by their parents – is on the increase. Exact figures are virtually impossible to obtain, like so many other areas of abuse, the traffic is woefully under-documented because of the clandestine conditions in which it occurs. But Italian child-care agencies believe the number of pre-teen children smuggled into Italy in 1989 was in excess of 10,000.

In 1988 sixty warrants for child trafficking were issued by the Milan police against *argati* bosses in the area. Fagin-like, they had taught the children to steal or prostitute themselves. In between assignments the children were kept in encampments outside the city. Those who failed to reach a daily 'target' of money from whoring, or the assigned amount of valuables to be stolen, were beaten and often tortured. Defence for Children International reported that a common practice was to administer cigarette burns to sensitive parts of their bodies.

In its own investigation, the agency discovered that 'when the bosses needed more children, they quite simply made a phone call to Yugoslavia in order to get a new consignment.'

In 1990 the traffic continues virtually unchecked.

Overall, Italy has a poor record over illegal child labour. While, again, no official statistics exist for the number under the age of fourteen working – indeed the Central Institute of Statistics in 1988 did not list a single child working under the age limit – the reality is that many hundreds of thousands of Italian children remain illegally employed.

They often work under conditions which amount to slavery. The worst areas are Naples, Milan, Turin, Genoa and the provinces of Apulia, Lazio and Sicily. A firm in Palermo still demands in 1990 that children must work five hours a day after school, plus eight on Saturday and four on Sunday. In Naples, the Italian Trades Union Congress estimates 50,000 children still working similar hours; in Sicily the under-age work force still tops 200,000.

All are paid well below adult wages, and most made to work at tasks only suitable for grown men – quarrying, hauling rubble or moving heavy mechanical parts in workshops. Many are forced to toil through the night. In the villages of Italy's central plains, they sew through the night. In Sardinia, children are even hired as scarecrows, standing from dawn to dusk in fields, flapping their arms in the blazing heat of a long summer.

The transition of Spain and Portugal from dictatorships to democracies was one of the great political success stories of the closing half of this century – except in one significant aspect. The exploitation of children in both countries remains a blight which the authorities do little to stop.

It is now more than twenty years since the Lisbon administration made it an offence to employ children under the age of fourteen. The penalty for doing so remains paltry. The average fine is no more than equal to £20 – about the selling price of a pair of shoes cobbled by an under-age boy working in one of thousands of sweatshops in northern Portugal. There, scenes of Dickensian misery exist, where many thousands of under-age and underfed boys and girls, some as young as six, work up to sixty hours a week.

Drawing upon the deepening pool of the young workless, employers can pick and choose. They prefer young girls to their elder sisters; the former are less likely to become pregnant. They prefer boys to girls, simply because boys can work longer and harder.

The men who hire them are usually former migrant workers, the *Gastarbeiter* returned from West Germany and France, often themselves brutalized by years of toil in northern Europe, they use the same ruthless techniques they learned in Lyons and Hamburg.

Portugal's government has all but given up trying to deal with the situation. Its Justice Minister said in 1989 that heavier fines and terms of imprisonment are not the answer for the exploiters: others will simply take their place. Some government ministers add that, without child labour, the already parlous economy will collapse. The unspoken hope is that sufficient financial help will come from the industrial members of the European Community to make it possible for Portugal's economy to begin to balance itself. But the political pragmatists in Lisbon say that even then it is doubtful if child labour will be completely eradicated, because the profits it provides are too

221

great to be given up. The children of Portugal remain on the treadmill of exploitation.

In 1973 Spain ratified the minimum working age as fifteen. Seventeen years later, child labour persists throughout the country, with minors working long hours. They are paid well below minimum wages, and have no social security, and few health and safety precautions.

Even more disturbing are reports that the country's Costa del Sol has become one of the main conduits to smuggle women and children out of northern Europe to the Middle East and beyond. Boats already used to bring drugs from America and Asia into Puerto Banus, the raffish marina near Marbella, are claimed by some child-care workers to be used to take out human cargoes. The Spanish police have conducted several investigations, but say they have been unable to find any evidence. The reports, however, persist.

Elsewhere in the Mediterranean Basin, it is equally hard to obtain evidence to support strongly-held suspicion of a general exploitation of children. One Anti-Slavery Society investigator found 'employers are generally reluctant to let visitors see working conditions. On many occasions entry was strictly forbidden and doors firmly shut. There was an obvious desire not to draw attention either to the number employed, or to their ages.'

Turkey is an example. With the opening of the country to tourism, its rulers have taken care that visitors see as little as possible of the way the country's child labour force is exploited. In 1989 there were six million children in Turkey of school age who had not received a lesson – but instead worked from dawn to dusk creating the bric-a-brac of package-holiday tourism: plastic beach bags and balls, sunglasses, sandals and T-shirts. Their hard labour made a significant input into the economy. Few adults complain. No one knows what the children think.

A similar story prevails in Greece. The conditions of many of the sweatshops of backstreet Athens makes a mockery of the birthplace of democracy. Thousands of children who cannot read – and therefore have no understanding of the few safety rules on display – work long hours, the latest victims of centuries of hardship for young Greeks.

While powerful industrial nations like the United States, West Germany and Great Britain continue to demand cheap imports from the Third World, child labour will continue.

In 1990, Bangkok, as well as remaining the global capital for sexual exploitation of children, produced the largest single pool of child labour for the world's clothing industry. Children who have barely learned to walk, toil endlessly in sweatshops behind interminable rows of sewing machines. Britain imports a hundred times more clothing in value terms from Thailand than it did a decade before. West Germany and the United States continue to show a similar increase in their textile trade with Asia. The reason, clothing executives readily admit, is the cheapness of the products.

The Government of Thailand, asked to justify child labour, produces the standard response of all Third World countries. A government spokesman reiterated in 1990 that

> economic necessity still forces parents to put their children to work at an early age. The rise in the standard of living will probably be the only solution to alleviate this problem. This can only be achieved by hard currency for our exports. In a competitive world, Thailand has to export as cheaply as possible – and that, of course, means using children to manufacture. It is a circle which can only be broken by importers paying more, so the manufacturers can create better conditions.

It is a forlorn hope.

Yet it is not a shame of the Third World confined to the Third World.

There are now more than 80,000 Mexican, Central and South American children – an unprecedented number – working alongside their equally impoverished families harvesting crops in the United States. Their conditions are often slave-like: pittances for salaries, living rough, forced from dawn to dusk to perform back-breaking work. The children cook and wash in unpurified water; in the fields they slake their thirst from used pesticide containers.

Child labour will continue to remain what it has always been – the creation of poverty, government social policies and the cultural values concerning the role of children. No one expects that with the arrival of 1992, it will come to a swift halt. It will remain a blight for the foreseeable future. The child slaves of today will become the adult cast-offs of tomorrow.

Three years after President Corazon Aquino declared 1987 as 'The Year of the Exploited Child in the Philippines' – a campaign primarily aimed at ending the sexual traffic in the young – their plight remains as bad as ever. Foreigners continue to travel to the islands in search of child sex. Children's rights advocates say that little note is taken by the Philippine authorities of the physical damage inflicted on young bodies through sex with adults, many of whom frequently resort to sadism. Still less do they consider the emotional confusion experienced by children plunged into sex while still discovering his or her own identity or of the distortion of values imposed on children who learn early in life that sex can be sold for survival.

In the Philippines, as elsewhere, turning the tide against child prostitution will never be easy. The only solution some experts say, is indeed an economic one: end poverty – end child prostitution. Strengthening the economic fabric of the family will provide a safety net for children. Child-care workers say any such move must begin at the grass roots, getting the children off the streets. There must be stronger legislation to deal with offenders. These are modest demands to deal with a situation which has reached crisis point in countries like Thailand.

There, Pattaya competes for the role of the world's raunchiest city. Beginning on Beach Road South and moving back from the shorefront of what was once a quiet fishing village, tens of thousands of under-age prostitutes continue to ply for hire. As estimated million visitors a year – from US sailors on shore leave to paedophile businessmen from Europe – visit this honky-tonk area which caters for every sexual requirement.

'Friends of Women', a Thai activist group, constantly patrols Pattaya, gathering evidence of under-age exploitation. The reports are graciously acknowledged by the Public Health Ministry, but no action is taken. The official Thai policy is that prostitution is illegal in the country – therefore, in the words of a government spokesman, 'it is no problem'.

The reality is that there are almost three million prostitutes in the country in 1990. Half are under the age of fifteen – Thailand's minimum working age requirement. 'Friends of Women' believe that, as AIDS spreads among existing prostitutes, the Thai sex industry will bring in ever-younger disease-free recruits from the virtually limitless supply of pre-teen girls and boys from the poorer northern provinces. Thailand could then become the first nation to see its future generation destroyed by the most virulent of all the sexually transmitted diseases. Given that the country primarily caters for the sexual needs of male foreigners – the prospect of global transmission of AIDS becomes ever greater.

In Thailand, says Alan Whittaker of the Anti-Slavery Society, it is still a tragedy in 1990 to be born poor. 'It is a double tragedy to be born poor and pretty. Poor children from the provinces simply become part of the juvenile labour force. The poor *and* pretty do their version of child labour in somebody's bed or brothel.'

Bangkok remains with the invidious distinction of being the world's only completely open market for the buying and selling of children. During the January to March dry season, train loads of children, prepubescent, confused, often alone, arrive in the capital, mainly from the north-east. Whittaker reports that 'as many as 500 of them arrive each week. They change hands for little more than the price of a watch. Once bought these children serve the rest of their time as slaves.'

Life for women in the Philippines has always been harsh. Discrimination means they had few equal employment opportunities and receive lower wages. Many women migrate.

Over 30,000 entered Britain between 1970-1980. They continue to be used as cheap labour for the hotel and catering industries, and as resident domestics in private homes. In 1989, the Commission for Filipino Migrant Workers in London reported that women were still often subject to physical and sexual abuse.

While new UK immigration laws bar foreign domestics from being allowed to work in Britain, the Home Office continues to admit the private servants of wealthy Arabs and other foreigners. In a submission to the Home Office, the Commission described how those 'employers' keep servants' passports in their own possession at all times. The servants do not understand the rules governing their status in Britain. If one escapes from their employer and tries to work elsewhere, she becomes liable for instant deportation.

The Commission believed that in 1989 there were hundreds of Filipina 'illegals' in Britain – living hand-to-mouth existences, and often battered and preyed upon by touts, pimps and procurers. The Commission asked the Home Office to look sympathetically at the plight of the women. The Home Office announced it was planning to deport the illegals.

Many Filipinos continue to enter into contracted marriages to avoid deportation. Alliances are usually arranged by marriage bureaux, many with names as exotic as the girls they market. They operate not only in Britain, but throughout Europe, North America and Australia.

For a while no one knew what had happened to the women. Then gradually, the stories of Utopian dreams being shattered surfaced; Filipinas suffering from isolation and cultural shock; husbands who had become unbearable when they discovered their wives were not as exotic and submissive as they had been led to expect.

The Philippine Women's Support Committee, based in London, has concluded

> The marriage bureaux make large profits from marketing women to cater to various demands and needs of men. Some of them are large businesses – demonstrated by their

incursions into the tourist industry. They actively promote false images and stereotypes to sell their services. Oriental women in general and Filipinas in particular are projected as completely subservient to men, whilst the Western liberated woman is portrayed as aggressive and unsuitable for marriage. On the other hand Western men are advertised as ideal husbands who will provide economic security and fulfil the dreams and hopes of Filipino women.

A blunter judgment came from Sister Margaret Healy, director of the Commission for Filipino Migrant Workers.

> Those men are either seeking a passing sexual relationship, or a concubine type of wife whom, they are assured, will submit themselves without question to their every sensual whim. We are dealing here with the exploitation of women in a very pernicious form which is not only racist and sexist, but often slavery.

In the United States the young have been kept in chains and received no income at all, only food for their labour. Until 1985 in the small town of Kerrville, Texas, a ranch in the hilly farming community run by a German immigrant family, kept 75 slaves. The family acquired them simply by cruising the nearby Interstate 10 highway. They picked up drifters, some barely into their teens, youngsters who would not be easily missed by family, friends or the authorities – the kind of person John Doe Sixty probably was. They were driven back to the ranch. They found themselves confronted by armed guards who chained them to other helpless slaves.

The captives were made to fell trees, used to make souvenir key chains sold to local tourists. The ranch is close to the birthplace of President Lyndon Johnson. The slaves worked to the accompaniment of Elvis Presley's *Jailhouse Rock*. The guards routinely tortured them using electric cattle prods on their tongues and genitalia; when they killed one, they burned him. The Texas Rangers finally raided the place and it took almost two more years to bring the case to trial. The maximum penalty the rancher and his sons faced was 99 years, one received 15 years, the other 14 and one was acquitted.

There are people in Kerrville who still say it is 'all a trumped-up case'; that 'such things' don't happen in the United States. They did – and continue to do so. Reading the trial transcripts of slavery in Kerrville, somehow makes more believable what Susan Davidson continues to claim is happening at the California ranch.

How many more ranches exist?

Satanism, and its attendant abuses, continues to grow. In May 1989, a German researcher suggested there could be as many as thirty million who are now actually involved worldwide in some form of Satanic worship. More certain, groups and sects are constantly being born, split apart and reformed. Some Devil-worship is what it says it is – essentially an anti-Christian, hedonistic and anti-moral view of life. For its followers, Satan has become an object of devotion.

However, the Turin scholar, Massimo Introvigne, director of the Catholic Church's Center for the Study of New Religions, is convinced there will be a significant upsurge in the number of cults who are 'sadistic, orgiastic and involved with drugs'. J. Gordon Melton, director of the Institute for the Study of American Religion at the University of California at Santa Barbara – the nation's main documentation centre for Satanic studies – estimates there could now be 5,000 full-time Satanists in the United States.

In 1990 Susan Davidson continues to insist the figure does not take account of the number who are termed 'lone Satanists', those who practise ritualism outside a cult. She continues to point out that many of the most notorious Satanic crimes in recent years have been committed by such Satanists, including David Berkowitz, who murdered six people in New York under the name of Son of Sam, and Richard Ramirez, the 'Night Stalker' of Los Angeles, who also murdered under Satanic influences.

Other researchers are cautiously beginning to agree with Susan that human sacrifices are on the increase. In April 1989, at a remote ranch close to the Mexican border with Texas, police found the remains of thirteen victims. Their skulls had been emptied of brains and limbs hacked off at the joints, cauldrons were filled with hearts and other organs cooked in human blood. The cultists believed that consuming the brew protected them from arrest and even made them immune to police bullets. A month later, in Mexico City, the cult's leader, Jesus Constanzo, died in a shoot-out with police.

It was soon established that the cult had survived for so long because of the protection of police and officials in the area; they were reported to have received 'substantial payments' to take no action. The allegations have an eerie similarity to those that Susan Davidson continues to make about high-level protection for the California Ranch.

In Turin, where Satanic ritualism remains rife, the city's chief exorcist, Father Guiseppe Ruarta, warned that a lack of faith may have allowed Satan to become

a surrogate of the need for the sacred which is in each one of us. Our independence and salvation makes us wish for someone who is greater, who is above us. It is probably the result of fears and insecurity never resolved which sparks this obsession with the Devil. It is an obsession which strikes most strongly against those who are psychologically most weak.

That is, perhaps, as good an *explanation* as any – but one which offers no *solution*. The Catholic Church, for one, shows little sign of actually setting out to confront the Devil. It has, for instance, little money available to conduct full-scale research into Satanic ritualism.

The traffic continues to grow in children and young adults kidnapped and murdered for their organs. Dr George Abouna, chairman of the organ transplant unit at the University of Kuwait is among those who are joining Susan Davidson in gathering evidence. In 1990 he is satisfied that an increasing number of wealthy renal patients from the Middle East, Europe and North America are travelling secretly to India, the Philippines and Thailand to obtain transplants at private clinics. Hundreds of such operations are estimated to have been performed in 1989 in India alone.

Dr Abouna reports that

facilities are often unsanitary and hospitals eager to discharge patients after operations without the crucial supervision for complications that often arise in the first three months after a transplant. In many cases hospitals do not screen organs for disease and some recipients have contracted hepatitis and AIDS.

Many of the organs have been removed from young prostitutes.

Dr Abouna believes it is now only a matter of time before organ trafficking is as professionally organized as the drug cartels, 'with doctors and hospitals and the underworld united by a common interest – the high profits from stealing people for their organs.'

In 1990 Rosalie Bentell of the Geneva-based International Commission of Helping Professions, which monitors human rights abuse by physicians, continues to collect reports of 'unearthed remains of children with missing organs, and fattening houses in Central America – where undernourished children are nursed back to health before being killed for their organs. It's a sellers' market.'

In January, 1990 further evidence of the pernicious trade emerged in Mexico City. There police recovered a stolen baby: Its body bore a surgical scar where a kidney had been expertly removed.

On the other side of the world, in Madras, India, one of the country's most respected physicians, Dr Krishna Reddy, was convinced that in countries like his, the traffic would continue to flourish.

Every year there are 80,000 new cases of renal failure in India – and only 600 dialysis machines.

> The simple law of supply and demand prevails. There are plenty of bodies. But not enough machines. So they take from the bodies. There are plenty more where they came from. It is appalling. It breaks a doctor's basic rule not to do any harm. But the reality is that it happens

said Dr Reddy.

Slavery in all its contemporary forms – officially United Nations - reorganized forms – remains today the largest form of human abuse. It continues to transcend race and colour. It flourishes equally among the God-fearing and the godless. It has been correctly identified as the product of greed and power which feeds off poverty and helplessness of others. Dr Roger Sawyer of the Anti-Slavery Society has said that the urge to enslave is fundamental to human nature. Given the Society's estimate in 1989 that the figure of 200 million slaves will continue to increase, it is difficult to challenge that assertion.

It is impossible to pretend otherwise than that the situation is a grim one. But it is not hopeless – not yet. Not if there is a collective will to act.

That requires each one of us using every means in our power to ensure that emancipation is the birthright of each man, woman and child who remains enslaved. We must protest their plight. We must protest against all those who exploit the enslaved: elected Governments, regimes and dictatorships. The multi-nationals who sell us cheap clothing and food produced by, and through, the suffering of slaves. Protest means action. It means writing to elected representatives. It means lobbying.

For a start each one of us should ask our parliamentarians to ensure that each nation on earth must abolish work by children under the age of fourteen. The International Labour Organization adopted this standard in 1973; in 1989 only 35 nations had ratified the minimum-age convention. The United States is one country that has not.

Third World countries must be made to raise the school leaving age. Education is the key to breaking the poverty cycle. Mandatory schooling is helping to eliminate child labour in Britain and the United States. Those countries and other industrial nations should look again at the proposal of Claude Cheysson, the former European Common Market Foreign Aid Commissioner. In the late 1970s he proposed that foreign aid and trade concessions should be withheld from countries with exploitive forms of child labour. The idea fell on deaf ears. It should be urgently re-examined.

229

It will require bold and innovative thinking. It will be financially expensive. It will be asking the First and Second Worlds to make their greatest and most far-reaching contribution to the future of the entire world.

A start must be made. Not all the voices of those 200 million will have the strength much longer to go on crying out for help.

EIGHTEEN
Explanations

In all, I spoke to over ninety persons in four continents who were, and mostly still are, involved in fighting the traffic in humans.

John Sullivan provided me with access to the network of Customs agents and attachés he controls across the world from his office in Washington DC. Sullivan had said that if ever I ran into trouble, his men would try and help, or would know who could.

In 1989, he was head of the US Customs taskforce responsible for dealing with child pornography, working closely with other government law enforcement agencies, within the US and around the world, especially those who dealt with adult pornography and drugs.

Sullivan sat me down in his office at 1301 Constitution Avenue, NW, in the very heart of Washington's bureaucracy, and said that in his view the population of the world was coming close to spending more money on the by-products of slavery – prostitution, porno films, magazines and books, audio cassettes, and 'just about anything in the sex exploitation line you care to name' – than it did on food and clothing, on medical attention and education.

Sullivan's approval allowed me, among other places, on to those access-restricted floors of American embassies, where his men often share space with the CIA, FBI and the agents of the Drug Enforcement Agency. There seemed to be an unwritten rule among them that if Sullivan spoke *for* me it was okay to speak *to* me, and to allow me to look into files marked with the bold red restriction, *CONFIDENTIAL*, and to read messages stamped *SECRET* or even *TOP SECRET*.

There were others, field agents, who are trained to keep away from the public view, who spend their days and nights moving with endless cunning and speed among the slavers. They are young and magnificently fit, with the wits of the streetwise and an unerring eye for the soft spots, the places where they could strike with maximum effect.

231

In Amsterdam one agent bedded me down in a brothel, where he himself regularly slept the night deeply to make a small profit on his government US $75 *per diem*. In Baghdad another showed me some of the secrets of his trade – informant cryptonyms and unlisted telephone numbers. At Bangkok's Don Muang Airport, an agent briefed me on the flights which carry slaves to the Middle East. In the lobby of the Manila Hotel, still another explained how simple it was to move young Filipinos to Europe.

Nor did all the pieces fit neatly. Men like *El Reyes* – The King – saw to that. I'd been told he had the best of contacts, a man with links to hot money, drugs and the grey world of intelligence. Some said he'd worked for the CIA; others that he still did. It took a couple of weeks to lock-up all the arrangements to meet him but I had become used to that. Finally, I'd taken an American Airlines flight from Dallas to Mexico City. I'd called a number from a payphone in the airport concourse and a young nervous voice, a boy's, after I identified myself, told me to take a taxi to an address in the Colonia Santo Domingo district.

It turned out to be in a street of shops selling cheap clothes and shoes, electrical equipment and records. *El Reyes* worked in a drug store. For a Mexican, he was a big man, with bad teeth and out-to-lunch eyes and it was easy to believe what others said about him. He took me to a back room, filled with unopened cartons. He locked the door behind him and spread out on top of a box a set of photographs, arranging them carefully, the way a stamp collector might do with a set of valuable first day covers.

He stepped back, so I could move in and get a closer look. The faces in the photographs were all of children, boys and girls, somewhere between the ages of five and ten, all with the dark skins of Central and South America. They looked starved and frightened. *El Reyes* explained, in the sharp voice of a born hustler, that the children were about to be sold to a man in San Diego who made porno movies. He shifted his gaze to look at me out of the corner of his eye. He said he could arrange for me to interview the children for US $1,000.

I studied the pinched faces. They all had the same hopeless look I'd seen on the faces of other children in the files of the Anti-Slavery Society, and other human rights organizations. That look on the faces in the photographs was compounded for me by the knowledge they were destined to be used in a particularly brutal and evil manner – and all to provide sexual gratification for others.

I forced down my own anger and disgust over being in a locked room with a stranger who traded in such matters. No matter how many times I brushed against the slavers, I always felt the same. I told *El Reyes* I was not interested in exploiting the children further. He shrugged and said that for $500 he would answer questions about the slaver's activities in Central and South America. It was money well spent.

There were others, like *El Reyes* whose paths, when I crossed them, made me never quite certain how they would react. They, too, were men without ethics or scruples and often displayed the killer instincts of venomous snakes. Sometimes they hid behind self-deprecating smiles, and were as trained to sidestep questions as to avoid physical surprise. I sat with them in Asia, the Middle East and South America, and they often made sure I knew they were carrying a gun.

Watching those closed faces and listening to voices that could be as chilling as damp mountain air was an unforgettable experience.

Nor was it always easy to tell by appearances who was who. Richard Rivera could pass for a *pistolero*, or a Mexican *indigenista* as if he'd spent all his life running from the *Federales*, while in reality he works with them. When we met he was an assistant US Customs attaché unconcerned about the price on his head after he had bust an arms operation in Nicaragua. He explained he was proud he had worked his way up, roughing and toughing it as a Federal undercover agent in Central and South America, fighting dopers, hit men and the gun-and-people runners. He talked for hours about things few would dream existed. Only occasionally, when he didn't want to answer a question, did he show a frozen stare, as he sealed himself in a remote place somewhere inside him, his mind-your-own-business hideout. Then, after a while, he'd start talking again, and the forbidding look left his eyes, and the smile returned.

For over a year I lived part of their lives with them, learning about their tradecraft, those skills no book can teach, and which depend on a cunning and ruthlessness that must try and match them. I cannot say I liked all the persons I met. Nor can I pretend that they told me everything I wanted to know. But between them they became a lens which allowed me to view the plight of the enslaved.

From the outset, I realized I faced a challenge unique in my thirty-seven years as a reporter and investigative author. It became clear that while this was a story of courage, and anchored in the United States, its focus must be on the children, teenagers and women who are enslaved. There *is* a special horror to their fate. They are truly the defenceless ones, battered and exploited, often subjected to unspeakable pain and horror.

Essentially, the story you have read is a report from the front line in the fight against slavery. Some people, for good reasons, have had their identities protected. Dialogue which could not have been recorded first-hand was recreated from memory.

That eminent modern student of human evil, Professor Noel Walsh of St Vincent's Hospital, Dublin, a deeply caring psychiatrist and

233

mentor, produced a *leitmotif* on how to write up the research. 'The preservation of confidentiality must take precedence over the full disclosure of irrelevant detail.'

The alteration, or elimination of such details – names, locations, dates – have not, in my judgement, in any way significantly distorted the truth.

When I started to set down the story, I discarded draft after draft. I was afraid that anyone who read them would find the contents still just too incredible. There were many people who helped me present the final story.

Officer Sandi Gallant of the San Francisco Police Department was reassigned in March 1989, to deploy her intelligence-gathering skills against drug traffickers in the city. After being divorced for eight months, she became once more engaged to be married. She had met her fiancé on a blind date shortly before she prepared to travel to Hawaii to continue the healing process from the emotional toll her divorce had taken. She hopes to remain with the police department until she retires in 1996.

Inspectors Earl Sanders and Napoleon Hendrix remain together in 1990 as the most formidable homicide investigators in San Francisco. Their evidence, together with the testimony of Bork, Eddie and Ricki, led to Clifford St Joseph receiving a thirty-nine-year sentence for the murder of John Doe Sixty. St Joseph is due for release in 2029. Bork remains 'somewhere' within the US prison system. The detectives occasionally see Eddie and Ricki, still working the streets.

Special Agent Jack O'Malley continues to formulate sting operations which reach out to all corners of the world. He remains, in 1990, the most active agent in the United States Customs Service in putting child pornographers out of business. Colleagues say part of his success is because he continues to regard his targets as personal adversaries.

Susan Davidson has moved the Center to another suburb in Orange County to reduce running costs. It still operates on a financial shoestring. However, a number of corporations in California promised donations which at least guarantees the Center's existence for the foreseeable future. Susan continues to gather evidence on the Ranch. Her success in healing young victims is as remarkable as ever. In a New Year's message in 1990 to her supporters, Susan reported more children than ever before were being helped by the Center. Pamela gave up counselling in May 1989 and moved from California, 'because this state is not the place I want to rear my children in.'

In April 1989, the Anti-Slavery Society was 150 years old. Maureen Alexander-Sinclair, its deputy director for the past quarter century, said that, given the Society's estimate of 200 million slaves in the world, and the number increasing daily, she expected – if the organization could financially survive – her successors would have to mark a 200th anniversary. She found it deeply disturbing that a world which by then would probably have colonized space will still not have eradicated all forms of slavery.

My wife, Edith, constantly reminded me that the very real danger in writing a book about evil was that it could actually help to propagate it. I have tried to be constantly mindful of that and never, I hope, presented evil simply to show it exists. The evil in this book is an integral element of a story of hope.

My children – Catherine, Alexander, Lucy, Nicholas and Natasha – continued to suffer from their father's workaholism: knowing they were there was a comfort. Never has the importance of a closely-knit family mattered more to me than it did during the research and writing of this book. In dedicating it to them, it is a small measure to mark the love they gave me.

David Jensen, a doughty American journalist who has worked on previous projects with me proved once more a valuable research source. Using his computers, he located material from all over the world; it was a remarkable example of how technology can be harnessed to tease out the truth. His suggestions were always valuable. Lucky the writer who has such a stalwart support. David was always at the end of a telephone or facsimile machine. Many a morning I came to my office to find that overnight from his base in California he had electronically mailed still more evidence of modern-day slavery. The book would be all the poorer without his input.

After I had made a dozen unsuccessful attempts to begin the story proper, it was he who suggested, 'lead your readers to the truth slowly. Give them time to adjust to what the story is *really* about. Why not start with the boy Shambu?'

How many Shambus have there been since then?

How many of you will say – here and now – this exploitation must stop? On that answer hangs, literally, the lives of all those others who have now joined the 200 million who were enslaved when you first began to read about Shambu.

Sources

Without the co-operation of the following this book would not have been possible.

Interviewees

Alexander, Peter J
Alexander-Sinclair, Maureen
Andrada, Ruben D
Asciende, Juan
Augusto, Orlando
Baker, Edward K
Baker, Stuart
Balabanovska, Bebe
Basaloong, Lap
Bath, Robert
Cameron, John K
Cartwright, Julie C
Coles, Dudley
Coles, Eva
Corcoran, George C
Cormier, Claude
Cortes, Virgie
Craig, Robert
Davidson, Lee
Davidson, Susan
Dispenzirie, Peter J
Donaldson, Iain
Dos Santos, Richard
Duarte, Jasmine
Edwards, Paula-Mary
Edwards, Sam
Fernandez, John D
Foster, Darylene
Franklin, William R
Gallant, Sandra D

Gregory, Al
Harris, Pamela
Hasim, Rachid
Healy, Margaret
Helmerson, John R
Hoffman, Peter
Hurley, John A
Hutchinson, Jim
Isa, Kamal
Jacobson, Viktor
Jankovska, Mirjana
Jarvis, Lee
Jarvis, Lyn
Joseph, Yvonne
Jupp, Michael
Kennedy, Peter S
Kroopman, Else
Laughton, James M
Lavery, William H
Leeman, Oliver
LeVey, Anton Z
Libid, Edmundo
Luksik, John
Lyne, Jacques
Matthews, John
Moore, Bram A
Muirhead, Arthur B
O'Malley, John
Opino, Mary-Louise
Orlando, Carlo

Panola, Marie
Pickett, Charles H
Preemansing, S
Preston, John
Salvalio, Enrigues
Sanders, Earl
Shaw, Clifton
Srisomwong, Sundharee
Strickland, Chris
Sullivan, John
Suman, Michael
Urbanski, Roger R
Uribe, Elene
Van-Neil, William G
Velmann, Arturo
Vratji, Dieter
White, Calvin G
Whittaker, Alan
Wilkie, James W
Wilson, Paul
Wilstead, Tom
Wood, Cy
Wrightman, Keith

Organizations

Adam Walsh Child Resource Center, Orange County, California
Adults Molested as Children, San José, California
Ampex Corporation, Redwood City, California
Asi Senden Home, Manila, Philippines
Child Find, New York City
Children of the Night, Hollywood, California
Children's Rights, Washington, DC
Children's Villages of India, New Delhi, India
Defence for Children International, Geneva, Switzerland
Hogares Providencia, Mexico City, Mexico
Interpol, Paris
International Association of Chiefs of Police, Maryland
Legal Services for Children, San Francisco, California
National Center for Child Abuse and Neglect, Washington, DC
National Center for Missing & Exploited Children, Washington, DC
National Children's Commission, Addis Ababa, Ethiopia
National Network of Runaway & Youth Services Washington, DC
National Runaway Switchboard, Chicago, Illinois
National Sheriff's Association, Washington, DC
Parents of Murdered Children, Cincinatti, Ohio
Project 'P', Toronto, Canada
Salvation Army, London
San Francisco Police Department
Scotland Yard, London
Stolen Child Information Network, Anaheim, California
Texas Child Search, San Antonio, Texas
The American Humane Association, Denver, Colarado
The Anti-Slavery Society, London
The Commission for Filipino Migrant Workers, London
The Foundation for Children, Bangkok, Thailand
The Hong Kong Christian Service, Hong Kong
UNICEF, New York, London, Switzerland
United States Customs Service, Washington, DC
Youth Development, Washington, DC
Youth in Crisis, Bridgeport, Connecticut

Bibliography

The regular publications of the Anti-Slavery Society demand special attention. They are models of reportage, and owe much to their editor, Alan Whittaker. For those who would like a lengthier introduction to the subject, then highly recommended is *Slavery In The Twentieth Century*, by Roger Sawyer (Routledge & Kegan Paul, London). It remains, so far, the only full-length comprehensive survey of many aspects of modern-day slavery.

Anti-Slavery Society Publications and Papers

(Published or privately printed in London, unless otherwise stated)

Anti-Slavery Reporter and Aborigines' Friend, Series V: 29–31 (1939–42) and 32–34 (1942–45), Klaus Reprint, 1969; Series VI: November 1976, vol. 12, no. 5, November 1979, vol. 12, no. 6 and November 1980, vol. 12, no. 7; Series VII: December 1981, vol. 13, no. 1.

Anti-Slavery Society Annual Report for years ended 31 March 1972, 1973, 1974, 1975, 1976, 1977, 1978, 1981, 1982, 1983, 1984, 1985, 1986, 1987 and 1988.

Child Labour Series

Child Labour in Morocco's Carpet Industry
Child Labour in India
Child Labour in Spain
Child Labour in Thailand
Child Labour in Italy

Indigenous Peoples and Development Series

The Philippines
The Chittagong Hill Tracts

Research Reports

Cronje, S., *Equatorial Guinea: The Forgotten Dictatorship*
Ennew, J., *Debt Bondage: A Survey*
Gretton, J., *Western Sahara: The Fight for Self-Determination*
Pool, D., *Eritrea: Africa's Longest War* (revised edition)
With Radda Barnen
(Swedish Save the Children), *Female Circumcision*, Geneva

Submissions to the United Nations Working Group of Experts on Slavery

Cronje, S., 'The Wall of Silence: forced labour and political murder in Equatorial Guinea'
Child Labour in Colombia
Child Labour in Hong Kong
Child Labour in India
The Exploitation of Child Labour, Oral Intervention by Leah Levin
Migrant Workers in the Dominican Republic
Child Labour in Sivakasi
Turkish Migrant Children in Germany
Bonded and Forced Labour in Peru and India
Child Domestic Workers in Latin America
Child Labour on Plantations
Sexual Exploitation of Children

Recommended Reading on Satanic Ritualism

Bubeck, Mark I., *The Adversary* (Chicago: Moody Press, 1975)
Bubeck, Mark I., *Overcoming the Adversary* (Chicago: Moody Press, 1984)
Koch, Kurt E., *The Devil's Alphabet* (Grand Rapids: Kregel Publications, 1971)
Koch, Kurt E., *Occult Bondage and Deliverance* (Grand Rapids, Kregel Publications, 1971)
Lindsey, Hal, *Satan Is Alive and Well on Planet Earth* (Grand Rapids, The Zondervan Corpn 1972)
Marrs, Texe, *Dark Secrets of the New Age* (Westchester: Crossway Books, 1987)
Stratford, Lauren, *Satan's Underworld* (Harvest House 1988)
Warnke, Mike, *The Satan Seller* (Plainfield: Logos Inter., 1972)
Wildman, Don, *Case against Pornography* (Wheaton: Victor Books, 1986)

Articles and Reports provided by United Nations Economic and Social Council

Allen, E.E.

'Testimony before the Committee on the Judiciary United States Senate Nov. 1981', Ernest E. Allen, Chairman of Jefferson County Task Force on Child Prostitution and Pornography, 1981

Aes-Milho E.

'El Problema de la Prostitucion en Iquitos', BA Thesis in Social Work, Catholic University of Lima, Peru, 1977

Abal, Ismodes C.

'Prostitution en Lima', paper presented to a UNICEF seminar, La Familia, Infancia y Juventud en el Desarollo Nacional, 1967

Anti-Slavery Society

'The Sexual Exploitation of Children'; report to the United Nations Sub-Commission for the Prevention of Discrimination and the Protection of Minorities; Geneva July to August 1984 (mimeo)

Barry, K, Bunch C. and Castley S.

(eds) *International Feminism*: 'Networking Against Female Sexual Slavery – Report of the Global Feminist Workshop to Organise Against Traffic in Women', Rotterdam, The Netherlands 6–15 April 1983, International Women's Centre, New York, USA, 1984

Buhdiba, A

'Exploitation of Child Labour, Final Report of the Special Rapporteur of the Sub-Commission on Prevention of Discrimination and Protection of Minorities', 1982

Carlsson B.

'Sexual Exploitation and Sale of Children', Mss for the Anti-Slavery Society and Radda Barnen, 1984

'Review of Developments in the field of Slavery and the Slave Trade in all their Practices and Manifestations'. Reports by States concerning the Convention for the Suppression of the Traffic in Persons and the Exploitation of the Prostitution of Others. Note by the Secretary General. E/CN.4/Sub.2/AC.2/1984/5/ 17 May, 1984 Geneva

Ennew J.

Liberated Vigilada, report for the Peruvian Probation Service Cambridge Social Consultancy Unit, UK 1982

Finkelhor D.

'What's wrong with sex between adults and children? Ethics and the

242

problem of sexual abuse', in *American Journal of Orthopsychiatry* vol 49 no. 4 1979

Fernand-Laurent J.

'Report of the Special Rapporteur on the Suppression of the Traffic in Persons and the Exploitation of the Prostitution of Others'; United Nations Economic and Social Council, 17 March 1983. Geneva

Government of Canada

'Summary of Sexual Offences against Children in Canada. Report of the Committee on Sexual Offences Against Children and Youths': appointed by the Minister of Justice and Attorney General of Canada, the Minister of National Health and Welfare, 1984

Karunatilleke K.

'Recent Trends in the Fight against the Traffic in Human Beings and the Exploitation of Prostitution'; paper submitted on behalf of INTERPOL to the 27th Congress of the International Abolitionist Federation, Nice, France, 1981

O'Grady R.

'Third World Tourism: Report of a Workshop of Tourism' held in Manila 12–25 Sep. 1980, Christian Conference of Asia, 1986

Ohse, U.

'Forced Prostitution and Traffic in Women in West Germany', Human Rights Group, Edinburgh, UK, 1984

Perpignan Sr. M.S.

'Philippine Women in the Service and Entertainment Sector', TWMAEW, Singapore, 1984

Spartacus

'Spartacus Holiday Help Portfolio': Sri Lanka Spartacus, Amsterdam, 24pp, 1987

Spartacus

'Spartacus Holiday Help Portfolio': Manila Spartacus, Amsterdam, 1987

Thitsa K.

'Providence and Prostitution – Image and Reality for Women in Buddhist Thailand', Change International Reports, Parnell House, Wilton Road, London, SW1, 1986

URSA

'Adolescent Male Prostitution; a study of sexual exploitation, etiological factors and runaway behaviour'; draft of Executive Summary; California, October, 1981

Vizard E

'The Sexual Abuse of Children – Parts 1 and 2' *Health Visitor* no. 157, UK, 1989

Wihtol, R.

'Hospitality Girls in the Manila Tourist Belt' *Philippine Journal of Industrial Relations*, vol IV nos. 1–2, 1984

Articles and Papers Provided by the International Abolitionist Federation

Bond, Tim

The Price of a Child, A Look at the Children's Market in Bangkok and a Tour of the North Eastern Province of Thailand (Sentinelles, Lausanne, July 1980)

Bouhdiba, Abdelwahab

Exploitation of Child Labour, report submitted to the Sub-Commission on Prevention of Discrimination and Protection of Minorities (E/CN.4/Sub.2/479 of 8 July 1981, E/CN.4/Sub.2/479/Rev.1 (United Nations Publication, Sales No. E.82.XIV.2)

Bridel, Renée

'*La Traite des Enfants*', *Revue Abolitionniste*, No. 44, fourth quarter 1981. Paper submitted to the 27th Congress of the International Abolitionist Federation, Sep. 1981

Holm, David

'Church and Tourism', Report on an International Conference in Stockholm, Nov. 2–6 1981 (Uppsala, Sweden), 81pp. Issued by the Church of Sweden, International Study Department

David, Kati and Casiraghi, Liliane

'*La Situation Sociale des Prostituées à Geneve*', thesis for the certificate in social politics of the Faculty of Economics and Social Sciences of the University of Geneva June 1981

English Collective of Prostitutes, New York Prostitutes Collective, US Prostitutes Collective

'*Nos besoins, Nos desirs, Nos revendications*' ... document submitted in French to the Twenty-seventh Congress of the International Abolitionist Federation 8 Sep. 1981, 2pp

La Prostitution en Afrique

'*Famille de Developement*', No. 13, Dakar, January 1978

Federation of Asian Bishops' Conferences
'Third World Tourism, Report of a Workshop on Tourism', held in Manila, Philippines, 12–25 Sep. 1980

IDOC International, Rome
'Tourism in South East Asia', No. 10, 1982

Deputy Secretary-General of INTERPOL
'Aspects recents de la lutte contre la traite des etres humains et de l'exploitation de la prostitution d'autrui', statement to the 27th Congress of the International Abolitionist Federation, Sep. 1981, *Revue Abolitionniste*, no. 43, 3rd quarter 1981

Levasseur, Georges and Richez Laurent
Professors at the Universities of Paris and Angers. *'Synthese des travaux du 27eme Congress de la Federation Abolitionniste internationale, 8-11 Sep 1981'*. *Revue Abolitionniste*, No. 44, fourth quarter 1981

Mancini, Jean-Gabriel
'Prostitution et Proxenetisme', (Presses Universitaires de France, Paris, third edition 1967), 126pp

Minority Rights Group
'Sex Tourism, problems and solutions', written report for the Working Group on Slavery, seventh session, Geneva, August 1982. Unpublished

Thitsa, Khin
'Providence and Prostitution – Image and Reality for Women in Buddhist Thailand'. Change International Reports, Parnell House, Wilton Road, London, SW1, Sep 1980

Juvenile Prostitution

Allen, Donald M
'Young Male Prostitutes: A Psychological Study', *Archives of Sexual Behaviour*, vol.9, no.5 (1980): 399–426

Benjamin, Harry and R.E.L. Masters
'Homosexual Prostitution' Prostitution and Morality (New York: Julian Press, 1964)

Bracey, Dorothy H
'Baby-Pros', Preliminary Profiles of Juvenile Prostitutes (New York, John Jay Press, 1979)

Bryan, James H
'*Apprenticeships in Prostitution*', Social Problems vol. 12 no.3 (Winter 1965) 287–297

Butts, William M
'Boy Prostitutes of the Metropolis', *Journal of Clinical Psychotherapy*, vol. 44, no.5 (1974) 441–451

Caplan, G.M
'Facts of Life About Teenage Prostitution', *Crime and Deliquency* vol.30 no.1 (January 1984) 69–74

Caukins, Sivan E and Neil R Coombs
'The Psychodynamics of Male Prostitution', *American Journal of Psychotherapy* vol.30 no.3 (July 1976) 441–451

Coombs, Neil R
'Male Prostitution', *American Journal of Orthopsychiatry* vol. 44 no.5 (October 1974) 782–789

Craft, Michael
'Boy Prostitutes and Their Fate', *British Journal of Psychiatry* vol.112 no. 492 (November 1966) 1111–1114

Davis, Kingsley
'The Sociology of Prostitution', *The Sociological Review* vol.2 no.5 (October 1937) 744–755

Morgan, Ted
'Little Ladies of the Night', *New York Times Magazine* (16 November 1975) 34–50

Child Pornography

Baker C. David
'Preying on Playgrounds: The Sexploitation of Children in Pornography and Prostitution', *Pepperdine Law Review* vol.5 no.3 (1978) 809–846

Burgess, Ann W and Marieanne L Clark
(eds) *Child Pornography and Sex Rings,* (Lexington, Mass: D.C. Heath and Company 1984)

D'Agostino, R.B
et. al. 'Investigation of Sex Crimes Against Children: A Survey of Ten States', *The Police Chief* (February 1984) 37–50

Dauber, Eric L.

'Child Pornography'. *Florida State University Law Review* vol. 10 no. 684 (1983) 684–701

Dudar, Helen

'America Discovers Child Pornography'. *Ms.* (Magazine) (August 1977) 45–47, 80

Guio, Michael V

'Child Victimization: Pornography and Prostitution', *Journal of Crime and Justice*, vol.111 (1980) 65–81

Heinrich, B

'Extent of Child Pornography in Texas'. Texas House Select Committee on Child Pornography, Interim Report (66th Legislative Session, 1978)

Houston, Judith, Samuel Houston and E. La Monte Ohlson

'On Determining Pornographic Material'. *The Journal of Psychology* 88 (1974) 227–287

Kutchinsky, Berl

'The Effect of Easy Availability of Pornography on the Incidence of Sex Crimes: The Danish Experiment', *Journal of Social Issues*, vol.29 no.3 (1973) 163–181

Rooney, Rita

'Innocence for Sale: A Special Report on Child Pornography', *Ladies Home Journal* (April 1983) 79–81, 127–132

Paedophilia

Bernard, Frederic

'An Enquiry Among a Group of Paedophiles', *The Journal of Sex Research* vol.11, no.3 (August 1975) 242–255

Cook, Mark and Kevin Howells

(ed) *Adult Sexual Interest in Children*' (New York Academic Press, 1981)

Peters, Joseph J and Robert L Sadoff

'Clinical Observations on Child Molesters', *Medical Aspects of Human Sexuality* (November 1970) 20–32

Rossman, Parker G

Sexual Experience Between Men and Boys (New York Association Press, 1976)

Tindall, Ralph H.

'The Male Adolescent Involved with a Pederast Becomes an Adult', *Journal of Homosexuality*, vol.3 no.4 (Summer 1973) 373-382

Tsang, Daniel

(ed) *The Age Taboo* (Boston: Alyson Publications, 1982)

Sexual Exploitation/Abuse

Bales, Richard H

'Sexual Exploitation as a Form of Child Abuse', *The Police Chief* (April 1979) 34–35

Finch, Stewart M

'Adult Seduction of the Child: Effects on the Child', *Medical Aspects of Human Sexuality* (1973): 170–187

Finkelhor, David

'Sexual Abuse of Children: A Sociological Perspective', *Child Abuse and Neglect* vol.6 no.1 (1983) 95–102

'What's Wrong with Sex Between Adults and Children?' *American Journal of Orthopsychiatry* vol.49, no.4 (October 1979) 592–597

'Risk Factors in the Sexual Exploitation of Children', *Child Abuse and Neglect* (1980) 265-273

Geiser, Robert L

Hidden Victims (Boston: Beacon Press, 1979)

Lewis, Ken

'On Reducing the Child-Snatching Syndrome', *Children Today* (November/December 1978) 19–35

United States General Accounting Office

'Sexual Exploitation of Children – A Problem of Unknown Magnitude', (GAO Report, 20 April 1982)

Index

John Doe Sixty; vampires
Blue Lightning Operations Command (BLOC), 119
Boise, 138
Boleyn, Anne, 136
Bolivia, 34, 76
Bonnie-Q, 65–6, 103
Borderline, Operation, 119, 120
Bork, Morris, 145–51, 186–99, 234
Boston, 158, 165
Brazil, 12, 73–4, 110, 213, 216
brickyards, 9
Brighton, 111
Britain, 99, 214; adoptions, 75, 113; and child labour, 222; Filipino immigrants, 225; Home Office, 225; immigration laws, 225; missing children, 47–8, paedophiles, 42, 111–12; Satanism, 111
brothels, 21; India, 3–4, 11; Middle East, 9, 216; Thailand, 12, 18; USA, 217; West Germany, 18
British Broadcasting Corporation, 91
Brussels, 116
Burma, 20, 76

Cairo, 21, 215, 216
Calexico, 116
Cambagna, Daniel, 218
camel-racing, 9–10, 42, 113
Cameo, Operation, 114–15
Campus, Angel, 75
Canada, 203; border with USA, 34, 165; and pornography, 203; RCMP, 193; and slave trade, 21, 138
cannibalism, 25, 26, 70, 102, 138, 143, 175, 202
Cantirino, Bill, 73
Canton, 75
Carlisle, Al, 176
Castro, Elsa Maria, 113
cemetery desecration, 27

Center for the Protection of Children's Rights, Bangkok, 113
Central Institute of Statistics, 220
Central Intelligence Agency, see United States of America
Chad, 212–13, 217
Charlene, 165–8
Charlie, 48–53, 77, 106–7, 114, 169–83
chattel slavery, 212
Cheysson, Claude, 229
Chicago, 16–23, 39–44, 90–5, 114–20, 138, 153–68, 203–7, 217, 234
Chicago Tribune, 43
child labour, 220–3
child pornography, see pornography
Child Search Inc., 176
children: sex with, see paedophiles
Childwatch, 111–12, 218
Chile, 34, 76, 213
China, 75, 161
China Lake Naval Weapons Center, 51
churches, 45, 111. *See also* Roman Catholic Church
Cincinnati, 117
'circuits', 33, 157–8
Ciudad Juarez, 116
Cleveland, Ohio, 117
Cliff and Clint, see Bork, Morris *and* St Joseph, Cliff
Colombia, 217
Commission for Filipino Migrant Workers, London, 110, 225, 226
Commission for Human Rights in Central America, 74
Common Market, *see* European Economic Community
Computer Pen Pals Club, 117
computers, 117, 218–19
Conneaut, 120
Constanzo, Jesus, 227
'coozie spot', 91